Life Stories

*The publisher gratefully acknowledges
the generous contribution to this book provided by
the following organizations and individuals:*

*Elizabeth Durein
Orville and Ellina Golub
David B. Gold Foundation
Moore Family Foundation*

*The author gratefully acknowledges
the following organizations and individuals:*

*Marion Rockefeller
James Compton
New England Biolabs Foundation*

LIFE STORIES

WORLD-RENOWNED SCIENTISTS REFLECT ON THEIR LIVES
AND THE FUTURE OF LIFE ON EARTH

Edited by Heather Newbold

UNIVERSITY OF CALIFORNIA PRESS
BERKELEY   LOS ANGELES   LONDON

University of California Press
Berkeley and Los Angeles, California

University of California Press, Ltd.
London, England

Library of Congress Cataloging-in-Publication Data

Life stories : world-renowned scientists reflect on their lives and the future of life on
earth / edited by Heather Newbold.
     p.   cm.
     Includes bibliographical references and index.
     ISBN 0-520-21114-6 (cloth : alk. paper) — ISBN 0-520-21896-5 (paper : alk. paper)
     1. Environmentalists—Biography.   2. Environmental sciences.   I. Newbold, Heather,
1947– .
   GE55.L485   2000
   363.7'0092'2—dc21   99-054133

Manufactured in the United States of America

09 08 07 06 05 04 03 02 01 00
10 9 8 7 6 5 4 3 2 1

The paper used in this publication meets the minimum
requirements of ANSI/NISO Z39.48-1992 (R 1997)
(*Permanence of Paper*).

In memory of Henry Kendall

CONTENTS

PREFACE

THIS BOOK IS FOR PEOPLE WHO WANT TO KNOW WHAT IS HAP-pening to life on Earth—and to us. This knowledge is so important for our survival that I invited prominent scientists who investigate the planet's life-support system to tell their stories for our benefit.

It is rare for scientists to discuss publicly their experiences, emotions, and beliefs because such expression is considered unscientific. This collection of personal and professional reflections is exceptional for its revelation of scientists' private lives and thoughts. Their profound understanding, appreciation, and reverence for life is inspirational and potentially transformative. We can experience it by following the development of their awareness, knowledge, and wisdom through their lives.

These leading scientists began their careers in different scientific fields—in chemistry, nuclear physics, engineering, astronomy, and meteorology, as well as in the life sciences. In the forefront of their disciplines, they researched diverse aspects of the biosphere, yet reached convergent conclusions regarding the plight of our planet. Their systemic perspective and global worldview prefigure a shift in the scientific paradigm and provide a prototype for our future. At this pivotal point in history, consequential decisions about our collective fate need to take account of the circumstances that enable life to exist—and the requisite conditions for its continued existence.

The individual stories in this book focus on crucial components of the global biosphere: the land, plants, forests, creatures, rivers, oceans, climate, and atmosphere. Just as we are dependent on all these systems, each planetary part depends on every other, and everything is interconnected within an integrative whole.

Thus each story relates to the others, and a single story evolves. From their origins in a particular person, place, and time, the stories expand to encompass the planet and the future of life on Earth.

———————

As the scientists do not have time to write about their lives, they discussed them with me. I composed our conversations as narratives, incorporating additional information, which they later reviewed, from their correspondence, speeches, and publications.

Gaia, Our Living Earth

JAMES LOVELOCK

I SUPPOSE THE BEGINNING IS RELEVANT because I am quite old. When I was a small child, the world was an incredibly different place from what it is now. It was far less mechanized. The cities were much smaller and more densely packed together. There were no cars, so people could not go out and commute from suburbs; they could only travel by train.

Even if you lived in a large city, as I did in London, it was possible to get out into untouched, heavenly countryside. I do not think that experience is as readily available anywhere now; it is something we have really lost. No longer can you hear the dawn chorus of birds. Even in the suburbs, it is nothing like it used to be; there were so many birds then that it was quite deafening.

It saddens me that few people ever see the stars at night. Although parts of London were so dimmed by the street lights that I could not see the sky, when I did see the stars, I was awed. The occasional meteorite was tremendously exciting. I could not help wondering what it was like out there and what was to be found in outer space. Of course, as a child, I never dreamed that in the future I would actually be involved in that kind of enterprise.

Things like that made life very different back in those days. There was far less in the way of material things, but much more of a feeling for nature and the world. You felt you were part of it. That more than made up for all the fancy things we now consider essential. Consequently, I do not worry about the loss of them should civilization collapse, as we would go back to a simpler and more natural lifestyle—assuming life endured.

Nature was a source of unending fascination and delight for me. I shared my father's instinctive kinship with all living things and enjoyed our relationship with the natural world during our walks through the countryside. I felt so strongly about being outdoors that I did not just dislike going to school—I loathed it. On a lovely day in the summer, being trapped indoors felt like being imprisoned. I was free to explore the countryside only in my imagination.

I lived in Brixton, a very rough part of London, equivalent then to Harlem in New York. Yet it had a wonderful public library where I learned most of my science. As a child, I would go there and get textbooks as well as fiction. Wade's *Organic Chemistry* was an early one that filled me with delight, and Dean's *Astronomy and Cosmography* was another. Of course, being so young, I did not understand half of it. But when you are inquisitive, any information soaks in like a sponge because the mind loves to be stimulated. Stuff went into readily accessible places to be retrieved later on in life.

Nobody was instructing me, so I roamed across the sciences. I was interested in them all and did not perceive them as being separate. I was fascinated by biology because I liked to go out and watch the small organisms: newts, frogs, snakes, insects, and birds. I wanted to know about them, so I read about biology as well as chemistry, physics, astronomy, and so on. There were no barriers; it was just one amazing universe.

It was so different from school, where the teaching of science is unbearably dull. Had I not stuffed my mind with it beforehand, I would never have taken any interest in it at all.

For children, there is no separation between knowledge and experience. Separation is something artificial that adults use to segregate subjects; it is like intellectual apartheid. When you are a child, all knowledge is interesting.

Outside, when I saw strange new things in nature, it was incredible. I remember seeing a pair of snakes, adders doing their dance. I did not know whether it was two males in a standoff or mates in a courtship ritual. They did circular dances on the ground and then suddenly came together, standing on their tails, looping around each other. It was just like the medical sign of the caduceus with intertwined snakes—the most wonderful sight. When I saw something amazing like that, I wanted to know more about it, so I went to the library to find out.

I also loved making things, even as a little boy. We used to travel by train in those days, and I was interested in how fast the train was going, so I made an airspeed indicator I could hold out the window to measure the speed of the train. I calibrated it using the second hand of my grandfather's watch to measure how long it took to go between mileposts along the track. If there was something to figure out, I would invent an instrument to do it, rather than ask someone. It always seemed like a great challenge. We had very little money, so I simply used whatever I could find and discovered I could make things out of just about anything. I used to ponder about being marooned on a desert island and making a radio with nothing but the vegetation and rocks. My father was like that; he was very inventive and could fix almost anything.

When I grew up to be an adult working in famous scientific institutions, if there was a question requiring an answer, there frequently was not the equipment available to ascertain the answer. Either we could not afford to buy it, or, as was more often the case, the equipment simply did not exist. There was nothing to do but invent it. Somebody once told me that inventions are exceedingly easy if you have a need; it is finding the need that is problematic. If you are a scientist, you always need to know something or other. It feeds back, because once you invent an instrument to make the measurement that leads to a new discovery, soon you will need a new instrument for that purpose and have to invent it.

I have more than fifty patents on my inventions, and I have been surprised by the scientific discoveries they have enabled. For example, one I invented in 1957, the electron-capture detector, is still among the most sensitive of chemical analytic methods in existence. It revealed for the first time the ubiquitous distribution of pesticide residues in the natural environment. This information enabled Rachel Carson to write her book *Silent Spring,* which initiated widespread awareness of disturbance in the environment and subsequently led to the formation of the environmental movement.

Later the same device enabled the discovery of PCBs in the environment. In 1971 I used it to determine the global distribution of chlorofluorocarbons, which are critical components in stratospheric ozone depletion. This evidence led to the discovery of the hole in the ozone. Most recently, the detector has made possible a system of atmospheric and oceanic tracer technology, enabling meteorologists to follow the movement of air masses. It is now being applied to ocean research.

My family was not prosperous, so there was no prospect of my being able to go to university. I knew I had to have a degree as a sort of union ticket to get into a laboratory and do science. Consequently, I went to work as a laboratory technician. That way I was able to work during the day and go to university in the evening. It was not discouraging, as only 1 percent of the population in Britain then was able to attend university anyway.

The firm I worked for was made up of true professionals. They would tackle almost any scientific problem within their area of specialization and anything to do with it. Chromatography covered a very wide range. The important lesson I learned from them was the necessity of doing science properly, never fudging or cheating in the least, even on little things.

I remember the boss telling me I was doing a difficult analysis, and if I got it wrong, to tell him, so we could do it together until I got it right. Getting it right was important because people's lives could depend on it. If we gave a wrong analysis, it could endanger people and ruin the firm. It impressed on me that science is a serious business, and I must get it right. In the year and a half I was with them, I too learned how to be a real professional.

When the opportunity of completing my degree became available, I went to the University of Manchester. Although it was a first-class science department, I was taught that it does not matter whether you comprehend the method or get results, as long as you understand what it is all about. That is the academic way. It dawned on me that students were being produced who were entirely unprofessional. They treated science almost as a business of passing examinations; it did not matter what you really did about it, whether it was right or not. In contrast, my work with the laboratory was a singularly formative time of having to do it right.

I left the firm because World War II broke out. In London the war was an incredible experience—bombs and rockets were exploding around us like fireworks! Yet I think people who stayed in London found it an inspiring experience. It was frightening, but it was not so damaging that it destroyed us all. It made you stop worrying about whether you could pay the rent next week, because you did not know whether you would be here. I can understand why people continue to live on the edge of volcanoes—it adds something to life.

During the war I worked at the National Institute for Medical Research. There were all sorts of problems, some of them related to the war: for instance, protecting troops against flash and flame. We devised quite a number of effective methods for that. There were also fearsome things such as working on the production of a vaccine to protect against a lethal virus expected to be encountered in Southeast Asia. It has a high mortality in people who are not used to it, so if you worked with it in the laboratory and caught it, you would die. It was extraordinary that in an institute in London, people were actually having to experiment with so deadly a virus. We had to help them devise methods to prevent the organism spreading and killing everyone. There was plenty of excitement.

As a youth my curiosity ranged over everything, including medicine and physiology, but there was no possibility of my family being able to afford my education for a medical degree, because it was too long and costly. So I was happy to get a job at the National Institute for Medical Research. While I was there doing work on cross-infection in hospitals, I obtained a Ph.D. in medicine. The doctorate is for research, not medical practice. I worked in all sorts of divisions of the institute: virology, physiology, biochemistry, experimental biology, and many more. In the twenty years I was there, I covered most fields of medicine.

It was one of the best laboratories in the world. On the floor where I worked, my lab was shamed by being the only one not to win the Nobel Prize. That shows the scientific caliber of my colleagues along the corridor. In addition to the wonderful people, the working conditions were desirable. The chain of command was a bit like the Quaker church: all members were equal and responsible only to the director, who was a marvelous man. There were no set hours, and we were able to work on whatever we chose. I could not have had a better place to work.

Yet, strangely, I found tenure stifling. The thought of life going down a railway track, straight to the grave, horrified me. I could not stand that, and I knew I would have to leave, but there were two problems. First of all, it was too good to leave. Besides that, the people were so extraordinarily nice that I did not want to cause offense by leaving.

Having read science fiction all my life, I used to say that science is the business of reducing science fiction to practice. Quite out of the blue came a letter from the director of Space Operations at NASA, asking if I would join the Surveyor mission as an experimenter. I was invited because some of my inventions were just what they needed to analyze the lunar surface prior to the astronauts' landing. I was thus honorably able to leave the National Institute of Medical Research to join the National Aeronautics and Space Administration.

As I was curious about the experiments to detect life on other planets, it was not long before I moved from the Moon Project to Life Detection on Mars. I was astonished at the low level of scientific activity going on in the biological side of the Mars Project. Eminent biologists who ought to have been taking part in the experiment were not interested. They were so obsessed with molecular biology and genetic evolution that they did not want to know about life. The discovery of DNA's double helix occurred at the Fitzer Institute when I was working there in Cambridge, so it was all part of our scene at the Institute for Medical Research.

It was such a stunning discovery that it shifted scientific focus from the big picture to the small. Scientists became intensely reductionist; they wanted to go down to the molecules and atoms to study life. It is an ultramicroscopic view. It assumes the whole is never more than the sum of its parts. Therefore, by taking things to pieces, we can figure out how they work. There is no looking outward toward life as a larger thing, a worldwide phenomenon. You need the physiological top-down approach as well as the microscopic bottom-up approach.

Science lacks wholeness of vision, so it is divided into separate expertises. The life sciences by their very nature necessitate synthesis, yet science is subdividing so rapidly that it is almost terrifying. At my last count, there were well over thirty different kinds of biologists, and they are all almost proud that they know nothing about the other branches of biology. Everyone is an expert in some specialized minutiae, so none of them talk to each other. With every year that goes by, new branches develop. Like those bifurcation diagrams in chaos theory, it is just going on into a complete miasma. This fragmentation is happening at a time when the need for synthesis is crucial.

As a result, the study of life itself is almost nonexistent. In order to study life, first you need to ask, "What is life?" Life is not even listed in the *Dictionary of Biology;* it is not defined. Once you know what you are looking for, then you have to ask, "How do you recognize it?" Unfortunately, we did not know the answer to that before we looked for it elsewhere.

There was a senior person at the Jet Propulsion Labs who was a nice but authoritarian man, whom people were a bit frightened of. One day, he called me into his office and asked, "What do you think of these life detection experiments?" I said I did not think much of them. Even if there were life on Mars, I thought there was a poor chance of finding it with the kind of equipment they were proposing to send. For the most part, scientists were just automating their own labs and sending them to Mars. That is not a good way of finding life somewhere else. I said so, and then he asked me what I would do. I replied that I would look for an entropy reduction on the whole planet. He laughed, saying that was a cop-out, because if the discovery of entropy reduction would indicate the presence of life, he needed to know how to do it. So I said, "Give me three days, and I will come back with an experiment for discovering entropy reduction."

I returned with the idea of analyzing the chemical composition of Mars's atmosphere. It was based on the premise that if there was life on Mars, it would be obliged to use the atmosphere as a source of raw materials and as a depository for wastes, thereby altering its atmosphere and disturbing its chemical equilibrium. In 1965 I had a little paper in *Nature* called "The Physical Basis of Life Detection" that proposed physical tests for the presence of planetary life. One was a top-down view of the whole planet, instead of a local search at the site of landing. Using it, an observer on a spacecraft beyond our solar system could recognize that Earth is the only planet in our system that has life.

My idea, when applied to what was known about Mars from infrared astronomy, suggested Mars was lifeless. Therefore it was not a popular experiment among scientists looking for life on Mars. NASA liked my approach, but the biologists did not. In the end, my experiment was never flown. The team thought they could get enough compositional analysis of Mars's atmosphere from a mass spectrometer attached to the Viking spacecraft. In fact, the instrument was too dedicated to analyzing the soil to look for life-characteristic substances.

NASA was tolerant even though I raised a lot of flak by saying that what they were doing was pointless. They easily could have fired me, but they did not. They kept me employed, mainly as an inventor. I continued working in Britain, traveling back and forth as a consultant. I still have two pieces of hardware sitting on Mars now, devices that enabled the gas chromatograph mass spectrometer experiment to work. I have three plaques from NASA in recognition of this, so apparently I was of some use to them, apart from ideas that were not exactly politically or financially advantageous for NASA.

The idea of "Gaia" was born in my mind in 1965 while I was at NASA in the Jet Propulsion Labs. It was a personal revelation, an idea that suddenly appeared like a flash of enlightenment. I was talking to Dian Hitchcock, an author-consultant there at the time, about the extreme difference between the atmospheres of Earth and Mars. As I was observing that Earth has such a reactive, unstable atmosphere, it suddenly dawned on me that an extremely unstable atmosphere could not stay constant unless something was regulating it. Somehow life keeps our atmosphere constant and favorable for organisms. Life on Earth not only created our atmosphere; it also regulates it.

The next morning, I discussed my idea with the man who shared my office, Carl Sagan. He did not think much of my idea but said there was one thing in favor of it: did I know the sun had warmed up by something like 25 percent since life had begun on Earth? Then I realized climate regulation might have occurred as well as regulation of biospheric chemistry. Although the sun's energy has increased 30 percent during the three and a half billion years life has existed on this planet, Earth's surface temperature has remained constant. According to standard physics, the planet's surface should have boiled in the rising heat, rather than cooling as it has.

Similarly, the chemical composition and concentration of gases in the atmosphere have remained stable. For example, the balance between oxygen and ammonia continues within the narrow range in which life can exist. Disastrous consequences would occur with minor shifts: an increase in oxygen of only 4 percent could ignite the entire atmosphere.

Life can exist only under limited circumstances, which have been actively maintained by necessity. Living organisms must regulate the atmosphere in order to survive. Examining our overall atmospheric stability, I realized it is created by the planet itself. The reason biospheric conditions on Earth are optimal for life is that they are an extension of the living systems on the planet.

When I first saw Gaia in my mind, I felt what an astronaut in space must have experienced seeing our home, Earth. I perceived Gaia as a single living entity consisting of Earth's biosphere, atmosphere, oceans, and land. Its entirety constitutes a feedback system that creates optimal physical conditions for life on this planet. It is a totality endowed with qualities far beyond those of its constituent parts. It differs from other living organisms in the way we differ from the population of living cells in our bodies. Gaia is the largest of living systems—it is our superorganism.

In my estimation the greatest benefit from space research is not what we have learned about space; it is what we have learned about our own planet. For the first time in human history we have had a chance to look at Earth from space. That distant perspective revealed the planet as a whole, enabling us to see it as a single entity in which air, water, land, and life forms all combine as one. The photograph of Earth from space has become an icon.

In addition to the image of Earth itself, photographs of other planets give us a new perspective on Earth. Mars appears to be a dead and barren place. It is so obviously lifeless, it looks like a slightly worked-over lunar surface. I used to argue quite a lot with my friend Carl Sagan, who would say, "How do you know there isn't life hanging on in an oasis somewhere?"

I asserted, but never convinced him, that a planet could not have only sparse life. Life cannot exist in isolation. The planetary life system either takes charge of its chemistry and physics, whereby life flourishes, or the system degenerates into a state like that of Mars and Venus, and life is totally wiped out. Mars and Venus are permanently dead; they lack organic molecules and can never bear life.

When it was first formulated, Gaia was just a hypothesis: "Let us suppose." It got better when I joined with the eminent biologist Lynn Margulis and we worked together on it. But when we tried to have our papers published, scientific journals refused to publish them. Scientists regarded our hypothesis as "dangerous," so we encountered strong resistance to our ideas. It is scientific heresy to propose anything that could be interpreted as teleological, that might imply the possibility of foresight, planning, and purpose in nature. As a result, it remained a hypothesis until about 1980.

From then on, it has become a theory, much more solid and sound, with quite a lot of supporting evidence for it. For example, if it were not for algae living in the ocean, there probably would be no clouds in the atmosphere, and our planet would be an enormously hotter place. The contribution of algal biochemistry to cloud formation is one of the geophysiological mechanisms involved in responsive climate regulation.

One discovery is based on a model I created in 1981 called Daisy World, which put Gaia on the theoretical map. The planet's climatic consistency is comparable to our body temperature remaining constant whether we are in a hot or cold environment. The temperature regulation of the planet operates similarly to our own. Physiologists have grown interested, and, to their great surprise, they have found that many of the physiological systems in our bodies that have puzzled them completely, such as the regulation of sugar in the blood by insulin, operate by a mathematical system very similar to my theoretical Daisy World.

The physiological system that regulates our own bodies is comparable to the one I postulated as regulating the whole planet. When the famous physiologist Walter Cannon came across the same thing in the human body, he named it homeostasis, the ability to regulate. He called it "the wisdom of the body." You might just as well say Gaia is "the wisdom of Earth."

It is perfectly natural that we should be similar to the planet on which we evolved. From the combined evolution of rocks, ocean, air, and organisms emerged the entity that is Gaia. Eventually we evolved within that entity. Organisms and their environment are so tightly coupled that they constitute a single system. This evolutionary system is an emergent domain of which the whole is more than the sum of its parts. It is emergent because the entire system working together has properties beyond a mere collection of its component parts.

The way I explain Gaia theory now is as an offshoot of Darwin's great vision. There is nothing in Gaia theory that is contrary to

Darwin; it just extends Darwin's idea of the evolution of organisms to include the parallel evolution of the environment. The Darwinian view was that life adapts to the environment it finds. The Gaian perspective is that not only does life adapt to its environment, but it also adapts the environment to itself, creating a home conducive to life.

The planetary perspective that Gaia provides stresses the crucial relationship of the planet's condition to our own. If life contributes to creating the conditions for its survival, then enhancing living organisms improves our shared environment. Naturally, when an organism's functions are beneficial to the environment, it flourishes as its environment thrives. Conversely, destroying organisms diminishes the conditions enabling our survival too. Inevitably, any species adversely affecting its environment is doomed. When damage to the biosphere is global, then our collective organism, Gaia, is at risk.

Unfortunately, my hypothesis is deliberately distorted by those destroying life to exonerate their behavior. They use it to claim that their destructive actions do not matter because "Gaia will fix it." But life cannot repair itself when it is dead!

The irresponsibility of those who misuse science to misinform the public is a serious problem for society. Scientists are revolted by the misrepresentation of my theory by those with malign intent. But they also have difficulties with its more benign usage. For over a decade, I have been urged to have nothing to do with the philosophical implications of my theory.

In the introduction to *The Ages of Gaia*, I give an account of a meeting we held in Oxford. I gave a talk about the planetary self-regulation going on at the moment. Toward the end of the talk, I simply said, "So, you see, it looks as if Gaia likes it cold." It was just a convenient way of saying the system operates better when it is at a low temperature. Afterward, a friend warned me, "You should never say things like that. It really upset the scientists around me, who said, 'Oh, he's gone back to all that mystical stuff.' "

I have been under enormous pressure from scientists to be "scientifically correct" (which is just like being "politically correct"). Scientists are intolerant of my mentioning anything nonscientific regarding Gaia. It has prevented me from expressing anything philosophical, as I did in my first book. I am not changing what I said in that book; I stick with it. So I say the first book, *Gaia: A New Look at Life on Earth,* is for the general public. And the second book, *The Ages of Gaia,* has been completely expurgated to take all such references out of it, for scientists who will not accept them. It is a dilemma. I have not departed from the general views expressed in my first book; but, speaking as a "scientist," I have had to turn aside from those views, or scientists will not listen to me.

I am an ordinary, old-fashioned, straight, hard scientist accused of being a mystic. When I was a student, I was asked if I had ever had a spiritual experience. I replied that living itself is a spiritual experience. A natural philosopher can be deeply spiritual; knowing the natural world intimately leads to a profound, loving relationship with it. People ask me about the philosophical implications of my theory, but I do not know. I think we live in a self-organizing universe. The formation of life was inevitable; it was not a chance accident. Gaia is a manifestation of life.

Which brings us to the question of whether life will continue to exist on this planet. If that is questionable, we have to ask, "What shall we do now?" I have pondered this an awful lot. I am not sure it is in our nature to do much. Most people just project this century into the next and get the same story as in the last: it might go on as it is, getting more polluted and more uncomfortable, but still livable.

On the other hand, I can think of lots of disasters that would change it totally. Natural disasters that did not matter as much one hundred years ago can now be devastating. To give a simple example, there is a volcano in Iceland that erupts every two hundred years, on average. When it erupted in 1783, it caused two years without any harvest in the Northern Hemisphere. In those days, there was only a fraction of the population there is now, some of whom could be fed on stored food. If the volcano erupted now, its effects would be devastating.

People do not want to think about that. They know the greenhouse effect is heating up the planet and terrible things are going to happen as a consequence, but they do not want to give up driving cars, because driving is convenient. Yet the ultimate effect of spewing noxious gases into the atmosphere is like sitting in a closed garage with the car engine running, asphyxiating from toxic air. We are polluting and poisoning the planet as well as ourselves.

People do not even do the simple things, like not eating fast-food burgers, which are made from beef raised on clearcut forest land. Rain forests are named so because forests are responsible for rain. Trees evapotranspire enormous volumes of water through their leaves, creating vapor clouds that condense moisture in the forest. Along with providing life-giving water, the cloud cover reflects sunlight back into the atmosphere, thereby cooling the climate. Without trees there is no rain. Without rain, the soil dies from erosion, and nothing grows.

Where humid tropical forests are being destroyed, soon there will be vast, arid deserts with mean temperatures of 120° F. This desertified land will encircle the globe, severely altering the climate for billions of people starving in the tropics. It will also damage the climate of the entire planet by destroying its natural cooling and air-conditioning system, causing drought, flooding, and famine around the world. This scenario is inevitable if we continue cutting trees and suffocating ourselves with greenhouse gases.

There is a pervasive feeling of an ominous calm like that preceding a coming war or a tropical hurricane. We know what to expect from a hurricane, but we have no idea what is coming now. There will be surprising events that cannot be predicted. In addition to the gradual changes becoming apparent, a stressed system undergoes a sequence of abrupt events increasing in critical magnitude. We will rapidly approach the critical level of degradation of all Earth's natural ecosystems—when the whole system starts to collapse.

It appears from our present behavior that we will not do anything about our problems until something awful happens. It has often been said that the only thing that could pull people together is a threat from outside. If we were to react to our internally generated threat (the consequences of what we are doing, instead of aliens coming in and attacking us), maybe we could save ourselves. Unfortunately, we would rather blame and fight the other guy, so I think it is going to take some dreadful catastrophes before people cooperate.

We need a connection with something larger than ourselves. We have a collective identity, but it is not comprehensive enough. Most people are tribal: they identify with their own culture, religion, nation, or whatever. They do not care about their nation as long as they are all right. But when they perceive that it is under threat, it is amazing how unselfish they become. In wartime, they even give up their lives. It is remarkable.

How do we draw on that strength to make it global? There is no use in talking about the human race or the United Nations, because, although such a union is a good idea, it does not move people the way their tribe does. Even environmental problems are blamed on other nations and used to score points in national politics. Such tribal conflicts are as dangerous and self-defeating as scientific and religious fundamentalism. The global environment encompasses us all, regardless of ethnicity, race, or nationality.

Now, at the close of the twentieth century, there is little time left to remedy real problems affecting Earth. Confronted with global catastrophe, we can only hope there will be some new response in the human species. Environmental ignorance could be replaced with ecological awareness. We could shift our focus from short-term gain to long-term consequences. Instead of trying to manage the planet, we could manage ourselves.

Our thinking could change from being human-centered to planet-centered. We could learn to live with Earth as part of it, by humbly receiving and giving the gifts that sustain all of us who live on this planet. Gaia could be a way to view Earth, ourselves, and our relationship with living things. To me Earth is alive, and I am part of it. People could think of Earth in that sense—we all belong to Gaia.

Further Reading

James Lovelock. *The Ages of Gaia.* Norton, 1994.
———. *Gaia: A New Look at Life on Earth.* Oxford University Press, 1987.

Life-Support Systems

PAUL EHRLICH

I WAS ALWAYS INTERESTED IN NATURE. MY
mother, who was a schoolteacher, was very helpful
with anything in which I had an interest. My parents sent me to summer camp when I was a kid, and I loved it because there was a nature program. I had been fascinated by snakes
and frogs, but the camp introduced me to butterfly collecting, which
I continued on my own. I learned not only about butterflies but also
about things like geography, because butterflies are found all over the
world.

When I was in junior high and high school, I concentrated on butterflies, tropical fish, and girls. I never lost my interest in any one of
the three. My room had thirty to forty tanks of tropical fish and
drawers filled with butterflies. I would still love to work in a big laboratory of tropical fish, but you can only do so many things at a time,
so I have not been able to pursue my interest in fish in my adult
years, other than through underwater research on coral reefs.

After traveling around the United States with a moving summer
camp when I was fifteen, I was introduced to Charles Michener at
the American Museum of Natural History in New York. He encouraged me to join the Lepidopterists' Society, which was just starting
up that year, in 1947. I joined the society and found I could exchange
butterflies with other collectors.

I was surprised and delighted with my first exchange. A collector in California sent me a lot of fairly rare and beautiful West Coast butterflies in return for some common, ordinary East Coast ones. I think he was just being nice to a kid in New Jersey, but I was overjoyed. That childhood joy has lasted a lifetime because some of them were Bay checkerspot butterflies—the organism on which I have done most of my research and the work for which I am best known.

We have been doing a long-term study of this beautiful butterfly, which is now federally listed as threatened. It says a lot about what is happening to wildlife, because that butterfly used to be very common in the San Francisco Bay Area. I can still remember when I was fifteen, opening up the envelopes with these wonderful butterflies from faraway California.

At that time, I could never have imagined I would personally handle tens of thousands of them, put marks on them, then let them go. Our study of their population, genetics, and ecology started in 1959 and has been continuous since then. In fact, our whole group is settling down finally to write a book about it.

My very strong interest in nature continued in my undergraduate years at the University of Pennsylvania, where I pursued my hobby of chasing girls more than anything else. When I was not tracking those fascinating organisms, I kept up my research on butterflies and fish, publishing a few papers on butterfly behavior. My unimpressive grades reflected the amount of time devoted to my favorite subjects instead of the required ones, but I applied to graduate school anyway.

In the winter of 1953, the Entomological Society of America met in Philadelphia, so I went to see Charles Michener, the man who had started me out in this field. By then he was a professor at the University of Kansas, in the best entomology department in the country. I went up to him and said I was applying to his department, and, since he had started me on this route, he should give me a chance to show what I could do in graduate school, even though I had not shown much promise as an undergraduate.

Maybe Mich felt responsible for all those years I had spent chasing butterflies, because he said all right and got me a graduate assistantship with Bob Sokal, who later became the "father" of the entire field of numerical taxonomy. At the time I met Mich, he was working on butterflies and moths. When he left the museum, he switched, and he has had a fantastic career working on the evolution of social behavior in bees. We have remained friends until this day, and although he is now over eighty years old, he is still working very hard.

My interest in environmental problems also developed when I was a kid. Trying to raise butterflies myself, I found it extremely frustrating because the plants I was feeding them were poisoned by pesticides that killed the caterpillars. So much DDT was spread around that I could not find food that was not poisoned. So, at a young age, I observed the effects of pesticides and realized things were being totally screwed over.

Later, in graduate school at Kansas, the assistantship with Sokal got me working on the evolution of DDT resistance in fruit flies, which revealed, to me at least, the futility of using pesticides. At Kansas I also made the smartest move of my career—marrying Anne. She has been my partner in research and writing and everything else ever since.

In 1958, when I was a postdoctoral researcher, Edward O. Wilson recruited me in the effort to stop the spraying of pesticides used in an attempt to exterminate the imported fire ant. The U.S. Department of Agriculture was indiscriminately spraying poisonous chemicals to try and exterminate these pests, although pesticides ordinarily wipe out everything except pest populations.

That was the first political battle for both Ed and me, as well as my introduction to political ecology. Although he is a bit older, Ed and I have had parallel careers working on insects. His work on ants is absolutely incredible; I wish I had written his book on them. It was especially nice that Ed and I shared the Craafoord Prize, which the Swedish Academy of Sciences developed for researchers in fields ineligible for the Nobel Prize (such as the life sciences, including ecology and the environment). Ed and I started out on the front line of ecological activism at the same time and ended up (accompanied by our mothers) meeting the King and Queen of Sweden in 1990.

After my postdoc, I was lucky enough to get a faculty position at Stanford—the best job open at the time, and still the best for me. I have turned down all other offers in order to stay at Stanford, because this is the best place for me to do what I do. The chair of the department that hired me said they would like me to teach a course in entomology and a course in evolution. So I started out with the evolution course, spending the first nine weeks teaching where human beings came from and the last week saying where we are going—which in my view is straight to hell. Those latter lectures got to be quite famous, even in those early years.

In the mid-sixties, I left for a year on sabbatical to work in Australia with Charles Birch, one of the world's most distinguished ecologists. I see him every couple of years and just returned from seeing him again. He is also over eighty years old and still swims in the ocean every morning at five o'clock, even during the winter.

After I returned from Australia in 1966, word about my "Where are we going?" lectures had reached a lot of the alumni, so I was invited to speak to the Commonwealth Club on that topic. At the time, I did not realize the speech was being broadcast on the radio. The title of the talk was "The 'Food from the Sea' Myth: The Biology of a Red Herring." I discussed the illusion that we could have an infinitely large population simply by feeding everyone seafood. This led to a lot of invitations to talk on radio and television. If you are a natural-born loudmouth, why just talk to fifteen in a class when you can address fifteen thousand or millions?

Dave Brower, who was doing books for the Sierra Club, heard me and suggested I turn my talk into a short book. Brower and the publisher, Ian Ballantine, wanted to produce it in time to "influence the elections in 1968," which shows how naive we all were in those days. So, with the help of my wife and some of my colleagues, I wrote it in about three weeks. I wanted to call it *Population, Resources, and Environment,* but the publisher chose the title *The Population Bomb.* That is where the bomb came from and how I got nailed as the "population bomber."

In 1968 I was at Yale visiting my old friend Charlie Remington, who started the Lepidopterists' Society and is a leading expert on butterflies and moths. He came with me to visit an attorney who was interested in starting a population organization, and the three of us founded Zero Population Growth. The attorney came up with the name, which I thought would never take hold—but that shows what I did not know.

At the end of the sixties, Arthur Godfrey gave a copy of *The Population Bomb* to Johnny Carson, who liked it so much he invited me on his show. He talked to me for half an hour the first time, in early 1970, allowing me to give the address of Zero Population Growth, which was in Los Altos. That resulted in the biggest delivery of mail to Los Altos in the history of the post office. Carson had me on a few more times that spring, giving me a lot of airtime.

By the end of the spring, ZPG had grown from six chapters and six hundred members to something like six hundred chapters and six hundred thousand members. That was the start of Zero Population Growth and the end of my private life. I was on the *Tonight Show* a lot after that, and I eventually went on to become an NBC correspondent for a while on the side, always pushing the same agenda.

The world desperately needs an overview, and the media is not providing it. The journalistic system is breaking down. What passes for news and comment in the media is mostly nonsense and trivia, which is why the public dismisses it. If you turn on the news, you are likely to hear about some celebrity who has been caught with a prostitute or killed his wife or whatever. The network news is no longer news; it is entertainment. Important issues are rarely discussed on the news. They are almost never addressed even on programs that purport to examine significant matters, where you get commentators who think they know everything and actually know little about how the biophysical world works. The standard media gurus and pundits are basically ignorant of what is going on in the real world.

The issues they discuss are not nearly as important to the world as the ecological and evolutionary relationships of human beings to the viruses, bacteria, and fungi that attack them. The growth of the gross national product is a trivial issue compared to the growth of the scale of human activities relative to the ability of natural ecosystems to support them. The problems of increasing our agricultural productivity are infinitely more important than who will be the next party presidential candidate.

Despite television's current failure to inform the public, past media exposure of our group's conclusions about population and the environment introduced me to a new group of people in the policy area, many of whom have become good friends of Anne's and mine, such as Tim Wirth and his wife, Wren. It also created long-term friendships with people such as Dave Brower, Garrett Hardin, John Holdren, and Peter Raven. Peter is a close colleague with whom I have published three papers, possibly the three most widely cited papers either of us has written. I still think of Peter and John as bright young scientists, although both are now distinguished senior academy members (which tells me something about what has been happening to my life.)

It is nice how professor-student relationships can turn into collaborative friendships over the years. One of the rewarding aspects of my career is that I now have many former students who remain friends and with whom I still work. They had a celebration for my sixtieth birthday where they toasted and "roasted" me, and it was wonderful to see how many of them there were.

I have continued to do research with many of my former students. Dennis Murphy got his doctorate with me over a decade ago, headed our Center for Conservation Biology, and now runs its counterpart at the University of Nevada. He is one of the foremost scientists in the field and is president of the Society of Conservation Biology. The governor of California asked him to be the chief science adviser for the state. Gretchen Daily, one of my more recent students, has become a leading spokesperson for preserving the ecosystems that support our lives. Her book *Nature's Services* was an instant classic. Tonight I am having dinner with one of my first two graduate students, Michael Soule, who is a pioneering conservation biologist. The other student was Harry Recher, whom I recently visited in Australia, where he is now one of the leading ecologists. In our field, we are a band of brothers and sisters fighting a rearguard action for life—and losing.

One of the great pleasures of my work has been building relationships with other scientists who are working on our dangerous predicament. Of course, it has also been a pleasure to work with my wife, Anne, on all this. Lately, she has received more recognition: she shared with me the United Nations' Sasakawa Environment Prize, the Heinz Prize for the Environment, and the Tyler Prize for Environmental Achievement, and she was just elected a member of the American Academy of Arts and Sciences.

It has always been clear to us, as it is to any biologist, that what happens to the environment is a function of how many people there are. You have a powerful emotional reaction when you see people building freeways and shopping malls on top of precious habitat and farmland. I have seen most of the places where I have done fieldwork destroyed in my lifetime. That gets to you emotionally.

What population pressures can do in a poor country became painfully obvious when Anne and I first visited India decades ago. We were just in India and China again recently, and China was shocking for a different reason. Their misguided rush to copy the mistakes of the West and become superconsumers is madly under way—which bodes ill for the Chinese and everybody else. We in the West are senselessly still going in the wrong direction ourselves, but there are not as many of us.

It has really hit home for Anne and me over the years because, unlike some economists, politicians, and other self-proclaimed "experts" who sit inside offices in cities, we spend our time out in the world. Anne and I have been on every continent, including Antarctica. We have watched areas where we were working in the tropics become deforested; we saw that happen in the New World tropics and the Old World tropics. We have worked extensively in Australia and also have been all over Africa, seeing the devastation happening in front of our eyes.

We have spent most of our lives out in the field, much of it in poor countries. We see runaway consumption and destruction of the environment creating incredible poverty. Attempts to emulate the West's destructive ways bankrupt poor countries. We know firsthand the dire problems that world agriculture is facing, so we work with the International Rice Research Institute and with agricultural economists.

What we have done is make a specialty of looking at the big picture. We are able to do that because we have this group of colleagues who are the best experts on the individual issues. For instance, John Holdren, founder of the Energy and Resources Group at the University of California, now at Harvard, is the physicist who understands more than anyone else about the environmental consequences of nuclear and fusion technologies. He is also a world expert in arms control and offers Anne his expertise because she works on a lot of the environmental problems of nuclear production and preparing for war.

When I need to find out about distribution of plants in the tropics, I talk to Peter Raven, who has that information at his fingertips. Peter Vitousek and Hal Mooney are key players on how to keep ecosystems functioning. If I want to know how soil systems work, I can talk to Peter because he is one of the top experts on that subject. Hal knows more about the physiological responses of plants, so I can ask his advice. We continually exchange data with Steve Schneider, the climatologist who came to Stanford from the National Center for Atmospheric Research. Gretchen Daily and I recently worked with Sandy Postel, who was with the Worldwatch Institute, on the problem of how much of the planet's freshwater supply will be available for human use in the future. We are basically buried in this stuff all the time, and the picture is perpetually grim.

Having this enormous capacity to tap the brains of experts allows our group to be synthesizers of what is going on in the world. What I do with one portion of our group is to focus on this global overview, utilizing both the biological sciences and the social sciences. As a result, I have written books with political scientists and with psychologists on diverse subjects. Other people in our group work on particular problems of conservation and biological diversity in specific places. Anne and I do fieldwork in the tropics on how to preserve what is left.

What makes our group unique is the global view we maintain, combined with the connections we make with local problems. I just hired a postdoctoral fellow who will be working entirely on the issue of food self-sufficiency: the problem of export crops grown for cash instead of for feeding local people. A colleague in the economics department is trying to get a postdoctoral fellow who is an economist to work with us on problems of how one best controls greenhouse gas emissions and things like that. I am working all the time with professionals in different disciplines, such as economists, political scientists, and law professors. We are particularly well situated here, both by being at Stanford and by having accumulated such a large range of colleagues. We have made a specialty out of being broad. That takes a long time and involves developing and maintaining a lot of relationships.

One of the meetings we had today with our entire group was on how to handle our information overload. For example, the book Gretchen Daily, Anne, and I did together, *The Stork and the Plow*, deals with how equity is going to affect the carrying capacity of the planet in terms of food production and human fertility. We looked at hundreds of books and thousands of papers to do it. We take in vast amounts of information and try to digest them all with the help of a bunch of colleagues who understand the ins and outs, but it is extremely complicated.

Nothing is more important for everybody than gaining a comprehensive view of this problem. To understand why, consider a little book that was put together for the twentieth anniversary of Earth Day, called *Fifty Simple Things You Can Do to Save the Earth*. If every human being did every one of them, it would not make a substantial difference, because the book did not mention the most critical factors: cutting consumption and reducing birth rates. Current trends in consumption and population cannot continue indefinitely.

We need to look at the scale of the enterprise relative to the ability of life's support systems to continue in perpetuity. The scale of the human enterprise is a product of the number of people, how much each one consumes, and what kind of technologies are used to supply the consumption. Until everyone comprehends that, we will not have the kind of political action we need in order to survive.

People need to understand that our survival depends on the life-support systems of the planet. Earth is the only life-bearing planet we know of, yet we know little about its self-sustaining systems. Most people are ignorant about them, so I will explain how they function. Ignorance of the laws of nature is no excuse for destroying it.

Life has existed here for around four billion years, evolving along with the planet itself. For most of these four billion years life occurred only in oceans. Life eventually altered the biosphere enough so that it could exist out of water and move onto land, but the land itself was moving around. As continents drifted, the geophysical environment and climate shifted too. The living passengers, transported on moving tectonic plates, diversified and adapted to continually changing conditions over long periods of time.

Besides gradual transformations over millions of years, sudden changes also occurred—just as they might again in the future. When the environment changed drastically sixty-five million years ago, the dinosaurs disappeared, along with countless other species of animals and plants. Climates changed so much that the balance among species was totally altered. When the dominant dinosaurs became extinct, mammals, which had previously been obscure, were able to diversify and thrive. One of those mammalian diversifications eventually developed into human beings. In the succeeding millions of years, all the species alive on the planet now evolved along with us.

While life was being transformed by changes on the planet, Earth was also being changed by life. The composition of the atmosphere is the result of Earth's organisms. Plants and microorganisms in the oceans and on land extract carbon dioxide from the atmosphere and expel oxygen. Other organisms inhale oxygen and exhale carbon dioxide.

Plants and some microbes convert sunlight into energy through photosynthesis, and other organisms gain their energy by consuming plants. All animals are dependent on plants and microbes for the oxygen they breathe and the food they eat. In addition to providing the energy that supports the rest of life, plants also cycle elements from the nonliving to the living. They absorb elements from air, water, and soil and combine them into carbohydrates, proteins, and other complex molecules. The elemental nutrients made available from inorganic matter by plants are needed by other organisms to survive.

Nutrients are cycled through living systems from one part to another in a continuous loop. Plants provide animals with nutrients, which they digest, utilize, and excrete. The resulting waste is broken down by decomposers, and the elements are returned to the soil and water, where they are again available to plants. This ongoing movement of materials through the biosphere continually renews nutrients, replenishes soils, and disposes of waste.

Plant producers, animal consumers, and organism decomposers form food chains. They are dependent on each other for their survival, having evolved together over a long time. Groups of plants, animals, and decomposers that coexist in one place are ongoing communities. Most natural communities are composed of so many different species that there usually are several potential food sources and predators for each organism. So it is relatively rare for any species to undergo a sudden great expansion in population size. In artificial communities created by human beings, such as agriculture, single monoculture crops and faulty pest control practices often allow insect pests to proliferate without predators.

The entire community in nature depends on its producers, and plants are always at risk of being consumed. Plants cannot escape from consumers, but they can hide. They might use camouflage or disperse their population as widely as possible, relying on wind, water, animals, birds, and insects to transport their seeds and pollen. They also hide inside protective outer layers and develop chemical defenses, becoming poisonous to protect themselves. Animals utilize some similar strategies to defend themselves against predators. They might hide, depend on camouflage, wear armor, or use noxious substances. They escape when they can and fight when they cannot. But for every defense that prey develop, predators evolve along with them, developing ways to overcome their prey's defenses.

Besides predator-prey coevolution, species that depend on similar resources adjust to each other's needs by evolving specialized niches, such as feeding on slightly different organisms, in different places, or at different times. Coevolution has produced another form of intimate relationship known as mutualism. Different organisms coexist in mutually beneficial ways, such as algae and fungi that form lichens; bacteria that provide nitrogen to legumes; and bees that exchange plant pollen for nectar.

The organisms within a biotic community and their interactions with the physical environment in which they exist form an ecosystem. Climate is part of a global ecosystem, and it is strongly influenced by the living parts of that system. For example, weather over land is moderated by vegetation, which alters surface temperature. And the amount of carbon dioxide in the atmosphere (and thus the entire climatic balance) is dramatically influenced by organisms.

Forests and plant communities also regulate the cycling of water from land to the atmosphere and back. Forests capture, retain, and recycle water. In forests, rainfall sinks into the soil, replenishing underground stores of fresh water and releasing it slowly in steadily flowing streams. In contrast, in areas of sparse vegetation water runs off the surface, taking the soil with it and creating floods.

Life-support functions are carried out continuously by self-sustaining, living communities. Natural ecosystems are actively engaged in maintaining the planet's habitability. To the degree we exterminate the organisms forming our ecosystems, we imperil Earth's capacity to support us. To the extent that we preserve our life-support systems, we increase our individual and collective chances of survival.

Further Reading

Paul Ehrlich, Anne Ehrlich, and Gretchen Daily. *The Stork and the Plow: The Equity Answer to the Human Dilemma.* Yale University Press, 1997.
Paul Ehrlich and Anne Ehrlich. *Betrayal of Science and Reason: How Anti-environmental Rhetoric Threatens Our Future.* Island Press, 1996.
————. *The End of Affluence.* Amereon, 1995.
Paul Ehrlich. *The Population Bomb.* Buccaneer Books, 1995.
Paul Ehrlich and Anne Ehrlich. *Healing the Planet: Strategies for Solving the Environmental Crisis.* Addison-Wesley, 1992.
————. *The Population Explosion.* Simon & Schuster, 1990.
Paul Ehrlich and Jonathan Roughgarden. *The Science of Ecology.* Macmillan, 1987.
Paul Ehrlich. *The Machinery of Nature.* Simon & Schuster, 1986.

Primary Producers

PETER RAVEN

MY FATHER'S FAMILY ORIGINALLY CAME TO California in the 1850s and lived in Walnut Creek, just east of San Francisco Bay. My mother was a Breen; her family came to California in 1846 with the pioneering Donner party, many of whom froze to death crossing the Sierra Nevada range. My mother's parents moved north across the bay to Mill Valley when the 1906 earthquake and fire wrecked their home in San Francisco. After the earthquake, houses were built in the area near Golden Gate Park. Our house was one of the first built in that part of the city, so there were still vacant lots in the area in the 1940s when I was growing up. The open spaces provided me with free territory to explore and discover what was around me.

When I was in kindergarten, I read a popular book on insects and then began looking around and collecting them. I started copying things about beetles from books, then wrote about butterflies and birds. I carted caterpillars around in my little red wagon, imagining how they were becoming butterflies—which I would eventually collect. Needing to know what to feed insects and where to find them, I learned about plants. Gradually, as I learned about more and more of them, my collection grew. When I found an interesting plant in flower, I took it home, taped it to a piece of paper, pressed it between the pages of the telephone directory, labeled it, and added the dried specimen to the expanding collection piled in my bureau drawer.

Fortunately I always lived near Golden Gate Park, even though we moved a few times. The California Academy of Sciences is located in the park, and I was taken there for the first time when I was two years old. At the age of eight, I was able to join the children's section. I was encouraged in my endeavors by being in a social group of supportive people who were interested in learning about and collecting insects and plants. The scientists there, especially Edward Ross in the entomology department and John Thomas Howell in the botany department, really helped and encouraged me.

I became increasingly interested in plants along the way. I was fascinated by the fact that in *A Manual of Flowering Plants of California*, which was written by Jepson in 1925, it was possible to have a description of all the plants and their ranges in California. You could learn where they were and why they were there. Given that information, you could go out looking for them and have a good chance of finding them. Sometimes you could find ones that were in places where they were not supposed to be, or, if you were really lucky, even find new ones. That was exciting and wonderful because it provided me with an existing framework. When you are dealing with insects or something like that, you do not have such a framework. If you want to identify them, all you can do is go into a big collection and compare what you have to what is there. It is more difficult to discover which specific creatures are supposed to exist in any particular location.

It was rewarding to be able to find plants wherever I looked for them. So I had an exciting and fulfilling time collecting plants while I was growing up. My interest in nature motivated me to explore as much of it as I could. Being too young to drive, I used buses to get around; but as I got up before the local buses even began running, I had to walk several miles to the Greyhound bus station. From there I took buses to interesting places where I could hike into the hills and collect plants.

One time I took the early bus down the San Francisco peninsula, but it was still so dark when I got to my destination that I could not see a thing. I stumbled along, collecting plants in the dim light of a signboard, which was kind of amusing. As it got lighter, I still could not see, because it was a very foggy day. Although I could only see about a foot ahead, I hiked up San Bruno Mountain anyway. I managed to get to the top without falling off and was relieved when I made it down the other side to Visitacion Valley. That was one of many youthful adventures seeking plants.

When I was twelve, I joined the Sierra Club, probably about the eighteen-thousandth person to do so, and I have continued as a member for the ensuing half-century. Two years after I joined, my mentor at the California Academy of Sciences, Tom Howell, was unable to go on a Sierra Club outing. He had been going on base-camp outings since 1941, using them as an opportunity to collect plants in different parts of the Sierra Nevada. Even though I was only fourteen years old, he asked me if I would go and collect plants for him.

On the trip there, I had the great fortune of sharing a ride with George Ledyard Stebbins, who is the most famous plant evolutionist of this century. He was then a forty-four-year-old professor at the University of California at Berkeley and moved to UC Davis soon after. At that point he was writing the definitive account of plant evolution, a book called *Variation and Evolution in Plants*. In the couple of weeks I was able to spend with him, he increased my enthusiasm immensely and taught me a whole lot. Most important, he introduced me to the idea of plant evolution and deeper studies related to that, which was truly inspiring. I was able to make a collection of plants there with him and bring them back. I wrote about the experience and published my first scientific paper, on collecting plants in the High Sierra.

Every year from then until I was twenty, I spent my summers working on Sierra Club base-camp outings in different places in the Sierra Nevada. One summer I also went to Mount Rainier, and another summer to Glacier Peak in the Cascades. I was really excited about the different kinds of plants, where they were, and where new ones could be found. Meanwhile, my personal herbarium moved from my bedroom bureau out of necessity. All the plants I collected as an adolescent went into the botany collection at the California

Academy of Sciences. I had added something like twenty thousand plant specimens to their collection by the time I went to the University of California as a junior.

Along with Tom Howell and Peter Rubtzoff, I worked on a project to collect and catalogue the plants in San Francisco, and we published a paper on the naturalized plants residing in the city. Right after my family moved to the Seacliff area in 1950, I was collecting plants nearby and discovered the single manzanita in the Presidio; there is one individual out near Baker Beach. I also discovered another plant there that was very important, a plant called *Clarkia franciscana*.

The reason that particular plant was so important is that botanists Margaret and Harlan Lewis, at the University of California in Los Angeles, had been working on the plant group *Clarkia* as a model of evolution. Although they had been studying *Clarkia* since World War II, that particular species had not been seen locally since 1902, when Katharine Brandegee, a botanist associated with the California Academy of Sciences, collected it. This particular plant is found only in the Presidio and in one locality in the Oakland hills.

Harlan and Margaret came to the California Academy of Sciences routinely to look for additional specimens of the group of plants they were studying. They found this one and saw that it had been collected by someone they had never heard of, so they wanted to know who Peter Raven was. When they met this sixteen-year old, they immediately asked me, "Where are the plants?" The only problem was that when I went looking for the plants, I could not find them. It was not until the following year, or maybe even the next, that I finally found them again.

I was a third-generation student at the University of California at Berkeley and had a wonderful time there. I was well taken care of and had some great teachers. But I had to decide whether to major in entomology or botany, and that was the point at which I decided to go into botany. My decision was based on the observation that there were a lot fewer majors in botany, so maybe I could make a bigger contribution working with plants than insects.

Between my junior and senior years at Berkeley, the Lewises invited me to come down to Los Angeles and work with them. We grew *Clarkia franciscana* in the greenhouse, hybridized them with other plants, and then studied their evolutionary relationships. Having done that, I published a paper on them, describing the new species. That got me started in botany, and of course the question of where to go to graduate school was answered by my involvement there.

My doctoral work at UCLA was on another group of plants related to *Clarkia,* in the same evening primrose family, but which grew mainly in the desert. I worked all over southern California, the Great Basin, and the Southwest. I had never been in the desert before, so it was all new and wonderful to me. Fortunately, 1958 and 1959 were both very good years for plants in the desert, which made it even more marvelous and rewarding. My postdoctoral work was in a very different climate, at what was then called the British Museum and is now called the Natural History Museum. I divided my time between London and the Royal Botanical Gardens in Kew, studying plants from around the world in the evening primrose family.

Soon after returning to California, I joined the Department of Biological Sciences at Stanford University, where I remained until 1971. There I developed a close friendship and working relationship with Paul Ehrlich. I was studying plants, and he was studying butterflies. We wondered why the larvae of certain butterflies fed on certain plants but not others, and how those patterns had evolved. Animals' choice of food affects and alters plants, which produce substances affecting and altering animals. Over time, multiple generations of mutual interactions transform species. Such complementary adaptations led us to devise the concept of coevolution to explain a process that was a major influence in creating the diversity of life on Earth. We just made up the word "coevolution" because it seemed natural, but it is a term that has generated thousands of scientific papers since.

My own outlook evolved enormously during that time. Until that point I had not thought much about conservation or the environment or the role of plants in general; almost nobody did. But the spirit of the sixties soon changed that. Paul and I, with other colleagues such as Richard Holm, went through it all together, getting more and more concerned about the environment, particularly the growth of the human population. We team-taught courses, and when Paul wrote *The Population Bomb,* we all worked together on it.

Thinking about world population growth and wondering how such rapidly growing numbers of people could be fed—in addition to observing the resulting decline in the organisms we were studying—shifted my perspective. Gradually it all began to flow together as I focused on what the global problems were. Within my own field, I contemplated how best to study plants around the world, the least well known of which were those in the tropics.

When I was twenty-two, I went on a summer student exchange program to study tropical plants in Colombia, and I was shocked by the mass poverty. By 1967, when I went and taught on the faculty at the Organization of Tropical Studies in Costa Rica, the relationship between population, poverty, and environmental degradation around the world had become obvious.

In 1971 I came to the Missouri Botanical Garden fully excited about this wonderful place, but still worried about population and global environmental concerns. This is the oldest botanical garden in the United States, in existence since 1859. We are generously supported by the people of St. Louis and are able to affect people here directly: eight hundred thousand people visit us every year, including over one hundred thousand schoolchildren, so institutions like ours are important for educating the public about the value of their environment.

As we were an organization that was predominantly focused on the tropics, it was natural to expand what we already had; a staff of about three Ph.D.'s and six support people has grown now to fifty-five Ph.D.'s and about a hundred people supporting them. Our scientific program in field-oriented botany is the most active of any botanical institute. We have research projects in many countries—mainly in the tropics, but also at other places around the world, where we send our field staff to work and live. In addition, the Center for Plant Conservation, with its headquarters at the Garden, is a national consortium of botanical gardens trying to preserve endangered plants of the United States. We have helped to establish similar consortia in other countries and would like to create an international network for global plant preservation.

A very important outlet for me in dealing with biodiversity and environmental issues is my involvement in the National Academy of Sciences. For much of the last two decades I have been on the council, and for over a decade I have been the home secretary. I am also a member of other academies of science in different countries and am on the President's Committee of Advisors on Science and Technology.

When the National Science Foundation asked me to convene a study committee here to consider the future of systematic and evolutionary biology and ecology, I convened about thirty-five scientists. Their conclusion, like mine, was that we needed to concentrate on the tropics. Their other major conclusion was that we needed to use modern methods of electronic data processing in order to deal with all the information becoming available about organisms.

The first study for the National Science Foundation led to another, on research priorities in tropical biology, which was a National Research Council study in 1979. I continue to coordinate interdisciplinary undertakings; for example, I recently helped plan a forum on biodiversity, which was jointly sponsored by the National Academy of Sciences, the Smithsonian Institution, the Library of Congress, and the American Association for the Advancement of Science. I try to keep all of those connections going all over the world, mainly by promoting collaborative international research. I am doing everything I can to strengthen the capacity of individual countries to deal with their own botanical and biological resources.

Eighty percent of the people in the world live in developing countries, which also harbor about 80 percent of the world's biological diversity. Altogether they have fewer than 5 percent of the world's scientists, and many of those are leaving for industrialized countries. For the majority of countries in the world, there is no scientific base at all for dealing with problems of sustainability and survival. I try to work on that problem directly. I have the great satisfaction of knowing that as a result of my own efforts and those of my colleagues in going to places like Russia and China and working with people there, these fields are taken much more seriously, and there is far more support for their scientists. This is not only good for them, it is good for us, too, because a healthy habitat in any country depends on capabilities of countries around the world to deal with their own resources responsibly.

I am still trying to promote a spirit of internationalism in the United States, a feeling that people all over the world are connected to us, even if we do not realize they are there. Americans feel that we should run our own economy in our own way with our own resources and that nothing much that happens in the rest of the world is important to us. Nothing could be further from the truth. The United States has less than 5 percent of the world's population yet uses 25 percent of the available resources. Among all the industrial countries, the United States is by far the smallest donor of international development assistance per capita, among other things. We really fear internationalism, yet our economy and our environment are definitely international.

Countries are so obsessed with increasing their economies that they exploit and consume their natural resources at the expense of their environment. Our former undersecretary of global affairs, Timothy Wirth, said that "the economy is a wholly owned subsidiary of the environment." It is, yet we talk about battles between the economy and environment as if they were equivalent. Our future is completely dependent on the way we manage our environment, yet the environment has been collapsing, becoming less and less sustainable with every passing year. We need to make a transition into something new, a new kind of economy that is not based on consumption but on sustaining, recycling, and renewing what we have.

Urban people are unaware of their dependence on nature. If you are walking down a city street, do you feel that you are dependent upon any natural productivity at all? Even when you go to the grocery store, you do not think of produce as growing, you just think of it as products. So although human beings are using or wasting about 40 percent of the total photosynthetic productivity of all life on Earth, we just do not experience it in any real way.

I have tried to do whatever I can to emphasize the importance of biological diversity, particularly the productive part. The three hundred thousand kinds of organisms that can photosynthesize include green plants, algae, and certain bacteria. Photosynthesizers are the sole source of real productivity; they are the only things on Earth individually able to generate products on a sustainable basis. Plants just keep growing and growing—without them, there would be no growth. They produce biomass by utilizing solar energy, transforming energy from the sun into chemical bonds that they use for their own life processes. The ten million other kinds of organisms in the world use them for their life processes. For the functioning of this planet and everything on it, plants are absolutely essential.

All of our food comes from plants, directly or indirectly. Ninety-three percent of our food comes from just 103 kinds of plants. Sixty percent of our food comes from just three plants: wheat, rice, and corn. The United States uses only ten varieties of wheat, six kinds of corn, and four types each of rice and potatoes. Yet there are thousands of kinds of plants that have been used as foods by people over the ages.

We urgently need to maintain the diversity of different kinds of plants. Agriculture's "green revolution" to feed the expanding human population was enabled by the scientific development of high-yielding varieties of major food crops. Nevertheless, monoculturing plants creates genetically uniform fields of crops—endless expanses of identical corn, rice, and wheat—susceptible to plagues of pests and diseases.

Corn blight destroyed 15 percent of the United States maize crop in 1970 and would have done worse had it not been for the existence of additional, genetically diverse corn strains. Fortunately, ancestral corn still existed in a tiny area of Mexico that had been scheduled for development but temporarily spared. Although their overall characteristics might not be attractive economically, these diverse, distinct strains might contain genes useful in the continuing struggle with pests and diseases.

Throughout the world, we are cultivating an aggregate area about the size of South America, and we need to improve our use of farmed land and to diversify it in order to produce food for the future. We have lost about 15 percent of our arable land over the last fifty years to urbanization and degradation of its fertility, at a time when we desperately need more land in cultivation. When humans began cultivating plants agriculturally around ten thousand years ago, there were only about five million people in the entire world. Now there are over six billion, and they are increasing rapidly. Already one-quarter of the people in the world are living in extreme poverty, and one-eighth of the world's people are starving. Simply feeding that population will demand increasing cooperation and a major change in the status quo.

Besides providing the food to keep us alive and healthy, plants also heal us when we are sick. Plants and natural organisms are the source of many of our medicines. Two-thirds of the people in the world are directly dependent on them for most medicines now. The other one-third of us, who use prescription drugs, are indirectly dependent on them in many cases. For example, the twenty top-selling prescription drugs in the United States contain a compound that originally came from a living organism or was improved or modified by using a natural product, or they are direct natural product derivatives that have been changed chemically after being produced, like steroid molecules that are chemically made into cortisone.

Plants produce an amazing array of natural compounds to defend themselves against diseases, insects, and other herbivores. The diversity of those compounds is incalculable, so there is no way of imagining what a compound would be without examining it. Plants' naturally occurring molecules have countless useful properties, which is why people are exploring plants for new kinds of potentially useful medicinal compounds all the time.

For example, taxol, which is derived from the bark of the Pacific yew tree (*Taxus brevifolia*), has been shown to shrink cancers of the ovary and the breast. The molecule was discovered in random testing of plants in the northwestern states. Artemisin, which is derived from a species of wormwood in China, holds promise as a new agent in the fight against malaria, a disease that afflicts 250 million people annually. Because the chemical structure of artemisin is unrelated to the chemical structure of other antimalarial medicines, its effect could not have been predicted in the laboratory. Because it attacks the plasmodium organism that causes malaria in a completely different way, artemisin or some derivative of it may become an effective defense against a dreaded disease. Only a fraction of the quarter-million kinds of plants have been fully examined, so there is a huge potential for additional medicines.

Furthermore, in terms of genetic engineering, we will be increasingly in need of plants' biological diversity. The nature of DNA has only been understood since 1953, when Watson and Crick posited that DNA was the genetic material. The first transfer of a gene from one kind of unrelated organism to another was made in 1973, only twenty-five years ago. We are starting to be able to transfer genes from one organism to another to improve the characteristics of the recipient organism.

In doing things like sequencing the human genome and the genomes of other kinds of organisms, we are beginning to know how genes differ. At this point we do not even know the difference between corn and human beings. We are trying to understand the functioning of genes so that we know the differences between them, as well as what characteristics are associated with which genes. This will increase flexibility in altering characteristics of organisms, which is valuable for practicing precision agriculture to cope with population growth and environmental damage.

Understandably, many people are concerned about the possible negative consequences of genetic technology, but it is not the technology as much as what you make with it and how you use what you make with it that has potential negative consequences. We cannot make genes; we can only transfer them. The ability to transfer genes between different kinds of organisms and then use the altered organisms in precise ways is something that could be very helpful. The question is, how intelligently are we going to do it?

When you lose an individual kind of plant to extinction, it is not like losing just one item from a grocery shelf. We are losing a whole repertoire of genes—individual organisms that have evolved along with all the rest of life for the past three and a half billion years and thus are unique. By driving countless organisms into extinction, we are losing the very elements we need for our own sustainability.

Extinction is happening so rapidly that we expect to lose as many as 50,000 of the 250,000 kinds of plants over the next few decades, and as many as two-thirds of all plant species over the next century. That is a scale of extinction as great as what happened when the dinosaurs disappeared. It would seriously change the character of life on Earth, of evolution, and of all our possibilities for the future.

If you think about the whole evolution of life on Earth, the Earth is four and a half billion years old, yet organisms have been on land less than half a billion of those years. Plants were among the first to colonize land. The organisms that exist on land evolved into communities, particularly during the last three hundred million years. They formed forest communities in which the interactions among the individual kinds of organisms shaped their destinies together. Since the last great extinction event at the end of the Cretaceous, about sixty-five million years ago, the number of species on Earth has been growing in a more or less continuous accumulation; when our ancestors, the genus *Homo,* evolved about two million years ago, the diversity of life was at a very high level.

Plants are the structure of nature's communities. They provide the base on which other organisms exist. Above ground, insects, birds, and animals feed on the plants, pollinate them, and disperse their seeds. Under ground, soil dwellers like earthworms, fungi, and bacteria decompose and recycle nutrients deposited by plants.

The aggregations of plants and organisms in communities, whether they are salt marsh communities, prairie communities, oak woodland communities, and so on, are what really keep the world sustainable and productive. They generate and retain soil, purify water, replenish watersheds, absorb pollution, regulate climate, and maintain atmospheric balance. It is only by preserving natural communities that we can have those benefits.

Communities collapse when their plant base is diminished. Tropical soils are infertile because the nutrients are held within the plants and other organisms. The roots of even tall trees are often very shallow, in part so they can quickly capture nutrients from fallen leaves and transfer them right back to the trees, and in part because the high rainfall causes rapid leaching of the soil. If the land is deforested, the soil cannot sustain its fertility, and it rapidly degrades into a biological desert.

In Europe and America, over 90 percent of the wetlands, meadows, prairies, and virgin forests have been destroyed by development or pollution. Plants cannot escape the conditions surrounding them; they thrive or decay with their environment. A tree that lives 150 years in a rural setting will last only 30 years in a typical city and just 7 years in a downtown area.

Cities depend on nature. For example, the water in New York City is largely purified by percolation through the various catchment basins in the Catskills. When the watershed became degraded by development, the water fell below EPA drinking standards. If the Catskills had not been protected and restored immediately, New York would have had to spend $6 billion to build water purification plants to provide the same services that nature provides free, plus an additional $300 million annually to operate them. Once those calculations were carefully made, the city moved quickly to protect its watershed in the Catskills by purchasing the land as a reserve, protected from industrial and agricultural development.

It is basically the communities of organisms that provide ecosystem services that keep the world functioning, pleasant, and enjoyable to live in. Plants are delightful. We like to have them around us—to see and smell and touch them. We love their flowers and express our emotions by giving them. They soften our whole environment, making our world beautiful and memorable. The spiritual satisfaction they give us makes our lives more meaningful and worthwhile.

Our first system of communication must have developed to deal with the variety of organisms that our ancestors encountered. Our brains and language evolved as our knowledge of the plants we depended on increased. They provided our original home on land as well as everything we needed. Our survival still depends primarily on plants.

Further Reading

Peter Raven and George B. Johnson. *Biology.* 5th ed. William C. Brown, 1999.

Peter Raven, Ray F. Evert, and Susan E. Eichhorn. *Biology of Plants.* 6th ed. Worth, 1999.

Peter Raven and Kunio Iwatsuki, eds. *Evolution and Diversification of Land Plants.* Springer-Verlag, 1997.

Peter Raven and George Johnson. *Understanding Biology.* 3d ed. William C. Brown, 1995.

Peter Raven, Donald Osterbrock, and Joseph Miller, eds. *Origins and Extinctions.* Yale University Press, 1988.

Peter Raven and Gilbert Lawrence, eds. *Coevolution of Animals and Plants.* University of Texas Press, 1980.

Biological Diversity

THOMAS LOVEJOY

IT REALLY ALL STARTED WHEN I WAS FOUR-
teen. The seeds of it might have been there before,
but I was not conscious of it. At that point, it was
time for me to go away to school, and there were a whole lot of
choices to look at. So we left New York City and went one hundred
miles to visit the first one. We did not get any further than the Millbrook School; as soon as I saw its zoo I did not want to look anywhere else! Without really knowing what I was doing, I said, "This
is where I want to go."

The zoo had been started by a wonderful, brilliant, charismatic,
eccentric biology teacher, Frank Trevor. He captured my interest in
biology and nature for life. It has just kept increasing ever since and
was helped along by subsequent mentors in my educational progression. One was Phil Humphrey, who was my freshman adviser at
Yale and is about to retire as director of the Natural History Museum of the University of Kansas. Another, Dillon Ripley, was director of the Natural History Museum at Yale and then came to
Washington to be secretary of the Smithsonian Institution. Loom-
ing large was my thesis chair, G. Evelyn Hutchinson, the great ecologist. They all cared about what was happening to nature. As Ripley put it, every biologist with a conscience should spend time on
conservation.

All I ever really wanted to be was a twentieth-century version of a nineteenth-century biologist, going to wild, exotic places to study weird and wonderful things—and coming back as infrequently as possible, just often enough to keep the funding going.

So it was destined, in a way, that I would go someplace; the only question was where. My junior year it was Nubia, in the middle of the Egyptian desert, where I collected birds, spiders, scorpions, lizards, and rodents. Later it was Kenya, where I collected birds for the Peabody Museum at Yale. So I first thought about doing my doctoral research in East Africa. But I was a little worried about the political transitions and insurrections going on there in the sixties. I did not want to get halfway through the research and not be able to finish.

Then I had the good fortune to go to the Amazon in 1965, an opportunity that Phil Humphrey arranged for me. I lived there from 1967 to 1969 while I did the research for my thesis. At that time, the Amazon was really isolated. You were cut off from what else went on in the world. In the few outposts that did exist, the telephones did not work; so what communication there was (and often it wasn't) was by mail or telegram. The Trans-Amazon highway had not been conceived of yet. The highway from Brasília to Belém had only been in place five years.

People were already exclaiming about colonization pressure, deforestation, and such ills. Then Daniel Ludwig came in with his wild scheme to develop the Amazon. The first conservation publication I wrote was about all that, "The Trans-Amazonica: Highway to Extinction."

We were sequestered. Living in the midst of the rain forest was like being enveloped in the great womb of the Amazon. My wife gave birth to twin daughters while we were there, although they were actually born in Rio de Janeiro because we were not so foolish as to try delivering them on the forest floor in the middle of the jungle. I sank into an existence of living and working in the wilderness: up at 3:30 in the morning, trekking through the forest to find birds before dawn, then catching and banding them until daylight faded.

The rain forest is very different from what people think it is; they imagine the rain forest alive with animals everywhere jumping on you. It is not. If you do not allow your mind to go racing off thinking about things that might do something to you, it is actually a benevolent kind of place. You really feel the peacefulness of it all. When you go into the forest, you do not see much, because everything is hiding from everything else. Much of what you do see is small stuff, insects of all kinds such as butterflies and ants. Once you begin to pay attention to them, they are utterly fascinating in their own right.

At first, the rain forest seems almost bewilderingly simple, that is, until you learn enough about it to be able to sense some of the difference. You do not notice individual things as much because each thing appears to be part of everything around it. Unlike temperate-forest plants, which grow separately, rain forest plants grow together. Every available niche is overflowing with living inhabitants: it is a giant green web of interlocking organisms.

Above you, layers of life are piled on top of each other. Shrubs, ferns, palms, trees of differing kinds and heights hung with huge vines, laddered lianas, and coiling creepers are intertwined together, meshed into an endless mosaic. Plants grow on plants growing on other plants. Flowering gardens cluster on terraced tree branches, orchids cascade in profusion, bromeliads perch like birds on branches. Epiphytic plants clumped on bark collect water and absorb nutrients from the air, providing homes and food for other plants and peculiar creatures. An amazing array of organisms resides at every level of the canopy.

Under this living umbrella, your senses are continually aroused. While winds whip the canopy above, tropical thunderstorms filter through the layered leaves, dissipating into mist in the still air below. The air is so humid that it is permeated with organic smells. Fertile scents drift down from above, and earthy odors waft up from the moist soil. Whatever falls to the ground is decomposed in weeks, compared to the years it takes in cooler, drier climates.

As well as being bathed in moisture and immersed in smells, you are always surrounded by sounds. At night sound is pervasive. In the darkness, it feels tangible. If it does not scare you, it can be entertaining and sometimes even amusing. The three senators I recently took there snored all night, accompanied by frogs improvising in response. It was quite a combo swinging in the hammocks.

While you are living there, you are so embedded in it that you do not know its full effect on you. Although I recognized the scientific importance of the forest while I was working in it, I did not realize what it meant to me personally. That moment of revelation came when I took my first bunch of senators to the Amazon in 1989. At that point, I had not been into the forest or to my research project for a year and a half. I was only a few steps down the path into my favorite camp in the forest when suddenly I had the feeling of coming home. That is when I realized the forest had come to mean something to me on a deeper level. I belonged here.

Now there are times when I want to go to the forest just for what I call a nature fix—restoration of my mental and emotional well-being. If I had lived and worked in Alaskan forests or African savannah, I would have had the same reaction there. You have to experience it yourself to know what it is actually like. That is why I take decision makers there and provide them with a real experience of the rain forest.

My first bunch included Al Gore, Tim Wirth, John Heinz, Peter Benchley, and Ben Bradlee, the executive editor of the *Washington Post*. It was quite a group. Two weeks before we arrived in Brazil Chico Mendez, the rubber tapper and activist who had brought attention to the destruction of the rain forest and the people dependent on it, was assassinated. With all the international media present, we were the focus of incredible attention and a tremendous amount of distraction. I have been told that our delegation's concern for the forest and its people actually began to change the way Brazil looked at all this.

I call them "my campers." One is vice president, one undersecretary of state, another secretary of the interior, and so forth. I have now had sixteen senators make the trip, which is a very positive statement about our Senate. It was their idea, not mine. As it has to matter enough for them to make it a priority and somehow fit it into their tight schedules simultaneously, it only happens sporadically.

They are given a big briefing book filled with information, but while we are going through the forest I do not talk much about it. I just add little bits and pieces as we are exploring the place and discovering things. We have discussions around the tables at camp. The ones who go are generally bright people who are curious, so they ask the right questions. I let them learn through their own experiences. An important part of this process is having something that has been an abstraction gradually become concrete to them. Immediate contact with their environment allows them to perceive it directly. They never forget the experience. And, of course, it is a great adventure they can talk about forever after. In exploring what is left of the largest tropical forest, they get the message that the rain forest is a necessary repository of diversity, that it is important for the world; yet it is being destroyed, and it is imperative to do something about it.

After returning from living in South America myself, I went to Philadelphia to work at the Academy of Natural Sciences, which is the oldest natural history museum in the country. The academy's honorary chair was another role model, Ruth Patrick. Like her contemporary, Rachel Carson, Ruth is a biologist who developed an ecological perspective and informed the public about the consequences of environmental pollution. Fifty years ago, Ruth pioneered the study of freshwater algae and other aquatic organisms to determine ecosystem health.

While it was inspiring being with Ruth, unlike her, I was not doing science. I did various administrative jobs at the academy, none of which was scientific. So I looked around for a job and wrote to everybody I knew. In response, a note arrived from David Challinor, the Smithsonian's assistant secretary of science, telling me that the World Wildlife Fund–US was looking for a project administrator.

Although it was a petty bureaucratic title, I went and met with the executive director anyway. They only had twelve staff then and were not looking for a Ph.D., but we ended up taking a chance on each other. I thought I would stay two or three years; instead I stayed fourteen and built the program of the WWF–US. Certain elements of that still remain: a strong science link, a Western Hemisphere orientation, and an emphasis on biological diversity, which meant tropical forests. I was fortunate to know a lot about tropical forests when the public first wanted to know what was happening to them.

When I was responsible for WWF–US's conservation strategy for Latin America, I started an ambitious research project looking at forest fragments over time. It is currently a joint research project of the Smithsonian and the National Institute for Amazon Research in Brazil. The Minimum Critical Size of Ecosystems Project has continued for the last twenty years and is now known as the Biological Dynamic of Forest Fragments Project, although locally it is called Projeto Lovejoy, and I just think of it as "my baby."

As with any long-term project, I did not envision all the things it would be. Originally I thought of it as answering a simple scientific question: with a given amount of land, is it better to have a single large preserve or a lot of separate, small preserves? The altered landscape in Brazil offered an immense natural laboratory in which to observe such an experiment. Beginning in the seventies, Brazil encouraged economic development of the Amazon basin through tax incentives. In exchange for rights to clear a plot of rain forest, developers had to leave half the plot uncut.

With the cooperation of everyone involved, including the Brazilian government, funding organizations, conservation groups, developers, ranchers, workers, and scientists, the plots were surveyed and sized effectively for research. We created a massive patchwork of different-sized plots of forest surrounded by cleared land. The plots ranged from one to ten thousand hectares (one hectare being about two and a half acres).

This extensive experiment proved that a large, intact area is much more viable than the same amount of land in smaller pieces. But answering this simple question led to further questions, such as what size does a reserve have to be to remain viable, and how do we manage areas smaller than the ideal? We need to find out what conditions are necessary to sustain ecological diversity in reserves. You cannot just put a fence around a forest fragment or set a piece of land aside as a park and expect it to stay the same.

Of course, the problem is much more complicated than anyone realized. Even the apparent size of a forest fragment is not what it seems. The perimeter of the fragment is exposed to outside stress and deteriorates rapidly. The normal conditions of a rain forest, dampness and darkness, are replaced with drying heat and searing light near the periphery. The tall canopy collapses, and the understory growth withers. Exposure to wind alone causes small forest fragments to lose from 15 to 30 percent of their biomass. The forest starts dying from the outside in. Edge effects at the perimeter wear away the forest, shrinking the fragment over time. The outer edge moves inward so quickly that small plots become completely edge within months. So the acreage needs to have an adequate buffer zone to protect the periphery and to be large enough to begin with to compensate for the shrinkage.

Species shrink with the forest. Amazonian rain forests are the most species-rich habitats in the world, with a million different species living tightly together. That includes the most plant species anywhere, which support one-fifth of all bird species, as well as many of the most colorful butterflies, beetles and other exotic insects. They are all crammed together in tiny ecological niches, so enmeshed in the surrounding network of species and so specialized to their specific habitat that they cannot survive outside it.

As the reserves degrade, species leave if they have somewhere else to go or eventually die if they do not. A census is taken of resident species before the surrounding trees are cut and then of what species remain afterward and how long they last. It is extremely time-consuming to account for species in the most biologically diverse place on the planet—and heartbreaking to see them disappear.

One of the worst problems with rain forest deterioration is the difficulty of regeneration. The fragile seeds need to germinate soon after landing in the poor, infertile soil, which is so thin that the sparse nutrients rarely reach more than an inch or two below ground. Thus the intertwined tree roots are shallow, hardly holding the forest together. When trees are removed, the exposed soil washes away in the frequent downpours, leaving a hard, bare surface to bake in the tropical sun.

The project is an ongoing provider of new insights. Since it offers an opportunity to study whatever forest regrowth might occur naturally, secondary succession has been added as another priority for the project. That investigation is useful for reforestation and recovery of degraded lands. The deforestation rate in the tropics is around one hundred acres a minute, so restoration will become increasingly important. Trees contain a lot of carbon, which turns into carbon dioxide when they are burned. If you burn the tropical forests, you increase atmospheric carbon dioxide by 50 percent and double the greenhouse effect. Conversely, if you plant trees, you decrease it because they take in carbon and fix it. If every country's forests absorbed its carbon dioxide emissions, we could help stabilize atmospheric composition and limit the greenhouse effect. The six billion tons of carbon dioxide we add to the atmosphere every year could be substantially removed by global reforestation.

Obviously fragmenting forests is not good for any species, including us. Waves of one hundred million more people on this planet every year crash against the rain forests, felling trees and the species they contain. We should shift from thinking of nature as something existing within human domains to realizing that humans exist within the natural landscape. Instead of islands of wilderness in a sea of humanity, we should have islands of humanity in a sea of wilderness.

I do not believe our problems can be solved unless everybody is engaged. One way to involve a lot more people is through the media. We were fortunate with our television series, *Nature*. Scott McVay, who was head of the Geraldine Rockefeller Dodge Foundation, arranged for me to go to Channel 13 in New York. Scott and I got into it at a time when there was no real nature or wildlife programming on television.

For the meeting, I took an old BBC film with a real conservation message. *Forest in the Clouds* is mostly about how the cloud forest works. It starts with tree trunks getting off the ground where they are lying, standing up, and turning back into trees. The film is actually being played backwards. In the end, when it runs properly, you see what really happened to the forest.

That is what created the *Nature* program. It just hit at the right time, and we found a formula that works, which is different from what we originally thought. We conceived of something hard-hitting about how the world is going to hell. But we could not do it anyway, because we did not have any money. So all we could do was buy British nature films and give them an American soundtrack.

The formula, which is really the right formula, developed out of that. The programs show people nature's wonders and intricacies, reminding them that it is all disappearing. But in a polite British manner (rather than a rude American way), it offers a rather gentle reminder. If we had stuck with the original concept, we would have been lucky to last a second season. As it is, the programs are still inspiring and educating people about nature.

People have learned a great deal from watching nature programs, but they still have a lot more to learn. Most people are ignorant of how many benefits, such as medicines, come from nature now and can come from nature in the future. Antibiotics and vaccinations account for half the people in the world being alive now. Yet people who are alive because of them do not realize that they were derived from looking at how nature works.

We have no idea what biotechnology might be able to do for us. It already generates $100 billion annually by using biological diversity. It is sustainable because the biological resource is not normally destroyed through use of its applicable molecule. The rapid pace of technological development will also provide new opportunities for biological processes. Biologically based businesses already exist, and others are starting up. Bioindustry uses microbes to manufacture products instead of using chemical processes. As industrial ecology grows, bioremediation, which uses natural organisms to clean up, can make the waste stream of one industry feedstock for another.

Our basic wealth is in nature. Biodiversity provides us with billions of dollars of resources harvested directly from nature. That figure does not include the incalculable benefits provided by processes of nature that perform public services for free, which Paul Ehrlich talks about.

The way we use economics is deceptive. There are a lot of things outside the calculus that should be inside. Economics only uses present value; anything long-term is not considered economic, so it is not included. But all economic growth is at the cost of natural capital. Society succeeds from time to time in setting some long-term goals despite the economic calculus, but, by and large, economic forces are working against us. We can change that. There are ways to harness market forces on behalf of the environment. It is a matter of defining the rules.

One innovative redefinition of those rules is debt-for-nature swaps. While sitting on Capitol Hill taking part in hearings on the international debt crisis, I figured there must be a way to deal with debt and help the environment by the same means. The current system forces debtor countries to obtain foreign currency to pay interest on their debt. Without an industrial base, the only way developing countries can pay is by selling off their natural resources and growing cash crops for export. Debt servicing is at the expense of the environment.

The world's environmental problems are so great already, and developing nations' problems are increasing so rapidly, that the only way to deal with the fiasco is through massive financial aid or debt restructuring. So, in 1984, on the op-ed page of the *New York Times,* I proposed swapping debt for nature. Simply put, nations should receive credits against their foreign debt for protecting their natural resources; their creditors should get tax breaks in return.

Predictably, the idea encountered a lot of resistance. No one objects to converting massive debt for commercial purposes, but using it for a socially useful purpose is unthinkable. They would rather throw billions of dollars of debt away than use it for anything positive and productive. In my estimation, it does not make sense for governments to write off billions of dollars of debt for nothing, when it could be used for long-term investment in the future, namely in nature.

The positive consequences would extend long after the debt disappears. A debt-for-nature swap would not require new financial infusions from outside, and it would help generate income inside the country by contributing to local economies and improving the debtor nation's ability to repay its international loans. Massive debt cripples a nation's ability to cope with its worsening social needs, so that its environmental problems are not only ignored but often compounded. Assisting a country's conservation benefits its natural resource base as well as the international community.

I am disappointed that swapping foreign debt for conserving nature has not become more extensive. So far only a couple of hundred million has come out of all those billions of dollars of debt. On the other hand, the $200 million gain for nature conservation is more than from anything else. And it is not over yet. There is still a lot of government-to-government debt. Heaven knows what Mexican or Asian debt is selling for now, and who knows what anyone's debt will go for later on. You have to keep coming back to it as things change.

Debt-for-nature swaps are not a solution to the environmental problem; they are just a financial mechanism. But they do help creditor and debtor nations by restructuring loans to poor countries rich in natural resources and biodiversity. The value allocated to nature helps limit its destruction and promotes conservation in developing nations. Among other things, the transactions have provided money for park reserves, as well as training in conservation.

Such local endeavors are helpful for assessing and preserving global biodiversity. We need to know what is happening to our natural resources. Biological diversity is the most sensitive set of environmental indicators we have. I am interested in a biological survey for what it adds to our natural knowledge. In addition, I am interested in what it can do for resource management, both in relation to conserving resources and for opening up doors of opportunity.

A distributed electronic network of biodiversity databases is beginning to develop here, in part spontaneously and in part through the Division of Biological Sciences of the U.S. Department of the Interior. It is also starting to happen at the international level, through the nations of the OECD (Organization for Economic Cooperation and Development) and their megascience forums. I am chairing a subcommittee on biodiversity for them.

I am helping the Department of the Interior organize the National Biological Survey, a new federal agency created to consolidate work in field biology. It combines research related to management of ecosystems by Department of the Interior agencies such as the National Park Service and the Fish and Wildlife Service. Management for select species, such as game or endangered species, is far simpler than ecosystem management. But it is much less effective than managing the ecosystem to care for all its species. That is what we are trying to do.

The National Biological Survey will also compile existing biodiversity data in federal and state agencies, botanical gardens, and environmental organizations. Then it will collaborate with them to collect additional data where needed to provide an increasingly comprehensive picture of America's changing biological diversity. Biodiversity databases are an enormous undertaking. The overwhelming problem is that most of the information has not even been collected yet; it is still out there in the wild.

One irreplaceable value of nature is as a living library on which to build the life sciences. Biodiversity is our collection of living knowledge. Each species is a unique set of solutions to a specific set of biological problems, equivalent not to a single book but to a series of volumes. If we lose a species, we lose that knowledge. Unlike information in books, once the species is gone, all the information goes with it.

The president of a major university once asked me what useful purpose was served by biodiversity. When I asked him how he felt about books and libraries, he was so puzzled that it was obvious he had never considered living species as analogous sources of information. Society places enormous value on books, data banks, and museums of inanimate objects, yet it devalues storehouses of live knowledge. We value libraries enough to pay for their support and to keep adding books to them. People want public libraries to have lots of books, even if they do not read them all themselves. If someone set fire to their local library, residents would be outraged. When the library is in flames, nobody doubts that books are burning.

Why is the public not similarly alarmed when rain forests are burned to the ground and biodiversity goes up in smoke? Recently, people around the world saw photos of the terrible fires deliberately set to burn Indonesia's forests. The smoke was so bad that citizens in neighboring countries could barely breathe. Yet no one even protested. Similarly, massive fires in the Amazon this year were worse than any before. But people do not know that, even though the smoke cloud was bigger than Brazil in the remote sensing image I saw. If you add those two together, in 1997 more of the world was burning than ever before in all of recorded history.

We are burning creation. It is going up in flames. The patriarch of the Eastern Church just said that causing an extinction is an "environmental sin." That is a good ethical summary. Every time we cause an extinction, we end something that has a lineage of billions of years. That should give us pause. But instead of pausing, we are speeding up the destruction.

So here we are at a time when the future of the flora and fauna of the planet is being decided. It is going to be in our lifetime. You can just say it is all going to hell, and do nothing—to make sure that you are right—making it all self-fulfilling. Or you can be optimistic to the extent that you think you can make a difference. If that is the case, you keep going. It is hard to keep your head and your heart, but you have to. Anybody who is still trying at this stage has that point of view.

My daughter is giving birth right now. By the time her child is my age, it will be halfway into the next century. What is it going to be like for my grandchild and all the other children being born now? How will they live?

Further Reading

Thomas Lovejoy and Richard Primack. *Ecology, Conservation, and Management of Southeast Asian Rainforests.* Yale University Press, 1995.

Thomas Lovejoy and Robert Peters. *Global Warming and Biological Diversity.* Yale University Press, 1994.

Thomas Lovejoy and Ghillean Prance. *Amazonia.* Pergamon Press, 1985.

The Nature of Things

DAVID SUZUKI

MY GRANDPARENTS IMMIGRATED TO CANADA at the turn of the century. They left their homeland reluctantly to come to a foreign place with an alien culture and an unknown language. As immigrants, they expected their children to be successful. Success, of course, was defined by making a lot of money. Being the eldest of six sons, my father was expected to be the first son to succeed. Yet, unlike his parents, he was born here, and his real love was for the land. He worked hard, but he loved gardening, fishing, and camping, which were absolutely alien to his parents. He was always a bitter disappointment to them because he wasted his time on such worthless activities instead of making money.

Most of my early memories are of camping and fishing with my dad. We bought our first tent when I was four, a little pup tent that I loved. Vancouver was surrounded with nature, so on weekends we would drive to a favorite place. Dad would put his pack on his back and me on his shoulders, and off we would go to camp in the woods. Sometimes we went to a river where dad borrowed a friend's horse, which we rode along the bank upstream. Then we let the horse go home, pitched our tent, and spent the weekend fishing our way back downstream.

We also went fishing during the week after work. One night when we were hiking around Loon Lake in the dark, we spotted large eyes staring at us, silently sizing us up. Fortunately, Dad had taught me to love and respect nature rather than to fear it, so encountering a bear was exciting rather than frightening. Those early experiences camping and fishing influenced the rest of my life. They were such an important part of my childhood that I began camping with my own children right after they were born.

We lived in Vancouver until I was six. When the Japanese bombed Pearl Harbor, the American and Canadian governments decided that people of Japanese descent were enemy aliens and constituted a danger. So they confiscated our property and moved us from the West Coast inland to a ghost town left from the gold rush. Unlike our American counterparts, we were not fenced in by barbed wire or armed guards; we were totally free. People cannot believe it when I tell them I was unaware of how bad the situation was. For me it was paradise because we lived in a cabin in the midst of nature. It was like living in a giant park; in fact, Valhalla now is a provincial park. It was an amazing setting in the Slocan Valley between the spectacular mountains of the Selkirk Range. The mountains were home to countless animals, including deer, coyotes, and bears, while the lakes and rivers overflowed with fish.

I did not have to go to school for a while because of a lack of teachers, so I was free to spend my time exploring the wonders around me, and I learned far more than I ever could have in school. My sisters and I wandered the hillsides gathering flowers and unusual rocks and discovering all kinds of fascinating creatures. For me the war years were a wonderful time of enjoying wildlife and wilderness.

As the war was coming to an end, the provincial government could not solve its "yellow peril" problem, so it offered us two choices. We could go to Japan, which for us meant going to a foreign country; or, if we remained in Canada, we had to go east of the Rockies. Exiled from our beloved British Columbia, we sought refuge in southern Ontario.

My dad and mom found work as laborers on a farm, and I worked along with them in the summers. My father made less than $1,000 a year (of course, inflation has increased values since then). Although we were very poor, we did not feel poor because we always had enough to live on and plenty to eat. Children today would regard the way we lived as primitive; for us it was an invigorating lifestyle that filled more than our stomachs.

My mother bottled fruits and vegetables in the summer for us to live on in the winter. We foraged for food everywhere, finding mushrooms in the orchards, nutritious roots underground, and edible weeds growing along the railway tracks. After work Dad and I went out on our bikes to catch fish. With a little net he made for me, we dipped in the ditches, creeks, and ponds, catching dinner and fascinating creatures to keep. Scrounged glass jars were filled with sunfish, catfish, and turtles, then carefully carried home to be my magical aquariums.

My parents also made me a butterfly net. Dad bent wire into a hoop that he attached to a wooden handle; then Mom sewed mosquito netting around it. Immediately I started insect collecting, which soon became an avid passion. I wanted my children to share my enjoyment of insects, but they do not want to kill them. My daughters have a different kind of sensitivity toward the environment.

We lived for four years in Canada's southernmost town, where Heinz ketchup is made. Leamington was a great place for me because it was a fifteen-minute bike ride from Lake Erie, which was full of fish. Fish was our major food, so I went down there all the time and brought home strings of fish such as perch and catfish for dinner. Now the fish are poisonous because so many pollutants have been dumped into the Great Lakes. Back then Lake Erie was so prolific that when mayflies hatched out of the water, their tiny three-centimeter bodies piled up four feet high on the beach. It was one of the most amazing biological phenomena I have ever seen. Within a decade that entire hatch was gone because pesticides and washing detergents sterilized the lake, which was declared "dead."

Later we lived in another Ontario town named London. I biked to my grandparents' farm and often stopped in a swamp to find frogs, reptiles, skunks, and foxes. At my grandparents' place, there were a creek and woods nearby, where I played for hours. I also spent a lot of time on the Thames River, the major waterway running through town. I knew every pool and where to catch different fish through-out the year, such as silver bass and pike coming in the spring to spawn. Other animals fished with me; I remember seeing a raccoon pull out a crayfish and then wash it before eating.

Today, if I said, "Let's go down to the Thames River and catch a fish," a parent would recoil in horror at the thought of their child wading in that river, because now it is a toxic sewer. There are hardly any fish left, and even if you caught one you could not eat it. The creek that I dipped in to get freshwater clams and fish now runs through culverts underground. The farm where my grandparents lived is a huge high-rise complex. The swamp where I spent so much of my time playing is paved over and is now an enormous shopping mall.

When I compare my childhood to that of children in that modern city today, I am shocked by the difference. They do not have the woods, river, and swamp to play in, so they hang out in what is there—shopping malls and electronic game galleries. They grow up in a biological desert, a concrete maze of roads, buildings, machines, humans, and the few plants and animals that are allowed to survive. Anything we do not want in our artificial environment, we destroy. Insects, for instance, are invaders to be killed. We teach children in cities that nature is the enemy; it is dirty, disgusting, and dangerous. So, rather than being curious and fascinated, children often recoil in fear when they see a wild animal. Urban inhabitants become so dis-tanced from nature that they forget they are still biological creatures.

A striking example of this is some friends who came from Japan to visit us. They told us that they love cities, and when we took them to our cottage on the island we realized they were comfortable only in artificial surroundings. Not only the children but the adults too were afraid to go outside, so they wanted to stay inside the whole time. The children were even afraid of the dog. When we did go out-side, they felt so uncomfortable that they did not know what to do.

They were not used to seeing anything alive and were repulsed by such simple things as rolling over a rock and seeing crabs, finding a clam, or catching a fish. Of course, all the food they buy in Japan is packaged, without any traces of blood, fur, feathers, or scales. Later

I met a teacher in Tokyo who told me that children in her class assume that everything brought home from the supermarket spends its entire existence in plastic wrap and Styrofoam.

I did not believe how common this notion was until I did a television series for children called *The Nature Connection.* One of the shows was about a farm, so I took two ten-year-old children from Toronto. We were there two days and had a wonderful time: we collected eggs from the chickens, milked cows, rode horses, and played with the animals. On the third day, I took them to a slaughterhouse. The boy burst into tears because it had never occurred to him that hot dogs and hamburgers are made from animals.

Such ignorance is not limited to children. A friend, a producer at the Canadian Broadcasting Corporation, took a woman out into the country and stopped at a pick-your-own vegetable farm. She had never been on a farm and was disturbed that the vegetables were growing in the dirt. She was a university graduate but did not know that vegetables grow in the ground. Like her, many people do not realize food is biological, because it seems so synthetic. Commercial food is processed to the point where it has no life in it. We destroy all the vitality and eat what is left.

The teacher in Tokyo does something interesting with her class. She asks them to write down all the things you need for your nutrition that were not once living. The kids mention all kinds of things such as miso soup, but it turns out that everything you eat has been alive. So they understand that the food you eat was a living plant or animal that gave its life for you and now makes up your body. That is a very profound lesson.

We are nourished by nature, but we are so disconnected from life that most adults do not even realize that. Living in artificial, manmade environments makes us forget our biological nature. We think our greatest achievement is independence from nature, but we are still as dependent on air, water, and soil as any other living organism. It is not technology that cleanses the air for us or manages the water cycle or gives us our food. It is the biodiversity of nature. We live in a finite world where matter is endlessly recycled through biological action. The variety of living things on this planet is what keeps it livable.

The more urban our environment, the more ignorant we are of how our world actually works. In Toronto, if you ask someone, "Where does your food grow?" or "Where does your water come from?" or "Where does your toilet water go?" they do not know. If you tell them that their toilet flushes into Lake Ontario, half a kilometer from the intake pipe for their drinking water, they are absolutely shocked.

We are under the illusion that technology controls the world around us and that therefore we are in control of the world. The farther we remove ourselves from nature, the more dependent we become on technology, and the more vulnerable we are to its failure. We can become victimized by the technological monster we depend on, just as we are already run by the speeded-up demands of our high-tech treadmill.

Trying to escape reality, we live in an increasingly illusory world. We are losing the ability to sense the real world. Being unaware of our biological nature leads to being out of touch with our own bodies, as well as those of others. We reject our animality, even though being with animals makes us more human. As the prevalence of pets attests, we have a natural bond with animals. Children are fascinated by animals from birth. The programs on my television series, *The Nature of Things,* that generate the greatest response from viewers are reports on natural history, particularly shows on animals.

When my family lived in Ontario, Dad borrowed a car so we could go to the Detroit Zoo, which was regarded as one of the great zoos. That was an amazing experience for me; I was overwhelmed by the sense of variety and abundance of living things. Actually seeing creatures such as a rhinoceros and a duck-billed platypus was unbelievable. Desiring to see the animals living freely in their natural habitat, I dreamed all my life of going to the Serengeti plain, Australia, and the Amazon. Essentially the Detroit Zoo aroused those dreams and stimulated my interest in studying zoology.

After I became an adult, I did travel to all those places. It is truly sad what has happened to them in my lifetime. When I was a child, the Amazon was an isolated place where outsiders had seldom gone. By the time I got there in 1988, there was no place foreigners had not invaded. The tribes had experienced extermination at the rate of about one a year since 1900. When I visited the Serengeti in 1985, there were more black rhinos in the Cincinnati Zoo than on the entire Serengeti plain. When I made it to Australia, there were still some duck-billed platypuses, but the remaining animals there were under siege.

We may not care about the deaths of millions of our fellow creatures, but they affect us anyway. These creatures not only share our home with us, they are our relatives. Ninety-nine percent of our genetic information is identical with that of our closest relatives, the great apes. Geneticists are realizing that all life forms evolved from the same original cell—which means that all living creatures are descended from the same parent cell, and we are all related.

In my lifetime the planet has changed from being incredibly abundant to being barely able to sustain life in many places. A few years ago, when my daughter was nine, I took her to the Toronto Zoo, thinking she would have the same response that I had as a child. When we got there, the first thing she asked was, "Daddy, are there many of these left?" At every exhibit she was worried that the animals were rare or endangered. For her, "extinction" is a constant word. It is tragic that whereas in my childhood the zoo was a chance to see what potential lies in nature, for children today, zoos are a reminder of the fact that creatures are disappearing and perhaps the animals in the zoo are the only ones left.

My father told me that when he was young, there was only forest where my house is now. Fishing right here, he caught sea-run cutthroats and sturgeon, things we would not imagine swimming around Vancouver today. My daughter and I used to go fishing out here and caught little flounders, which we ate. A few years ago we caught one that had lumps on its fins. I thought it was a parasite, so I cut it open, expecting to see a worm, but it was cancer. So we stopped fishing here.

In a world of such rapid change, we have marginalized the very people who could provide us with the perspective to counter the whole thrust of this change: women, children, elders, and indigenous people. One of the first things I learned from the aboriginal peoples

I have met around the world was to take your elders very seriously, respect them, and listen to what they have to say.

As I crossed Canada from one end to the other countless times, I talked to our elders. I asked fishermen in the Maritimes, "What was the fishing like when you were a kid?" I asked loggers in British Columbia, "What were the forests like years ago?" I asked farmers in the prairies, "What were the crops like then?" I asked them, "What were your neighborhoods and communities like then; how did you care for each other?"

Our elders tell us that all across Canada, the country has changed beyond description. In the span of a single human lifetime, we have radically altered our country. In North America, we have always said, "There's plenty more where that came from." But there is not plenty more anymore, and there will never be any more if we continue in the same way.

We are using up what rightly belongs to all generations. We have received this abundance from the past, and we have a sacred obligation to keep it intact for future generations. Just look at the change that has happened in the lifetime of our elders and project that rate of change into the future. What are we leaving for our children? Parents have always tried to ensure the security of their offspring, but the future fills us with fear for them. One of the reasons I do what I do is so I can look my children directly in the eye and say to them, "I'm doing the best I can." If we all do our best, we might be able to reassure them with more confidence that "everything is going to be all right."

The most frightening phrase I hear today is, "There used to be." I hear younger and younger people saying, "There used to be a creek here . . . there used to be woods over there . . . there used to be birds and animals around." We act as if all this is just lost somehow, and it is no big deal. We are passively observing this in our lifetime as though we could wipe these things out without any consequences. I do not think you can go on saying about the planet, "There used to be . . . ," or we are going to end up with, "There used to be people."

We have a seasonal ritual that our family celebrates. Every summer we go to the Okanagan Valley to pick ripe, luscious fruit off the trees.

Visiting it annually, we have seen astounding changes over the years. A development binge has resulted in such rapid construction that the water supply is insufficient for the houses. Orchards have been buried under strip malls, destroying Canada's most fertile fruit-producing area. One of the country's loveliest and most productive places is now a concrete wasteland, just like everywhere else.

It does not matter where you go—it is the same boring uniformity all over the world. I travel a lot for my television programs, and when I get off an airplane in Nairobi, or Beijing, or Tokyo, it all looks the same. You might as well stay home. As we monoculture the planet into a global marketplace dominated by international economics, we diminish a tremendous amount of human and biological diversity.

We increasingly revel in what human beings do: our computers, our buildings, our transport. In our worship of human beings and achievements we have lost our inspiration from the natural world. The real inspiration, the wonders, the diversity, the life, are in nature. Without those, we will attempt to make the planet over and thereby lose it.

If you go to a place where we have done that, such as New York, and see how people exist, you notice that they not only breathe polluted smog; they also live under a cloud of fear. They cannot escape it even inside their apartments: they have multiple locks on the door, plus all kinds of alarms and security devices, in addition to the guards downstairs. People exist in a state of war with their surroundings. That is no way to live.

Can't we create communities where you know the people in your local area because you live, work, and play there? Places where, if you are in a jam, you can just call your neighbor up and say, "Can you help me out?" It is clear that we have lost a sense of community, place, and belonging. We need to re-create those kinds of communal values.

Unfortunately, the opposite is happening. Everything that governments and corporations are doing now, for example free trade—NAFTA and GATT—is hell-bent on globalizing the marketplace, which is ultimately destructive of local communities. If citizens here will not give up their societal benefits and sacrifice medical care, pensions, and social security to cut costs, then companies will go to Mexico or some other "undeveloped" country where they do not have to pay such expenses. You see it happening all across Canada and the United States: local communities are being trashed by the multinational corporations.

Communities can be the counterforce to corporatization. In order to withstand corporate forces, they need to become independent and self-reliant. To avoid exploitation by the global economy for short-term profit, they must care for their own human and natural resources for the long term. Being locally based, they are the social sector that can best adapt to and protect the immediate environment.

Communities could be the survival unit of the future. This challenge has led me to establish a private foundation to create sustainable communities based on the grassroots support of ordinary people. We are trying to empower people by giving them a vision of a way of living that is sustainable. A sustainable society lives within the planet's productive capacity and protects the fundamental sources of life: air, water, soil, and biological diversity. We believe that when people understand that we are threatened with global environmental collapse, they will transform society from the bottom up. (Obviously it will never happen from the top down.) Our foundation is committed to that process of transformation.

Bioregions are fundamental to creating sustainable communities, so we have an expert bioregionalist, Doug Aberly, in our group. If you look at maps of counties and countries, you see that they are drawn in straight lines, ignoring topographic features. Bioregional areas follow natural boundaries along the tops of mountains and valley bottoms. British Columbia has about twenty bioregions, which follow major watersheds. The bioregions correspond almost exactly to the lands of the original native tribes throughout North America. Indigenous people lived bioregionally all over the world.

In contrast, our ecological "footprint" extends far beyond our local boundaries. In our crazy economy, rather than get food from farms a few miles away, we buy stuff that has crossed continents and oceans. We are using nonrenewable resources like oil to ship food over long distances. Wendell Berry told me that in North America food travels an average of about two thousand miles from where it is grown to where it is eaten. Food flows in from all over the world throughout the year, as though the planet were just one endless market. We have lost our sense of nature's rhythms and act as though the seasons no longer affect us. Our foundation encourages buying local, seasonal food because food that comes from where we live is the best for us. We should be aware of the rhythms of nature; we are of the earth and intimately connected to it through the food we consume.

I wrote a book called *Wisdom of the Elders* about native perspectives. When I did a book tour, I ended up at the Six Nations reserve in Ontario. The elders welcomed me into their longhouse, where they said, "Today's a holiday; we're celebrating the first day of the sap which is starting to run through the trees, and we are putting taps in for maple sugar. We take around thirty days a year as holidays to celebrate events: the first snowfall, the last day of ice, the first buds, the coming of the winds." Throughout the year, aboriginal people are celebrating the things that keep them alive and honoring their sense of connectedness to life. We do not do that. Like our ancestors, we need to create festivals to celebrate our relationship to nature and begin healing our souls.

Aboriginal people have lived on their land for thousands of years. Every rock, tree, river, and mountain is sacred in their culture because it is part of them; it is their identity. When natives struggle to preserve their land, they are protecting what it means to them. We just say, "Here's a million bucks; give us your land." We have overemphasized the material, economic things. We need to recognize that there are fundamental spiritual values that are important for us.

When I say this, people look at me as though I am weird: "What are you talking about? Are you a religious nut?" Yet when I tell them the story about my home, they can relate to what I mean. I bought our house when my wife was in graduate school. She was away when I found it, so I just went ahead and bought it, even though I was scared because we could not afford it.

We have had it now for more than twenty years, and during that time we have made it over. The garden was created by her father, who lives upstairs. The place has such a prime location, right on the water, that we get letters from real estate agents saying, "It's a hot market for foreign speculators, so sell your property!" Finally I got so mad that I assessed the personal value of my house. First, every aspect of this house has my wife in it. When she was away in graduate school, and when she taught at Harvard for five years, I could be anywhere in the house and feel that she was here. No one can see that, but I know it.

My dad is a cabinetmaker, and he made the kitchen cabinet for our apartment when we first got married. When I bought this house, I ripped out the existing cabinet and put dad's here. It looks odd because it does not fit, but every time I open the cabinet door, I think of my father. My best friend came from Toronto and helped me build the fence; then he carved a handle for the gate. Every time I open the gate, he is here too.

I like asparagus and raspberries, so my father-in-law planted them beside his beloved flower garden. When I eat them, I picture him in the garden he tends with such care. In the dogwood is a tree house I built and then enjoyed watching the children play in as they grew up. Underneath it, our dog is buried in his favorite digging hole, with the other family pets that followed. Along the back fence climbs a clematis where I scattered my mother's ashes when she died. After my sister's daughter died, we put some of Janice's ashes there too. When the beautiful purple flowers of the clematis bloom, the pain of their loss is lightened because I feel that they are still here.

Family and friends are a palpable presence, intermingled with the experiences and memories of a lifetime. That is what I put on my list, and when I finished it, I realized that those are the things that make this place far more than a piece of property—that make it my home. To me they are priceless, but on the market they are totally worthless.

We all have memories and experiences that matter to us. We have sentimental things that we keep: a letter from a parent who is dead, or from a past love. When my children were born we made an album for each one and filled it with things like the little ID bracelet from the hospital, the baby shower gifts, and, as they got older, their first attempts at art and other such mementos. We have a record of our children's lives. I have often thought that if there were ever a fire in our house, the only thing I would rush to save would be those albums. Yet economically they have no value. There are many things that are beyond price, but they are so devalued by the economic system that we do not even recognize them. We need to rediscover them.

Since 1970, per capita consumption in the United States has increased by nearly 50 percent. During that time, the United Nations indicators of quality of life in the United States have dropped by over 50 percent. Americans have bought the idea that having things makes them happy, but look at the indicators. We are less and less happy, yet we are still in this frenzy of buying because we believe it makes us happy. Our addiction to consumption is like a drug, a need that we have to satisfy. We always need another fix because nothing fulfills us. We have this vacuum, this empty hole inside us, and we think stuffing things into it will fill it up, but it does not. We just go on and on trying to fill what is fundamentally a spiritual need.

Economists think they are going to manage the planet by assigning an economic value to everything. A Chicago economist who won the Bank of Sweden Prize in Economic Sciences (the so-called Nobel Prize) claims that he can evaluate everything in the world. If you are married, that has an economic value. If you are divorced, there are economic consequences. (In their divorce settlement, an economist's wife demanded half the Nobel Prize money if her husband ever won it. He did, and she got it.) He has a factor for everything. There is no spiritual connection between you and another person, or between you and a place, only what can be factored in economically. I think that as long as we act on that basis, we will ensure the death of the planet.

The fundamental unreality of economics was clear to me from my initial exposure. When I was an undergraduate student at Amherst, I went to my first class in economics and left almost immediately. The professor began by stating: "Caring, sharing, and cooperating are emotional, irrational acts. Only acting in self-interest is rational. That is the basis on which modern economics is constructed." Personally, I cannot accept any system that is based on the assumption that selfishness is the way the world works and therefore is how we must construct our society. If that were true, none of us would exist, and neither would anything else.

I was ready to leave the class at that point, but then the professor started drawing graphs mapping it all out. I asked him, "Where in that diagram are air, water, soil, and the other living things that keep our planet livable?" He replied, "Those are externalities; they are not part of equations in economics." That is when I walked out; there was absolutely nothing to learn. You can make the diagram anything you want, because it is not grounded in the real world. Economists have "externalized" the very things that make the planet habitable and keep everything alive.

Economists give no value at all to natural capital. A tree left standing in a rich vibrant forest provides all kinds of natural services, including exchanging carbon dioxide for oxygen, holding vast amounts of water and releasing it slowly by transpiration, maintaining soils to prevent erosion, and providing living space for countless organisms. All those services are performed by a living tree in the forest. Nevertheless, foresters claim that the tree has no value until you cut it down. That is the economic mentality at work; natural capital is totally devalued.

In British Columbia we have some of the richest forests on the planet. Investors say they add fiber, which means they grow, at the rate of about 2 or 3 percent a year. If you cut down fewer than 2 percent of your trees, you could have forests forever. The problem is that it does not make economic sense to do that. If you clearcut the forest and put the profits in something else, you can make even more money. When the forests are gone, you invest in fish. When the fish are gone, you put your money in whatever is left.

It makes no difference how necessary anything is for life or how much you destroy, because all that matters is money. Economics ensures that we trash the planet because currency is not based on anything real. The economy fundamentally disconnects us from the things that sustain us and give us our quality of life. The belief that progress is to be measured in how much money we make, and how fast our economy grows, is the root of the problem. We showed that self-destructive cycle in our television program *A Planet for the Taking*.

There is nothing rational about economics; it is not science. The market has never been rational, and it is becoming increasingly irrational. There was a time when currency represented something tangible, things that were taken out of the earth. Money represented a real transaction. Now that money represents only itself, we can print as much as we want without it having any relationship to anything else.

We have reached the state of absurdity when you can buy and sell money and make money doing that. Every day over $1 trillion is exchanged in currency speculation around the world. The spiral is out of control, and nothing can stop it, because it is more powerful than governments. When the French franc dropped, the French government bought back billions of francs, but the franc kept falling, because speculators are stronger than governments. We saw the same happen recently with the Mexican peso and the American dollar, and then in the Asian financial markets. It is frightening.

We distort this unreal construct even further by creating measures of so-called economic health, economic indicators such as gross national product (GNP). Governments will turn somersaults to try and keep GNP going up. GNP only adds; it never subtracts. If you pollute the water, then, when people downstream drink it and get sick, GNP increases because they need hospitals, doctors, and lawyers. In 1992, America's GNP rose by $2 billion because it cost that much to clean up the *Exxon Valdez* oil spill. By the criterion of increasing GNP we should pollute everything and all get sick. What kind of an indicator is that? GNP is rising, but the quality of life is falling.

One of the really destructive aspects of our economic structure is its demand for steady growth. Growth is an absolute necessity. If you come to a plateau in business, you are finished. Economic growth in our society is equated with progress, and nobody wants to stop progress. So if growth is progress, we can never admit that we have enough. We always need to have more. The destructive impulse of the economy is immense, and its appetite is insatiable. This monster is intent on consuming the world. As Paul Ehrlich points out, there are only two systems on the planet that aspire to endless growth: cancer cells and economists. In both cases, the inevitable result of un-stoppable growth is the same—death.

Our denial is so total that we completely ignore all warnings about our situation. The Union of Concerned Scientists, including over one thousand scientific experts around the world, signed and released a document after the Earth Summit in Rio de Janeiro in 1992 giving an urgent warning to humanity. It stated that we are on a destructive path that has to be changed immediately, or within ten years we will no longer be able to make the necessary changes. It was a very stark warning from the world's leading scientists.

The major newspapers and television stations did not even bother to cover it. The *New York Times* and *Washington Post* rejected it be-cause it was not "newsworthy." Two years later, in 1994, the collective academies of sciences in the world, representing the leading scientists in every country, released simultaneously a document in nearly sixty countries, timed for the United Nations meeting on population. Es-sentially that document reiterated the concerns of the Union of Con-cerned Scientists, and again it was ignored.

Scientists, the experts who have the highest credibility in our soci-ety, claim that we have a crisis of monumental proportions and a very limited window of opportunity in which to act on it. Although we are dependent on the products created by science and technology, we are not willing to take seriously the warnings of scientists themselves.

There is an unwillingness to face up to the magnitude of the prob-lem. In part this denial is understandable: nobody likes bad news. If there is a way of not having to confront it, we would all like to avoid it. So we blame the messengers and discount the credibility of people—scientists and environmentalists—who are facing our prob-lems. I know this from personal experience because strangers grab me and say, "Who the hell are you? What do you want?" They are full of fear because they do not know what lies ahead, and they do not want to know.

My greatest difficulty has been in trying to convince people that there is a real crisis affecting all of us. The longer we ignore it, the worse it will get, and the more difficult it will be to change and sur-vive. Humans have never had to face the collapse of the whole system that keeps us all alive. The planet is a ticking time bomb waiting to go off, with precious little time left.

It is hard to gain perspective on this brief moment in human existence. As a scientist, I feel that scientific activity is exacerbating the difficulty of realizing what is going on. Foremost are the problems of lack of accountability for the consequences of science, interlinked with its financial relationship to private industry, its dependence on military support, and its control by political powers.

But there are also problems intrinsic to scientific methodology. Scientists aspire to look at nature "objectively" in an attempt to erase any kind of emotional attachment, because it can influence the way they look at things and interpret their results. But when you objectify and distance yourself from things, you eliminate emotional value and no longer care. And you lose any sense of why this really matters.

Furthermore, scientists operate on the assumption that if you concentrate on a minuscule part, eventually you will understand the whole. In my area of genetics, that is certainly the assumption. Geneticists manipulate a single gene without having any idea what it will do to the entire organism and its environment. Presumptuously, they think that if they can know the three million letters in the genetic blueprint, they will understand everything there is to know about what it means to be human. But the rest of us are not convinced that we are just genes.

The scientific method fragments nature. Scientists take an object out of its natural environment, isolate it in a laboratory, and control the conditions around it in order to make observations that are not connected in time or space to anything else. The purpose of science is to discover universal principles that apply anywhere, anytime, and are therefore predictable. But in disconnecting a fragment from nature, we lose its historical and ecological context.

Outside the artificial conditions of the laboratory, everything interacts synergistically. Natural interactions among complex systems produce new phenomena that cannot be predicted from the existing properties of the parts. It was certainly unpredictable that we would evolve from a tiny tree shrew. Emergent properties evolve from synergy within the whole. This evolutionary process has created the amazing variety of life on Earth.

Rather than study interconnected systems, science has fragmented the whole into unrelated, disconnected pieces. Science's focus on the part and lack of perspective on the whole system is the reason why neither scientists nor the public recognize science's ultimate discovery—that everything is interconnected.

Our interconnection really hit home as I watched the reports come into the television newsroom after the nuclear reaction in Chernobyl. It was Swedish scientists who announced that something had happened in Russia. Within minutes after Chernobyl, radiation started falling over Sweden. Within hours, Canadian scientists detected radiation over the Arctic. Within days, the world was blanketed with radiation. It was a striking demonstration of the fact that air does not remain within national boundaries. There is no Russian air, Swedish air, or North American air. Air is a single system that goes around quickly. The notion that we can spew stuff into the air and the wind will blow it away, so that we do not have to worry about it, is nonsense.

Recently, when we were filming in Banff, I picked up the newspaper and saw the headline, "Fishermen in Jasper warned not to eat fish." Fish in the Rockies had been contaminated by pesticides that had blown over from Russia. When we look at smog in Los Angeles and say, "I'm glad I don't live in L.A.," we forget that L.A.'s air goes everywhere, including into our lungs.

Everything is a part of the same whole system. The cycle of life was taught to me by aboriginal people. I keep trying to remind everyone that the most fundamental things connecting us to all other living beings are air, water, and soil.

Air is not empty space. It is a substance that comes out of my nose and goes into yours. What I have contributed to that air goes into your lungs, and some of those atoms become part of you. People are astonished to realize that we are linked by this common body of air. You and I have absorbed atoms that were breathed by dinosaurs one hundred million years ago, along with all the plants and trees, creatures and people that have existed throughout history.

Like air, water is a matrix that connects us together through time and space. Water, which makes up over 70 percent of our bodies, evaporates off the oceans and transpires off the forests. Similarly, the food we consume depends on the circulation of air and water, is grounded in the soil, and needs the assistance of living creatures to grow. Air, water, soil, and life are not separate; they are all part of the same system.

We are part of them, just as they are part of us. We do not end at the edges of our bodies; we are intermixed with everything else. When you realize that you are part of this living skin of life, it is very comforting, because it means you have this kinship with all other living things. When Lovelock came up with "Gaia," we knew it was right. It makes sense that there is something bigger than us and that we are part of it. Our spirituality comes from the realization that there are things beyond our comprehension greater than us. Our lives unfold in life's endless process of creation.

Further Reading

David Suzuki. *Earth Time*. Stoddart, 1998.

———. *The Sacred Balance: Rediscovering Our Place in Nature*. Prometheus Bound, 1997.

———. *Time to Change*. Stoddart, 1993.

David Suzuki and Joseph Levine. *The Secret of Life: Redesigning the Living World*. WGBH, 1993.

David Suzuki and Anita Gordon. *It's a Matter of Survival*. Harvard University Press, 1992.

David Suzuki and Peter Knudtson. *Wisdom of the Elders*. Stoddart, 1992.

David Suzuki. *Inventing the Future: Reflections on Science, Technology, and Nature*. Stoddart, 1989.

David Suzuki and Peter Knudtson. *Genetics: The Clash Between the New Genetics and Human Values*. Harvard University Press, 1989.

David Suzuki. *Metamorphosis: Stages in a Life*. Stoddart, 1987.

David Suzuki and A. J. F. Griffiths. *An Introduction to Genetic Analysis*. 2d ed. W. H. Freeman & Co., 1981.

Toxic Food Web

GEORGE M. WOODWELL

George M. Woodwell chose to focus on a single segment of his life because of its importance to this book. See the list of contributors for his other relevant accomplishments.

MY SCIENTIFIC EXPERIENCE WITH TOXINS began when I was a young plant ecologist, a new professor in the botany department at the University of Maine. I was there because it was an ideal place for my research on forests, but the boreal forests I was studying in northern Maine and New Brunswick were being doused with DDT sprayed from airplanes.

The aerial spraying of pesticides was done to control a single insect, the spruce budworm. The budworm is a natural inhabitant of those forests that periodically reaches densities in stands of balsam fir and white spruce sufficient to kill all the trees. Balsam fir and white spruce are rapidly growing successional species over much of this region, and commercial interests dependent on the forests felt threatened enough to persuade the governments of Maine and New Brunswick to use DDT to control the outbreak.

Spraying half a pound of DDT in oil per acre reduced the budworm population by 95 to 98 percent, but the remaining population would explode the next year and create the problem all over again. Year after year DDT was sprayed, and the population crashed and then exploded again. The net effect was to preserve the insects' food

PHOTO © GABRIEL AMADEUS COONEY, 1996

supply and thereby perpetuate the outbreak. After watching the cycle repeat itself, I could see that while spraying was protecting the trees, it was prolonging the outbreak and the need for spraying. It was also having many other effects.

DDT sprayed on the forest was carried far and wide. Wind carried it to nearby pastures, where it was eaten by animals and then by humans consuming milk and meat. Water and wind dispersed the poison throughout natural systems. Fish in the water, birds in the air, and animals on the ground were susceptible in varying degrees to DDT, and all were affected.

"Silent spring" became a reality. I watched it happening in the late 1950s in Maine, when, not far away, Rachel Carson was working on her book. Others were observing similar symptoms elsewhere. In New Brunswick, for instance, in one year there were no young salmon in the Miramichi, one of the world's most famous salmon streams. Toxins drifted into adjoining waterways and lakes, killing other fish and birds.

Reading through the existing literature on DDT, I learned that more than a decade earlier wildlife experts had conducted extensive research on the hazardous effects of DDT. They showed that DDT stayed around for a long time, and during all that time it continued to accumulate in animals. More than half a pound per acre killed fish, birds, and occasionally mammals. So the hazards of DDT were well known in the middle and late 1940s, when DDT use became common.

People concerned about what was happening to wildlife, and potentially to people, wanted spraying stopped and the pesticide banned, but powerful commercial interests were determined to continue. In Maine, the forest industry declared there was no other way to preserve the trees, and, as the trees constituted one basis of the region's economy, they claimed they had to spray to guarantee a regular income from forestry.

I was watching all of this from the standpoint of a scientist developing programs in plant ecology. A small grant from the National Science Foundation enabled me to study the hardwood forests of the area. Then the Conservation Foundation, a fairly new conservation agency based in New York, came to see me at the university in Orono, in central Maine. As an unknown young botanist, I was mightily flattered. They wondered if I would be interested in investigating the collateral effects of the DDT program on the trees. Already curious about that myself, I welcomed the opportunity. They provided $10,000 (at that time a good bit of money) to support my modest research program.

My first task was to examine how much DDT was falling in the forest. I used a simple technique for measuring how much landed after the planes sprayed. My little traps consisted of big sheets of aluminum foil. Collecting them immediately after spraying, I learned that only half the amount of DDT nominally emitted from the plane actually landed below—the rest "disappeared."

During the period that I was taking measurements in Maine, I found places in New Brunswick that had been sprayed systematically to calibrate the spray equipment on Canadian planes, so that the Canadians had data on how much DDT had actually been applied. I sampled the sprayed areas for DDT residues by carefully collecting soil samples from various places and various depths of soil, but I had not realized the difficulty I would have in reentering the United States with Canadian soil. No one is allowed to bring in unsterilized soil samples because of the possibility of plant disease, so I had to talk myself across the American border with a carload of contraband. The agent was, finally, generous. He extracted a promise from me that the soil would be sterilized at the end of our work. It was.

Once I had my samples safely imported, I engaged a chemist to work out techniques for measuring the amount of DDT in the soil. The technique used at that time was the Schecter-Haller method, which relied on a measurement of color in a treated extract of the soil. That method was displaced in time with much more accurate thin-film chromatography and, later, gas chromatography. The data allowed me to plot the distribution and persistence of DDT residues in the forest. The New Brunswick soil samples showed the residues had a half-life in excess of ten years: in other words, after ten years more than half of the original DDT deposit was still present.

We established the long life of DDT residues in the soil and the fact that about half of the residues were dispersed widely in the air at the time of spraying. We also looked into the mystery of what happened to the pesticide that disappeared. DDT, a fat-soluble crystal, is normally dissolved in oil for use as a spray. Apparently the sprayed solution instantly dried into tiny crystals that drifted away in the wind and were eventually deposited elsewhere. Some were blown higher into the atmosphere and carried a long way, so DDT residues were appearing in places remote from where the spraying was done. It was these residues that were appearing in mountain lakes, in the tissues of the crabeater seal in the Antarctic, and in the oceanic abyss, although we could not prove it at the time.

When I left Maine to go to Brookhaven National Laboratory on Long Island to set up a research program on the ecological effects of ionizing radiation, I took the DDT project with me; it was so promising that I did not want to drop it. Brookhaven agreed to support it, so I was able to pursue it and publish my findings on pesticide persistence in soils as well as other studies on effects of the spray on plant tissues.

On Long Island the extensive salt marshes were being sprayed from the air to control the salt marsh mosquito. Strong public objections were being voiced by those who did not wish to live in a poisoned environment. In fact there had been a lawsuit in the mid-1950s, brought by Robert Cushman Murphy and colleagues when pesticide interests (actually the Department of Agriculture) decided they could "eradicate" the gypsy moth by spraying the whole island. When their program was announced, some ornithologists and other naturalists thought it was not only unwise but actually dangerous to spray everything and everyone with a broad-spectrum poison. They took the issue to court and lost. The case set a bad precedent.

So the Department of Agriculture sprayed all of Long Island with the assurance that they would "eradicate" the gypsy moth once and for all. They failed, of course. No one has ever eradicated a pest in that way. It just popped back the next year and has been there ever since. Despite failures everywhere, big spraying programs were advocated to "eradicate" noxious insect outbreaks, large and small, all over the country. And, however misleading, the word is still used to justify major spraying programs.

My colleagues and I focused on the salt marshes because they were clearly being impoverished. The bird populations in particular were conspicuously affected, but evidence of the cause was entirely circumstantial. By 1965 osprey populations on Fisher's Island at the mouth of Peconic Bay crashed from around three hundred nests to three. Our hypothesis was that the decline was due to the use of DDT and its accumulation in the food web. As carnivores at the top of the food chain, ospreys and other avian predators were ingesting large quantities of DDT. Their reproduction was clearly failing, but we were not quite sure how. During the years we worked on it, ornithologists eventually discovered that the birds' calcium metabolism was interrupted, making eggshells too fragile for eggs to be incubated and hatch successfully.

With my colleagues, I set up a research program and hired an assistant to collect samples from the food web of the salt marshes and bays on the south shore of Long Island. He did an excellent job of sampling the salt marsh soils, water, algae, shellfish, fish, and birds. We had samples representing all the various trophic levels of the food pyramid in the salt marsh and estuaries.

By that time we were using new chromatographic techniques for determining DDT and other residues. I had been fortunate some years before in meeting a superbly talented chemist interested in the pesticide problem, Charles Wurster, who had moved recently from Dartmouth College to join the faculty of the State University of New York. He was also a brilliant ornithologist. He provided the techniques to measure DDT residues in almost anything.

Together we showed that DDT was accumulating throughout the food web on Long Island. The level of contamination was surprisingly high. Although we had collected living organisms, our experience and experimental data published earlier led us to recognize that the DDT content of their tissues was at the threshold of mortality at every level in the food web. Of course, if there is mortality, the organism is not there. The populations were in all probability suffering selective, continuous mortality in addition to the reproductive failures already observed.

It seemed clear that high levels of DDT were devastating the top carnivores, which were obviously disappearing. Even though the losses were not as obvious further down the food web, smaller organisms were failing too. The top carnivores could apparently tolerate the toxin up to levels of tens of parts per million; the herbivores carried burdens of only about one-tenth of that, in some instances one-hundredth of it. Acute lethal exposures for them were considerably lower than those for the top carnivores. Other experimental data confirmed these differences in vulnerability. At every level of the food web, the accumulation in living organisms was equivalent, just below an acute lethal concentration for that species.

Ascending each level of the food pyramid, pesticide concentrations appeared to increase by a factor of ten. The difference between the concentrations in the water and the single-celled organisms at the base of the pyramid and in the tissues of the carnivorous or scavenging birds at the top of the pyramid was 100,000-fold or more. Within a single species, however, the differences observed were as much as tenfold, so it was not surprising to find tenfold differences between trophic levels. Most living organisms in the marshes were within a factor of ten of acute lethal concentrations. The research we did then is probably still one of the best studies showing the accumulation of toxic residues at different levels in the food web.

DDT spraying in the salt marshes had to stop. The problem was how to stop it. While we were thinking about that, a brash young lawyer named Victor Yannacone filed a case in Suffolk County Superior Court. (Suffolk County occupies the eastern two-thirds of Long Island.) He filed it in his wife's name, claiming that her health and well-being were being violated by aerial spraying. He did not know about our work, but after talking with him we decided to support his lawsuit. We had just completed our research on the poisoning of the food web and had substantial evidence of the accumulation of residues toxic to birds and fish.

The court case was spectacular, because the newspapers were there to report our scientific testimony challenging the powers that be. We began by questioning the use of DDT to control mosquitoes, contesting its effectiveness and disputing its necessity. In doing research on the mosquito problem, I had stumbled on a scientific paper written by a botanist named Taylor who had done a botanical study of the salt marshes on eastern Long Island in 1939, before the use of DDT. In his research paper, Taylor's final comment was what a pleasure it had been to work in the salt marshes that year because of the absence of mosquitoes—due to the effectiveness of the new Suffolk County Mosquito Control Commission.

In court, the mosquito control commissioner, a man named Williamson, claimed there was no conceivable way to control mosquitoes without aerial spraying of DDT. Williamson, interestingly enough, had also been the commissioner in 1939. The technique used then (and still employed today) is drainage of marsh pools by ditching. So we introduced Taylor's evidence to contradict the commissioner's claims.

Our own research was shown with beautiful artwork. Dennis Puleston, a naturalist and artist on Long Island, illustrated the food web, showing the concentration of DDT residues in organisms and the role of each organism in the food web. We won an injunction from the court that prevented the use of DDT in the salt marshes that year. The injunction was later dissolved, so they were free to resume spraying, but by that time they had gone on to other techniques. In addition to stopping DDT spraying, our court case offered an opportunity for the public to learn about ecology and for ecologists to get a lesson in the use of the courts.

We had learned a few lessons in courtroom procedures ourselves and realized the potential of legal remedies. We looked around for other egregious misuses of toxins. We did not have to look far. Along the shores of Lake Michigan, the Department of Agriculture was proposing an aerial spraying of dieldrin, another chlorinated hydrocarbon pesticide, to control the Japanese beetle. The contamination of soil, farms, and Lake Michigan were all at issue. We decided to see if we could have it stopped.

Again there were interesting developments as the case progressed. When it came to testimony as to how the spraying program was started, our lawyer, Victor Yannacone, managed to extract from a Michigan entomologist that it was he who had discovered there were Japanese beetles present. How many were there? Three, he said. Incredulous, Yannacone inquired as to whether instead of airplanes and poison he had considered a hammer and block of wood. The exchange made the newspapers, of course.

We had good support from people in Michigan. The Conservation Department of Michigan was on our side, which was important; we would not have been there without them. But then the Department of Agriculture weighed in with a lot of money. We were defeated in our quest for an injunction. But we made the newspapers, and there was no doubt that aerial spraying of general poisons along the shore of Lake Michigan was unwise. All kinds of predictions came out of this court case, including one that the concentration of pesticide residues was high enough in the waters of Lake Michigan and its tributaries to stop reproduction in the coho salmon. Even as we were in court, news reports confirmed that, indeed, the fish were not reproducing. Although we did not win the court case, we certainly won in the public's estimation.

Of course we had also attracted the attention of the pesticide industry, which was trying to make life difficult. I had already been exposed to their opposition at the University of Maine, where entomologists were concentrating much research on the commercial removal of insects using pesticides. Universities were rashly testing toxins on every crop they could think of because of the money to be made selling pesticides and the funding received for research.

When the toxics industry noticed we had been successful in limiting the use of DDT, they became very interested. I recall defamatory articles by a man named Louis A. MacLane, who worked for the Montrose Chemical Company in St. Louis. He labeled people who were averse to pesticides as "peculiar" in many ways, which he proceeded to list. It was bizarre, and even more so in that his articles were widely published, even in scientific journals. There were all sorts of scurrilous activities, many of which have been chronicled in a commendable recent biography of Rachel Carson by Linda Lear.

As a result of our experiences in court, we established the Environmental Defense Fund, which has continued those battles ever since. There were many fights with the opposition along the way; the multibillion-dollar industry definitely did not want to lose. But EDF took on the toxic substances issue very aggressively, with the help of many others, and ultimately eliminated use of DDT in the United States in 1972. To achieve that, we all testified in a series of hearings run by the Environmental Protection Agency. William Ruckelshaus then was the EPA administrator, and it was his decision in the end that DDT had to go.

When it became clear that DDT was accumulating in the body fat of organisms all over the world, I wrote a paper for the *Scientific American* that was widely used, called "Toxic Substances and Ecological Cycles." In addition to my research on pesticides, I included findings from work on the ecological effects of ionizing radiation and the circulation of radioactive debris from nuclear weapons. I pointed to parallels in the circulation of DDT and radionuclides, which were circling the world as a result of nuclear bomb tests. After nuclear explosions, massive radioactive residues continued circulating in the atmosphere, so we were all exposed to the same radiation several times. When it eventually precipitated out of the atmosphere in rainwater, the radioactivity accumulated significantly in living systems.

We had at that time, and have had ever since, two global contaminations. We were being bombarded by radiation from nuclear fallout, including radioactive isotopes of strontium, cesium, and iodine, plus a series of other heavy metals. In addition, we were being flooded with chemical toxins, especially the pesticides used in agriculture, which were being carried around the world in the air and rained out far from their places of application. DDT was the primary example, but there were other chlorinated hydrocarbons, many of which are still around. Like radiation, the toxins were transported by air currents, but the ultimate repository of long-lived toxins is the oceans.

It is easy to see that toxins released into the environment are noxious, a hazard to people but also a hazard to life in general. The conclusion I came to at the time was that if we were meticulous in protecting people from ionizing radiation, nature would be protected. But in the case of other toxins designed to be effective in agriculture, the challenge is more difficult. We must protect nature to protect people. That rule is still true today.

The reason for the differences is important. People are sufficiently susceptible to ionizing radiation that if we keep the environment clean enough for people to survive, the radiation level does not pose a hazard to other life. That means, for example, that we must keep radioactive strontium from accumulating in milk, iodine from accumulating in thyroids, and cesium from accumulating in meat. If we can do that, there will not be enough radiation in the general environment to affect other organisms, which are all more resistant as populations than humans are.

But the toxics problem is one that affects insects, fish, birds, animals, all life; and if we protect all life, we shall protect people. In fact, if we do not protect nature, we cannot protect people. That is why the recent evidence of developmental aberrations and sexual abnormalities in wildlife, resulting from chemical exposure, is so alarming.

Observing the general pattern of circulation and deposit of hazardous substances, I learned enough to know that if we are serious about living in the world for a long time, we have to eliminate the possibility that such substances will circulate. As I thought through the problem, it became clear to me, and it is still clear today, that the general rule has to be zero release of toxic substances into the environment. Otherwise, if we have more and more people and more and more toxic substances, the world becomes progressively more contaminated.

It is fascinating at the moment to see that people now thinking about industrial development are beginning to realize that industries have to be held to a zero-release standard. Similarly, agriculture has to be weaned away from pesticides into practices whereby agriculture no longer contaminates the air, water, and land—and ceases to poison the food as well. The era of toxic substances in agriculture and industry has to end.

As a young scientist, I realized that the changes we were creating in the structure of nature were systematic. Disturbances from whatever source all lead to systematic biotic impoverishment: a reduction in the structure of nature to the point where small-bodied, short-lived, rapidly reproducing organisms prevail and large-bodied, long-lived ones (like us) are lost. That is a general description of what happens as the environment becomes poisoned and diminished.

That is about where we are at the moment. We are realizing that our overall environment is poisoned and becoming impoverished in the process. Once that accumulation occurs, it is substantially irreversible. The contamination of the oceans with pesticides can never be reversed in any period of interest to us. It is time for a revolution in our relationship to the environment. Our interest lies in clean air, water, and land that will support not only people but all other organisms. What is most important is to keep the normal living systems of Earth functioning, because they are what support us all.

Further Reading

George M. Woodwell and Fred T. Mackenzie. *Biotic Feedbacks in the Global Climatic System: Will the Warming Feed the Warming?* Oxford University Press, 1995.

George M. Woodwell and Kilaparti Ramakrshna, eds. *World Forests for the Future: Their Use and Conservation.* Yale University Press, 1993.

George M. Woodwell, ed. *The Earth in Transition: Patterns and Processes of Biotic Impoverishment.* Cambridge University Press, 1991.

George M. Woodwell and Erene Pecan, eds. *Carbon and the Biosphere: Proceedings 1973.* United States Department of Energy, 1973.

George M. Woodwell, R. K. Severs, J. E. Lovelock, et al. *Ecological and Biological Effects of Air Pollution.* Irvington, 1973.

Water Pollution

RUTH PATRICK

ALTHOUGH MY FATHER WAS A LAWYER BY PRO-
fession, he was a botanist by preference. His undergraduate degree was in botany, and he main-
tained an intense interest in natural science throughout his life. He
shared his love of nature with us, and as soon as my sister and I could
walk, he took us along on his Sunday treks through the woods to the
park. We collected flowers, ferns, mosses, nuts, and crawlers, such as
snails, worms, and caterpillars. When we arrived at the nearby
stream, he used a tin can on a pole to scrape the rocks and then
poured the contents into a glass bottle to carry back.

When we got home, we examined our treasures in detail. After we
had named the larger organisms, father opened his rolltop desk,
which housed four microscopes. He made slides of our collection,
and then we climbed on his knee and looked into a microscopic
world.

When I was seven, he gave me my first microscope—the one he
first had as a boy. It was simply a tube I could pull up and down to
focus, but I used it to examine everything I could find. This en-
trancement with the microscopic dimension of nature has continued
my whole life.

Being older, my parents escaped the northern winters by heading
south to Florida, so we took our assignments with us in lieu of

attending school. Father instructed us in science and math, and mother in reading and writing, in preparation for our exams when we returned to school in the Midwest. In the interim I learned what I could of the natural world by exploring the southern seashores and swamps.

During adolescence, we went to a private school in Florida, but father continued his scientific instruction. He shared his delight in diatoms by giving me slides of diatoms intricately shaped like jewels—but much more interesting and precious to me. I spent weeks trying to identify them before learning which ones I had gotten right. Between father and my high school botany teacher, I was well educated in science.

At a time when most women were fortunate to be able to finish high school, father was preparing me for graduate school. But first we had to deal with mother, a typical old-fashioned lady. Unlike my sister, who went to Smith College, I did not want to go to a "girls' school." I managed to go to coed Kansas University, but that only lasted a year because of mother's concern about the men I might be dating. Insisting I go to an all-women's school, she sequestered me at Coker College in South Carolina.

Despite its academic excellence, father was concerned that Coker's science curriculum was not extensive enough, so during the summers he sent me to study at biological laboratories—Mountain Lake in Virginia, Cold Spring Harbor on Long Island, and Woods Hole Oceanographic Institute in Massachusetts. While I was at Woods Hole, Ivy Lewis, the foremost algae researcher in the country, invited me to become his graduate student. As father offered to send me wherever I wanted, I went to Virginia to study with Professor Lewis.

The University of Virginia had no women undergraduates then, although there were a few women graduate students—all of us trying to be inconspicuous, studying instead of socializing. I managed to complete my research on the diatoms of Southeast Asia and received my M.A. and Ph.D. by the time I was twenty-six.

In 1931, while still in graduate school, I moved to Philadelphia to marry Charles Hodge, a graduate student at the University of Pennsylvania, whom I had met at Cold Spring Harbor one summer. A direct descendant of Benjamin Franklin, he was also an aspiring scientist, but during the Depression we both had to work as well as study.

Being a woman, I could not get a job at a college or university as a scientist, so I worked as a volunteer at the Academy of Natural Sciences of Philadelphia, serving as unpaid curator of the Microscopical Society and associate curator of the Microscopy Department for more than a decade. The academy has one of the world's finest diatom collections, so I continued my own research, but a young woman trying to be a scientist was an anomaly.

Women were assumed to be inferior, mentally as well as physically, and thus incapable of intellectual achievement. Why waste education and training on them that otherwise could be utilized by men? So the few women who tried to enter science's closed club attempted to appear and act as much like men as they could. If I exhibited the slightest sign of dressing up, I was immediately dressed down: even a little lipstick was met with derision. Fortunately, my father believed that women were as capable as men, and he continued to support the training he had initiated in my childhood. He also taught me that I should leave the world a better place than it was when I came into it, so I sought ways to utilize my knowledge of diatoms to solve social and environmental problems.

Innumerable microscopic diatoms exist in every body of water, from ponds to oceans. In marine waters, these single-celled algae float together, forming plankton, the primary food of many fish. Because different species of diatoms live in different water conditions and feed on different nutrients, identifying species within a water sample indicates the water's chemical condition.

In 1945 I gave a talk on diatoms at the American Association for the Advancement of Science. Afterward, an Atlantic Refining Company official in the audience, William Hart, approached me and said I had discovered a way to recognize the presence of water pollution, so he would be coming to see me soon. When Mr. Hart visited me at the academy, he explained his concerns about water pollution and its effect on aquatic life. We discussed the possibility of studying shifts in diatoms to determine what pollution was present and how it was affecting aquatic life. This incident was remarkable because it took place long before there was public awareness of water pollution.

A year later, he returned to the academy with an astounding gift. Unknown to me, Mr. Hart was head of the chamber of commerce of Pennsylvania, and amazingly he had managed to raise the equivalent of a million dollars, in today's terms, to do research for which there was not yet any public perception, never mind support. He told the academy's president, Charles Cadwalder, that he wanted to give the money to the state of Pennsylvania to donate to the Academy of Natural Sciences for diatom research.

The academy had never had so much research money, so the president was elated—until he was told that the money was for me to lead a research team. At that point he was aghast and said they could not possibly allow that, because I was a woman, and women waste money. When Mr. Hart insisted that the academy would not be given the money otherwise, the president reluctantly allowed me to undertake the research.

Nevertheless, Mr. Cadwalder was so upset about me being in charge of the project that he asked Charles Stein at DuPont, one of the codiscoverers of nylon, to come in periodically and check up on me to make sure that this woman was not wasting the academy's money. So Dr. Stein came in regularly to see what I was doing. Even though he was not familiar with the science of limnology (the study of freshwater ecosystems), he was a skilled scientist who asked interesting questions.

I soon realized that diatoms could not provide all the information necessary to analyze the water's condition, so I decided to study all the plants and animals living in the water and the overall structure of the aquatic community. Recognizing that I needed a lot of help with such a project, I organized a team of scientists composed of graduate students and young professors specializing in chemistry, algae, bacteria, insects, invertebrates, crustacea, fish, and so on. As the students' professors were also interested in our work, we enlisted their expertise when necessary. I also asked friends who were renowned lake and river specialists and water chemists to be my advisory committee.

In addition to being an innovative study on water pollution, the project was challenging because almost no one had studied rivers. We chose the Conestoga watershed because it contained both untainted natural streams and tributaries affected by organic wastes from agriculture, milk wastes from dairy farms, sewage, and industrial wastes. Within its area of nearly five hundred square miles, we created almost two hundred survey stations to collect all the aquatic species we could find.

This was pioneering, and the members of my team were so motivated by the opportunity to make an original contribution that we collected specimens all day and stayed up half the night trying to identify them before sending them to specialists for verification.

Our research revealed for the first time that the population and distribution of aquatic species indeed indicated the water's condition. The healthier the stream, the greater the diversity of species; the more polluted the stream, the fewer the species; and in the most polluted areas, no life existed.

In 1949 I published the results of our study and introduced the principle that natural streams are characterized by highly diversified species belonging to many different phylogenetic groups. This was one of the first papers written on why organisms live where they do in a river habitat. One of my chief advisers and my inspiring mentor, G. Evelyn Hutchinson, later told me that our study was a factor in writing his landmark paper "Homage to Santa Rosalia: Or, Why Are There So Many Kinds of Animals?"

Many scientists were interested in our results, including my overseer, Charles Stein, who informed the president of DuPont that I had discovered something that could be helpful with their water pollution problem. Long before there were any pollution control laws, DuPont's president, Crawford Greenewalt, had informed the company that they should know the condition of the water into which they were planning to discharge wastes and the effects of those wastes on aquatic species. Since that was exactly what we had done, DuPont gave us the task of determining the condition of rivers and the effects of their waste on rivers where they had manufacturing plants.

Without DuPont we could not have continued, because many trustees thought my research was unworthy of the academy. Fortunately, a few trustees, including Dr. Stein and my second husband, Lewis H. Van Dusen, thought I should be given a chance, so I was allowed to use the facilities for research but denied any academy funding.

DuPont kept us afloat until other companies, such as Sun Oil and Eastman Kodak, recognized the value of our studies and hired us too; then additional groups, including the Environmental Protection Agency, drew on our research as well. Other methods for defining the effects of pollution were developed, such as improved toxicity testing, and the diatometer, a means of measuring shifts in the structure of diatom communities, was created.

Wanting to know how to restore a polluted stream to health, I created a completely new stream to observe its progression and the succession of species that would inhabit it. A channel about ten feet wide and nearly one hundred feet long was excavated off an existing creek, simulating its normal flow patterns, including sections of white water, slow water, and a natural pool. I sterilized the stream bed by scrubbing it with disinfectant, then I let the water in and watched how the communities of aquatic life were established.

Microscopic organisms were first: bacteria, algae, and protozoans. Once the invisible base of the food chain was established, visible organisms could survive by feeding on their microscopic meal. Insects that filter their food from water were next, then other insects, worms, and snails. After two years, most of the small species from the original creek inhabited the new one. But the new stream's habitats were not extensive enough for fish, so those that swam in to explore the surroundings swam out without staying.

Continual research on associations of aquatic species in streams has shown that in natural streams there are many species functioning in each stage of nutrient and energy transfer. For example, primary producers, herbivores, carnivores, and omnivores utilize the nutrients and ecological conditions in various ways at different times of the year.

In 1955, I led a scientific expedition to the headwaters of the four-thousand-mile-long Amazon River. I wanted to know whether tropical waterways were as diverse as tropical land and whether they supported greater biodiversity than temperate zone streams. Examining streams similar to North America's, we found that while each pool might have around the same number of species as temperate pools, each tropical pool harbored different species, so the total number of species in all the tropical pools was greater than in temperate pools.

In addition to being useful for studying water conditions all over the world, diatoms can be used to interpret how water conditions change over time—even far back in time. When I was a graduate student, Professor Lewis had me examine peat samples from the 750-square-mile Dismal Swamp in Virginia and North Carolina to see what diatoms would reveal about the interruption of plant succession indicated by the sudden disappearance of existing tree pollen and the appearance of pollen from invasive plants.

Looking at fossilized diatoms in the peat samples, I was surprised to discover that they were saltwater diatoms, which could have been present only if a tidal wave had hit or the coastline had sunk. Absence of sand in the samples indicated a lack of tidal wave deposit, so we postulated that the forest died when the coastline sank. This was prior to the discovery that coastlines shifted in elevation during earlier geologic periods.

I was amazed by the realization that diatoms could reveal so much about what was happening around them and provide information for historical analysis. The success of this stratigraphic research motivated me to examine samples from the Great Salt Lake that had been sent to me by Dr. Eardley at the University of Michigan, who wanted to know whether it had been severed from the sea or was a freshwater lake salinized when its streams diminished. Diatoms suggested that the Great Salt Lake originated from freshwater sources.

Even when my research began to be accepted, some scientists did not consider the work important or even legitimate, so scientific recognition, when it did come, really mattered to me. In 1970, I was elected to the National Academy of Sciences, only the twelfth woman in over one hundred years of its existence. A few years later, I was given the John and Alice Tyler Award in Ecology, the largest financial award for science at that time. I invested the $150,000 and over the years used the income to fund research that otherwise I could not have afforded to carry out. In 1996, The National Medal of Science was presented to me by President Clinton.

In the more than fifty years I have been at the Academy of Natural Sciences, I have seen the Limnology Department that I founded in 1947 expand to become the Environmental Research Division, which includes over half the academy's scientific staff. As department chair I was able to establish two field laboratories, and as chair of the academy's Board of Trustees, I pushed them into adding a new research wing to the old structure built in 1875.

Today at our laboratories scientists not only perfect methods of determining the effects of pollution on aquatic life but also teach children and adults how to recognize pollution and how to mitigate it. At the University of Pennsylvania, where I teach, and at colleges where my colleagues teach, as well as at high schools and grade schools, students are involved in classes and research on rivers.

After half a century of expressing my concern for "the health of the environment," the response is heartening.

Further Reading

Ruth Patrick. *Rivers of the United States.* 6 vols. Wiley, 1999. Vol. 1: *Estuaries,* 1994. Vol. 2: *Chemical and Physical Characteristics,* 1995. Vol. 3: *Rivers of the East and Southeast,* 1996. Vol. 4: *Mississippi River Drainage,* 1998. Vol. 5: *Rivers of the West and Southwest,* 1995. Vol. 6: *Pollution and Environmental Management,* 1997.

Ruth Patrick, Emily Ford, and John Quarles. *Groundwater Contamination in the United States.* University of Pennsylvania, 1987.

Ruth Patrick and John Cairns Jr., eds. *Managing Water Resources.* Praeger, 1986.

Ruth Patrick. *The Diatoms of the United States (Exclusive of Alaska and Hawaii).* 2 vols. Academy of Natural Sciences, Philadelphia, 1966.

Marine Biodiversity

ELLIOTT NORSE

I WAS BORN IN THE POSTWAR WORLD OF RAPID
change and uncertainty, a time when a war had
just been fought that involved the whole globe.
The standard of civility was lowered and has never recovered. World
War II caused the breakdown of things we cherish about being
human, as entire categories of people were marked for annihilation
and civilians were specifically targeted for mass bombing. It was a
war in which we treated other people with the kind of callous disre-
gard that has heretofore been reserved largely for the way we treat the
other species of this Earth.

I was born in a country that had triumphed because we were so
economically powerful that we outproduced our enemies. The Germans and the Japanese outdid us in some ways: the Germans invented the first jet aircraft, and the Japanese produced torpedoes that
actually worked. Nevertheless, with a combination of technology and
phenomenal industrial capacity, we overwhelmed our foes. I think
that victory induced a euphoria about our economic power and our
ability to produce our way out of any challenge, any crisis.

That assumption of infallibility was extended to science. During
the war, scientists developed our military technology, and this formidable apparatus continued to proliferate afterward. An enormous
proportion of scientific funding was military—and still is. Even

today's computers are a direct outgrowth of the machines used to calculate trajectories of naval gunfire.

By 1947, when I was born, we were beginning to rise from the emergency economic footing of war and starting to worship the god of prosperity and sanctify the belief that we can all have everything. This is a compelling message to people who have known want, either because their country is poor or because it has allocated all of its resources to war. The war shaped my family and my world.

My father had grown up after World War I and left school after the eighth grade because he had to make money to help support his family. As a fourteen-year-old just out of school, like many kids he sold pencils on the street. Living in New York, he found his way into the fur industry and made coats for people much wealthier than we were. Dad was fascinated by mammals. He taught me about their ways and told me how much it hurt to make his living exploiting creatures that he cared for. It did not bother him to work on pelts of farmed mink, but he did not like using lynx or other wildlife. He worried about wild species that became less and less abundant in his lifetime.

My mother had a high school education. She made bombsights early in World War II and then became a military police officer at the Brooklyn Navy Yard. But whereas Dad was authoritarian (being in the army during the war was the defining event of his life), for Mom this work was just doing her duty. She was indulgent and loving, and she preferred baking cookies and teaching me to read to being an MP. What I loved most when I was little was when she sat me on her knee and sang to me. My favorite song was "Nature Boy."

I aspired to be a Nature Boy who was wise and kind, as Mom's younger brother Elliott had been. His absence was an unhealed wound she lived with every day. Elliott had been patriotic, funny, an animal lover, and an avid camper, which was tough for someone living in Brooklyn with no means to get out; but even in the city there were places he could find bits of nature. Three years before I was born, he was killed on a beach in Italy while fighting the Nazis. He was just eighteen. I think Mom conceived me so that there would be another Elliott to do what he might have done. My love for nature was a gift from my parents and my namesake.

Until I was seven years old, we lived in a little house in Brooklyn located on an estuarine canal in Gerritsen Beach. We called it The Canal because it was our whole world. It was bulkheaded and did not have a natural shoreline, but at low tide the estuarine mud flats were exposed. In my neighborhood, nearly everybody's work or recreation focused on the water. My focus was even stronger because the other kids did not play with me; we were the only Jewish family in a neighborhood of Irish, Italians, and Norwegians. The few people who would have anything to do with us were either other outcasts themselves, with no more opportunities than we had, or those who enjoyed such high status that they could afford to interact with us. Mostly my sister and I played alone, or with each other. She devoted herself to art and music; I immersed myself in biology.

The dock that projected from our backyard into The Canal was my one true haven. Lying on the planks that blocked the sky's reflection, peering through the cracks, I could look right into the water and see mussels, sea anemones, sea squirts, killifish, shrimps, and blue crabs. They became my friends.

I almost never wore shoes during the summer. I had a rowboat with no oars (my parents did not want me going out into the middle of The Canal, as I did not really know how to swim). So I pulled the boat along the bulkheads, listening to the herring gulls and catching blue crabs (which we called blue claws or blooies) on the way. At high tide, to fend off would-be rivals, males cradling females in their legs climbed up the pilings nearer the surface, within range of my long-handled net. I became a good crabber. With the blooies scuttling around the bottom of the boat, I stood on the seat to prevent the enraged crustaceans from pinching my toes.

I learned some hard lessons. A friend of my mother's brought me a killie trap. The first time I used it, I caught four young eels. After putting them in a bucket on our lawn, I went to get Mom, but somehow I forgot about them. When I came back, all the eels had jumped out of the bucket and died on the grass. Previously I had killed snapper bluefish as food and killies as bait, but I felt horrified at having killed these eels because I was careless; it was a lesson I never forgot.

More than anything else I wanted to learn about living things in the sea, so my mother took me to the library. That is how, at five, I decided to be an ichthyologist, one who studies fishes (I did not hear the term "marine biologist" until junior high school). The other kids in my neighborhood wanted to be policemen, firemen, cowboys, nurses, or mommies—the acceptable occupations in Gerritsen Beach. I was the only aspiring ichthyologist. I never doubted who I was or wondered whether I should change to fit in with everybody else. I knew what I loved and what I wanted to be. I have not changed my mind. What happened to that little person matters because this big person is built around him: he's still in there. Devoting my life to learning about and protecting living things seemed to be destined right from the beginning.

Not all the living things I came to love were marine. I can trace my love of forests to one tree on our block, a gnarled old poplar much too big for its yard. I still remember the way its leaves shimmered in the breeze. When it was unbearably hot, its cool shade and moist air offered the only comfortable place anywhere (air-conditioning had not yet arrived in homes). That wonderful old tree ultimately led me to write *Ancient Forests of the Pacific Northwest.* My career in marine and forest conservation biology came from that one block where I spent my first seven years.

My family broke up when I was seven, so we moved away from the home I cherished and the organisms that I caught, studied, and loved: the killifish, striped bass, snapper bluefish, and blue crabs. I never forgot that they shared their secrets with me when nobody else would.

Other fortunate influences followed later. At Brooklyn College, my invertebrate zoology teacher, Priscilla Pollister, saw something in me and helped to launch me into a life of learning. She became my mentor, providing me with heaping measures of encouragement and interest but also what would now be called "tough love." When it came time to apply for graduate school, she informed me that she would not write me a recommendation for any university near New York. With my scant financial resources, I had hoped to live at home and commute, but she insisted that my graduate education should be about learning and expanding my world, not just about marine biology. With her encouragement, I spread my wings (actually I hopped on a plane) for the first time.

I landed on the other side of the continent, at the University of Southern California. I soon felt so different from the natives that it might as well have been another country. Like many New Yorkers, I had never learned to drive. I became an alien in Los Angeles, where going anywhere is impossible without wheels.

My major professor at USC, John Garth, became my next mentor. In my first year at graduate school, on the way to Thanksgiving dinner, he suggested a dissertation topic for me: blue crabs. This was one of those times in life when something was totally right, an absolutely perfect fit. I studied the diversity of blue crabs in the Caribbean and the tropical eastern Pacific, including the species I had played with during childhood and other variations on the same theme.

In 1969, an oil well blowout off Santa Barbara became a mobilizing event in the environmental movement, as *Silent Spring* had been in 1962 and Paul Ehrlich's *Population Bomb* in 1968. It was a catalyst for the first Earth Day the next year, and there was money galore at USC for graduate students to work on the effects of oil spills. Despite the lure of this funding, I was determined to work on blue crabs in the Caribbean. Eight months of fieldwork in the Florida Keys, Jamaica, and both coasts of Colombia consumed all my savings. Yet every hour I had spent as a stock boy at Cheap Charlie's on Flatbush Avenue, delivering dry-cleaned clothes, tutoring kids in chemistry, and working as a Borscht Belt waiter in the summers brought me the freedom to follow my dream.

There are about sixteen species of blue crabs, and I had the privilege of studying all but one of the thirteen species in the Americas. Readily identified in the field if you get to know them, they are large, colorful, and relatively easy to catch. Their fascinating anatomical, behavioral, and ecological changes as they grow make them engaging subjects for research. The fact that as many as seven species occur in the same geographical locality is advantageous for studying how closely related organisms partition their environment and is useful for studying diversity. For the ten years I worked on them, they taught me to understand the relationships among species in their physical environment.

After I finished my doctorate, I was a postdoc for three years at the University of Iowa and did blue crab research in Curaçao. I wanted to get a faculty position at a good university, since I loved doing research in tropical marine ecology and teaching interested students, but such jobs had become scarce shortly before my search began, and the result was disappointing. I came in second at several good schools and was offered faculty positions only at places so bad I figured my brain would die; one I visited seemed like a high school for college-age children.

With my postdoctoral fellowship ending, I was about to be kicked out of married student housing when I learned that my mother had died. While I was away at her funeral, a call came offering a summer job I had applied for on a whim at the U.S. Environmental Protection Agency. A two-month position there turned into eighteen months of work. I learned how policy is and isn't made and how important science is and is not in that process. It was a real education.

The most wonderful marine ecosystems in the U.S. part of the Gulf of Mexico are two underwater hills called the Flower Garden Banks. At EPA I worked to encourage establishment of a national marine sanctuary and ensure that it was protected from insults, including oil and gas drilling. Believing that I was hired by EPA to protect, that is what I tried to do. But, not getting the cooperation I needed within EPA, I turned to two conservation organizations. Of course they needed information to help me, so I provided it. When it was discovered that I was talking to the enemy—the environmental community—I was told my job would be ending at EPA. Worse, my first environmental fight ended in defeat. But I learned a valuable lesson: in a country that guzzles oil and a region that is politically dominated by it, not one square inch of the Gulf of Mexico was biologically important enough to merit protection from oil and gas drilling.

Fortunately, one of the environmentalists I helped told me of a newly open position as staff ecologist on the President's Council on Environmental Quality. Later, when I asked Malcolm Baldwin, the man who hired me, why he gave me the position, he said it was not my credentials that had impressed him as much as my philosophy and willingness to put it all on the line for what I believed in. It was reassuring to find that doing the right thing is not always fatal. Of course, Malcolm was a wonderful mentor too.

When Americans talk about "the government," they do not understand that we are really governed by competing agencies with different agendas and constituencies. Moreover, the laws and regulations that shape policy in various agencies are different. At CEQ we worked for the president, and, because of the particular president we worked for, we had the ability to accomplish things I could never have done at EPA.

Working with Michael Weber, a brilliant environmentalist at the Center for Environmental Education (now the Center for Marine Conservation), I convinced council member Jane Yarn to encourage her friend and fellow Georgian Jimmy Carter to triple the number of national marine sanctuaries from two to six. The ones established were in California, Florida, and (of course) Georgia. It is heartening to have been involved in saving them and to have drafted the signing statement in which President Carter declared them to be "the marine equivalents of Yosemite, Big Bend, the Great Smokies, and the Everglades." When I fly over Point Reyes, north of San Francisco, or the Santa Barbara Channel Islands and see sanctuaries free of oil and gas platforms, I know my Uncle Elliott would smile.

I also had an opportunity to help save the intermountain valleys of the Great Basin in Utah and Nevada, where the air force wanted to put two hundred MX missiles on railroad cars and shuttle them constantly among 2,600 colossal hardened concrete shelters. Three of us studied the environmental impact statement (over two thousand pages long), realized the project would be an environmental disaster, and helped derail it. When the United States ultimately produced one hundred MXs, they were put in existing missile silos, saving tens of billions of dollars as well as those valleys.

Those are concrete (I couldn't resist) accomplishments, but the achievement I feel best about is an idea, the concept of biological diversity. I was assigned to be the senior author of a chapter in

Environmental Quality 1980, CEQ's annual report on a topic so broad that it had not been examined comprehensively: what was happening to life on Earth. Realizing that our planet was losing diversity at all levels of biological organization, I called it biological diversity. Actually Tom Lovejoy had used the term months earlier in two publications to mean species diversity, but I had not seen them. Later, in *Conserving Biological Diversity in Our National Forests,* I offered the three-level definition that is used today, the diversity of life at the level of genes, species, and ecosystems. We were losing diversity at all of those levels for much the same reasons.

The prevailing conservation ethic when we wrote the biological diversity chapter was utilitarian. There were only two kinds of organisms that mattered: useful ones and bad ones. Useful ones are those you can shoot, hook, or saw; bad ones eat things you can shoot, hook, or saw; and the rest are irrelevant.

A more Earth-friendly conservation ethic, which was recognized in law in the 1970s with the Endangered Species Act, holds that all living things are important whether they are known to be useful or not, so we should not cause any one of them to go extinct. The problem with this approach is that it requires species to be at death's door before you pay attention to them, like a health care system based on emergency care rather than preventive care.

Conserving biological diversity requires maintaining the parts and the processes, the integrity and interactions of nature. You do not subtract or add to it. By maintaining all the parts, you allow the processes to continue operating. This is a deeper environmental ethic because things do not have to be useful or about to disappear before you act. It also has political benefits because it unites different groups of people working to conserve genes, species, and ecosystems. Biological diversity has become the driving force in conservation worldwide.

In 1981, the entire professional staff of the President's Council on Environmental Quality was fired by Ronald Reagan. His term was a dark time, the most antienvironmental years in our nation's history. Before we left, we worked together to save CEQ by creating such political embarrassment that, although we were all still fired, the institution was saved. We had to save it from Reagan again in 1983, and then again in 1993, when President Clinton tried to eliminate it.

I landed at the Center for Environmental Education and then opened the Washington, D.C., office of the Ecological Society of America to give a public policy voice to my profession. It was a frustrating and difficult experience because most of my fellow scientists are uncomfortable about trying to influence the political process. Politics is seen as a dirty business, and the people who succeed in it are usually very different from those who succeed in science. Unfortunately, when experts fail to speak up, nonexperts make policy.

While at ESA, I wrote my first book, *Conserving Biological Diversity in Our National Forests.* When the Wilderness Society asked me to do it, I said I was a marine ecologist and did not know anything about forests, so I recruited scientists who did as coauthors. When forest activists found the book useful, the Wilderness Society hired me to write another book on forests in the Northwest.

That experience fulfilled a promise I had made to myself. When I was a graduate student at USC in 1974, I gave my dad a retirement gift, a tour of the West. He had fought for America in Italy, France, and Germany, putting his life on the line for a country he had hardly seen. After the tour, my fiancée and I went to Olympic National Park and spent two magical days falling in love with the Hoh rain forest. But when we emerged, I was shocked by the horrific clearcuts in Olympic National Forest and Washington State Department of Natural Resources land. The forests were devastated, with boles of trees stacked up in piles reminiscent of photos I had seen of human bodies at Auschwitz. I promised myself that someday I would do something about this, even though the idea was preposterous because I was a marine biologist who would never get to work on forests. But life had some unexpected turns in store.

Just as I was about to leave D.C. for Seattle to do the book, my father died. After his funeral in New York, I drove across the country. Now my parents lived only in memory.

During my first week in the Wilderness Society's Seattle office, I realized that the pejorative logger's term "old growth," like their terms "overmature," "senescent," and "cellulose cemeteries," made these forests sound disposable, and that a more evocative name recognizing their importance and majesty would be "ancient forests." I knew the term had real power to capture people's imaginations because the environmental community and the public adopted it immediately—and the timber industry never uses it.

My purpose in *Ancient Forests of the Pacific Northwest* was to examine the ecology of these forests in a way that created a case so compelling that nobody with a heart and a soul would harm them. I wanted to reach beyond the Pacific Northwest, to get people to see these forests as a national and world treasure. Fulfilling my heartfelt but hasty pledge, we succeeded to a degree that I still find amazing.

While researching the book and talking to experts on various aspects of ecology, I spent eight marvelous months in the ancient forests. It was a transforming experience. I realized that for the first time in my life I was home, recalling John Denver's song "Rocky Mountain High," in which he sings of coming home to a place he had never been.

Saving the sea is my full-time occupation now, and I do not visit my ancient forests often; but when I walk among the towering western hemlocks, Douglas firs, and Sitka spruces, I have a sense of belonging and rightness that I feel more strongly there than in any other ecosystem on this planet. It is like being in my wife's arms— it's just right.

In 1989, after *Ancient Forests* was at the printer, Roger McManus, president of the Center for Marine Conservation, asked me to return to CMC as chief scientist, with the goal of making marine biodiversity a public issue. That was a bold step, because the approach to marine conservation was scattered. Small groups of people were working to stop pollution, establish marine sanctuaries, and save the most charismatic species (great whales, dolphins, and sea turtles) and were becoming more involved in fisheries, but nobody had looked at the bigger picture. So I pulled together a comprehensive examination of marine conservation, *Global Marine Biological Diversity*, with 105 coauthors.

While we were doing the book, it became clear that one of the most urgent needs in marine conservation was a more integrated understanding of the living sea. I realized that the young science of conservation biology could create a multidisciplinary synthesis among marine sciences relevant to conservation, just as Michael Soule and others had done for the land. I proposed to CMC's president that my job should be to make the science of marine conservation biology happen, and he agreed. But after I negotiated with the University of Victoria and the Society for Conservation Biology to hold the seminal event in this effort—the first Symposium on Marine Conservation Biology—CMC backed out.

It forced me into an agonizing decision. Should I stay in a comfortable job where I was not accomplishing much or take the largest risk of my life by starting a new organization dedicated to helping the birth of marine conservation biology? With advice and encouragement from my friends and funders, Mark and Sharon Bloome, and the unwavering backing of my wife, Irene, I decided to quit and follow my dream. I founded the Marine Conservation Biology Institute in May 1996, and good things have happened since then.

Now MCBI is a six-person organization headquartered in Redmond, near Seattle, with offices in Washington, D.C. We organized the first Symposium on Marine Conservation Biology, and over one thousand scientists came from around the world. We have held a half dozen scientific workshops looking at the hottest emerging issues in the field. Our statement, *Troubled Waters: A Call for Action,* signed by 1,600 marine and conservation biologists from seventy countries, became the first marine environmental news hit of the International Year of the Ocean.

The sea is so vast that it seems invulnerable, a boundless cornucopia of resources for our appetites and a convenient toilet for our wastes. But humankind is more powerful than we realize, and the living sea is in real trouble. By applying scientific understanding about marine biodiversity and how humans affect it, we can make better decisions. Knowledge does not guarantee that we will do the right thing, but we will make better decisions with it than without it.

There is just one ocean, the world ocean system. The Black Sea flows into the Mediterranean, which flows into the Atlantic, which is connected to the Arctic Ocean, and through that to the Pacific and the Indian Oceans. They are all connected to one another through aquatic pathways. The herbicide sprayed onto a golf course in Chicago's suburbs is washed into streams, then the Illinois River, then the Mississippi River, which carries it into the Gulf of Mexico, then into the Atlantic Ocean, and from there into all the world's oceans.

Not recognizing this unity, we draw political lines on maps that have nothing to do with marine ecosystems. We divide Georges Bank between Canada and the United States; Canada manages its part one way and the United States manages it another way, so we screw up things for the Canadians, and they screw up things for us. We fail to protect, restore, and sustainably use the bounty of the living sea in Georges Bank and elsewhere in part because of political divisions that have no relationship to ocean circulation, submarine topography, and biological processes such as dispersal and migration.

Generally, a marine area is imperiled to the extent that it is influenced by what happens on land. The flow of materials, including sediments, nutrients, and toxic materials, is usually downhill from land to sea, so the sea is the collecting basin for much of what people do on land. Consequently, the marine places in the worst trouble are those adjacent to and thus most affected by activities on land. The Black Sea, for example, is surrounded by six nations—Turkey, Georgia, Russia, Ukraine, Romania, and Bulgaria—which have a long tradition of enmity and noncooperation. They do, however, have a strong incentive to work together to protect the Black Sea's living resources, which provide them with seafood important to their people; but there is one further complication. In addition to effluent from these six countries, rivers flowing into the Black Sea, such as the Danube, carry wastes from many more, including Switzerland, Austria, and Yugoslavia. These nations pay no penalty for destroying the Black Sea, whereas the Russians, Turks, and Bulgars, who also mess it up, pay for it when the Black Sea does not yield them the benefits that it used to. The six Black Sea coastal nations have no way to prevent the nations lining influent rivers from polluting them. We need an international agreement that recognizes that every place in the sea is downstream from every other place.

Like our political constructs, our economic systems work against us. One pernicious effect of a free-market economy was originally pointed out by Colin Clark, a mathematician at the University of British Columbia. He explained how our economic system ensures the destruction of natural resources, including long-lived species such as whales, sea turtles, and fishes. If you manage them for maximum sustainable yield, and they yield, say, 3 percent per year, that is a lower return on investment than the 5 percent you might get in a bank account. Thus, it is more profitable to liquidate them and invest the capital in something that pays a higher yield. The game becomes "take the money and run." Further, people who use natural resources have a strong incentive to maximize their returns by passing the costs of doing business (the harm they do to fish habitat, for example) to the rest of us while pocketing all the profits.

That reasoning helps explain why the world's fisheries are collapsing. Economic forces motivate fishermen to eliminate what could be a sustainable resource, and political forces prevent regulatory agencies from regulating them. We are liquidating our marine capital: most fish stocks are depleted, overfished by three and a half million fishing vessels around the world. National governments spend $125 billion dollars every year to catch $70 billion worth of rapidly declining fish. Subsidies for fleet expansion lead to more and bigger boats chasing fewer and smaller fish. As Daniel Pauly and coauthors noted in a landmark paper in *Science* last year, we are fishing farther down food webs. That is, increasingly we are eating what we formerly used for bait. This is eliminating the bigger fishes at higher trophic levels, such as shark, swordfish, tuna, grouper, and cod.

Once people used the power of their arms or the winds to take small wooden boats with gear made of natural materials into the trackless opaqueness of the sea. Now we use huge steel fossil-fuel–powered boats with durable, nondegradable gear that is all but invisible to fish. We have turned the sea transparent with precision fish finders, global positioning systems, and daily Internet downloads precisely locating temperature conditions in which certain species feed. Hotspots can be fished until they are emptied. The sea is still dangerous for fishermen, but it is far more dangerous for fish; technology has stacked the deck in favor of the eaters against the eaten.

Fishing is the last major commercial hunt for wildlife. Aside from depleting targeted fish populations, commercial fishing reduces biological diversity in other ways. It catches huge numbers of unwanted organisms in towed nets, in gill nets, and on longlines, then throws them overboard after they die on deck. Shrimping is even worse than other kinds of fishing. I have been on shrimpers where only 5 percent of the catch consists of shrimp. The other 95 percent of marine life— sponges, starfish, crabs, and a wide variety of fishes—become bykill. Recently two Canadian biologists reported that a large, long-lived fish that is not targeted in any fishery, the barndoor skate, is nearing extinction because so many have been caught incidental to commercial fishing operations.

MCBI's first scientific workshop on emerging issues examined the worldwide effects on marine ecosystems of trawling and similar fishing methods that tow heavy gear across sands, muds, gravel, boulders, and other bottom types. With my workshop cohost, Les Watling of the University of Maine, a marine benthic ecologist, we compared trawling, scallop dredging, and similar kinds of towed fishing techniques with a more familiar kind of disturbance on land—clearcutting. It put my years of work on forest conservation biology to good use.

Clearcutting and trawling are remarkably similar kinds of disturbances. Of course, there are differences—after all, the gear varies, and loggers clearcut to get the trees, not the birds and mammals living among them. But they both disturb most of the structure-forming organisms that provide habitat for many other species. And both of them cause a substantial nutrient loss from the affected site. Yet the difference in area is astounding: whereas the forest loss due to clearcutting each year is about one hundred thousand square kilometers (the size of Indiana), the area trawled each year is vastly larger.

We calculated nearly fifteen million square kilometers (twice the area of the contiguous United States). Even if we overestimated, trawling is still the greatest disturbance in the sea worldwide.

Fishing is only one of the major threats to marine biodiversity. The sea is filled with signs that things are getting worse, quickly. A century ago, Chesapeake Bay oysters cleaned the bay by filtering its water and supported a fishery one hundred times larger than today's; now oysters have been laid low by a lethal combination of overfishing, nutrient pollution, and diseases. The northern right whales that Captain Ahab and his real-life counterparts pursued to the ends of the earth have almost disappeared; the few that remain have failed to recover in number more than sixty years after whaling for them ostensibly stopped. Some are struck by ships; some are drowned in fishing gear—that we know. But is noise pollution preventing them from hearing the sounds of potential mates, are potent chemical pollutants inhibiting their reproductive and immune systems, or have we so changed food webs in the sea that they no longer have enough to eat? Coral reefs above a depth of 50 meters (165 feet) in the Indian Ocean have been devastated in the past year by increases in temperature. It has just been reported that there are no live corals left in the Maldive Islands: they are gone, which does not bode well for the thousands of other species that lived in them. These are all indicators that the sea is in trouble.

We are destroying the living sea and the biosphere it supports. I believe we have it in us to be wise, compassionate, and loving of our home, just as we can be stupid, greedy, and destructive. Which we choose will determine whether we survive or eliminate ourselves (and take countless other species with us). It is definitely happening, as evidenced by all the signs that our ignorance and lack of concern about the environment are coming back to haunt us.

As one of my heroes, David Ehrenfeld of Rutgers University, points out, we humans think we are all that counts. But we are just one among millions of species on this planet. Every bite of food we eat, every drop of water we drink, every breath of air we breathe comes to us courtesy of biological diversity. Living things are our essential resources and life-support systems, and our existence depends entirely upon their existence, functioning, and well-being. Even if we are not touched with wonder by the beauty of other living things, it is in our own interest to save them because without them we cannot exist.

Further Reading

Elliott Norse. *Global Marine Biological Diversity: A Strategy for Building Conservation into Decision Making.* Island Press, 1993.
———. *Ancient Forests of the Pacific Northwest.* Island Press, 1990.
Elliott Norse et al. *Conserving Biological Diversity in Our National Forests.* The Wilderness Society, 1986.

Nature Conservancy

MAX NICHOLSON

IF NATURE BECOMES IMPRINTED POWERFULLY during childhood, it endures throughout life. Early, vivid experiences in nature prepared me for a visit to the Natural History Museum in London when I was seven. I entered a wondrous new world in the bird gallery, where superbly realistic habitat displays captivated and carried me away. Finding these fascinating creatures in the wild became my driving desire; I lived to learn their secrets. Their calls and songs inspired me to try to understand them, so I sought them out, and, without anyone knowledgeable to help me, recorded my observations in field notes modeled after Gilbert White's 125-year-old *Natural History of Selborne.*

Wherever I went birds interested me most; but insects, mammals, and other creatures also excited wonder and an eagerness to experience more. My family's frequent moves across southern England created a nomadic response in me, a readiness to shift to unknown environments and be receptive to what they offered. The pangs of separation from earlier favorite haunts were assuaged by the opportunity to explore new and different kinds of country.

I was enchanted by the magic of nature's kaleidoscopic changes around me: falling snow, swirling mist, budding blossoms, and the eagerly anticipated return of migrating birds. The dynamic workings of nature ensured that I did not take it for granted; it was so vigorously alive that I was enlivened by being immersed in it. I was constantly alert to discover the fascinating activities of particular animals or the chosen habitats of luxuriant plants.

Unfortunately, my enjoyment of the natural world was broken when I was ten years old. In 1914 World War I started, and I watched thousands of boys only a few years older than I marching off in new uniforms to their foreign graves. This was a deep horror. What kind of world was I living in? The war preoccupied me with the sad state of mankind, so inferior to the natural world.

The postwar slump forced me to leave school early, but, fortunately, I found I could make a living writing about nature. That enabled me to continue self-directed fieldwork, sharpening my perceptions and understanding. Writing about nature stimulated greater insights and appreciation, and intense observation of bird habits and habitats led to population counting and then to ecology.

By the time I was twenty-one, I was writing books about birds. In quick succession, I wrote half a dozen, all on different aspects of birds, in addition to a number of articles and scientific papers. In the process, the ornithologist became an ecologist. My first book, in 1926, *Birds in England,* argued that an ecological perspective should determine policies of bird protection. The first line of my second book, *How Birds Live,* was "There is a flourishing science, Ecology. . . ."

My obsession with birds was, however, being matched by growing concern about the mismanagement of human affairs. Some commentaries that I sent to Geoffrey Dawson, the editor of the *Times,* led him to press me to revert to an abandoned intention to study at Oxford, so I went there in 1926. By great good fortune some of the original leaders of the environmental movement were there at that time. I met A. G. Tansley, our new professor of botany; Charles Elton, who was staffing the first Animal Ecology Unit; and Julian Huxley, who, although no longer teaching at Oxford, returned frequently and became a close friend.

After enrolling in the Ornithological Society, I organized the Oxford bird census and the first national bird census of heronries in

1928. Thus I shifted from independent and isolated activity to organizing teams for fieldwork, eventually reshaping field ornithology in Britain. Then I helped set up the Edward Grey Institute, the first ornithological research center at a British university. In 1932, I was involved in creating its twin, the British Trust for Ornithology, a pioneering project for national cooperative research. It still exists, continuing to do bird censuses and advising the government on factors affecting changes in bird populations.

Soon after arriving, I founded the Oxford University Exploration Club to undertake ecological expeditions. I went with it to Greenland and in 1929 to the Amazonian rain forest, where I spent some time up in the treetops, studying wildlife over a hundred feet above the forest floor. I was keen to study in territory that had not been disturbed in any way, a goal that was already becoming difficult because of so much human interference.

As time passed, I found myself becoming drawn increasingly into the sorry state of human affairs and giving less attention to nature. After finishing at Oxford, my work on public affairs took me into editorial journalism. I drafted "A National Plan for Britain," which became the basis of a socioeconomic research group called PEP (Political and Economic Planning). It attracted a lot of wonderful members, including Julian Huxley and other intellectual leaders. Working with them gave me a tremendous education in public affairs and management over a broad field.

When World War II broke out, Cyril Hurcomb recruited me into the Ministry of Shipping, where I became head of allocation of tonnage. I was surprised to find that managing the carrying capacity of British cargo shipping was not too remote from analyzing the carrying capacity of bird territories. Shipping involves systems analysis, just as ecology does. To fulfill crucial shipping needs during wartime, I had to attend strategic conferences in Cairo, Quebec, Yalta, Potsdam, and other places. In the process I became familiar with intergovernment business at the highest level.

During the war I had to travel frequently to distant locales, but the glimpses of foreign wildlife were fleeting and frustrating. I tried to snatch a moment to seek out the local birds while grounded on some airfield in Labrador, Newfoundland, or North Africa. Nevertheless, while flying long distances at lower altitudes than normal, I had extended periods of observing forests, wetlands, and mountains below. The highly personal experience of seeing nature up close at eye level was replaced with an impersonal panorama of vast natural realms of living creatures.

This broader perspective provided an overview of different biomes and the effects of varying local factors. It offered a view of both small-scale and large-scale variations, which proved helpful when I later assessed issues of international conservation management. The influence of such great synoptic ecologists as A. G. Tansley and W. H. Pearsall reinforced this shift of my interest from the micro to the macro scale.

When World War II ended, I hoped to have time to pursue bird studies in the field. Instead I was prevailed on to construct institutions to strengthen and broaden the precarious base of ecology and conservation. As postwar chair of the British Trust for Ornithology, I had to build up an efficient organization for ensuring the future expansion of field ornithology.

At the same time, Julian Huxley got me to serve as the ornithologist on the Wild Life Conservation Special Committee he was setting up. Its mission was to look at whether we could create a governmental nature conservation organization. The committee was admirably staffed with gifted and far-seeing ecologists. One of our tasks was to make field visits to sites that might require scientific conservation to find out what was still there and what needed to be done to safeguard its future.

Then I was appointed by the powerful new deputy prime minister, Herbert Morrison, lord president of the council, as head of his office. He was, among other things, minister of science. It was extraordinary that I became the official who would take delivery of the Wild Life Special Committee report I had contributed to and advise ministers what should be done about it.

Before my ascendancy to an advantageous position, ecology and conservation had been completely outside the corridors of power. With my place at the center of things, I could bring them right into the midst of it. This was an astonishing stroke of luck for ecology and conservation: one of their supporters was not only specially qualified to carry through their plans but also in the key official position to do so.

After some years in this dual function, I was pressed by my colleagues to head the national nature-conservation organization that the Wild Life Special Committee had initiated. This meant leaving the civil service to become director general of the Nature Conservancy. All my civil service colleagues thought I was absolutely mad to do this, because as a leading senior civil servant I was in line for a top promotion. While they regarded my departure as sheer lunacy, it was very advantageous for them because I was a strong rival. Word immediately went around that whether I was crazy or not, everybody should be very kind to me and to conservation. Nothing must be done to frustrate or move me to come back to the civil service.

This curious historical accident led to conservation suddenly acquiring a much more important status. Previously nobody had taken any notice of it. They still did not know what it was and did not take it very seriously. Yet the facts that I was director general of the Nature Conservancy and that they wanted to keep me there made all the difference. Thus not only did ecology and conservation measures sail through with full statutory and charter powers, but we also were assured of an unexpectedly high place in the priorities of the Whitehall pecking order.

People often assume that conservation just happened: there was this report, and its recommendations were carried out. But in fact all sorts of obstacles had to be overcome. I managed to steer our plans through bureaucratic mechanisms that would normally have buried them. First, in 1949, we had to negotiate the Nature Conservancy's royal charter as an official research council. We also had to draft and put through an Act of Parliament: The National Parks and Access to the Countryside Act. Its statutory powers were very unusual; for example, they included compulsory purchase of land for nature reserves and powers to make by-laws restricting what people could do on the reserves.

At the same time, we had to devise all sorts of new inventions, such as management plans for nature reserves, which no one had ever heard of. These involved all kinds of surveys of what was on the reserves and what the problems were in protecting them. Hardly anybody knew anything about this kind of work. I got universities to train postgraduates in order to create a strong professional cadre. Fortunately, many gifted experts in the life and earth sciences were inspired to team up within the Nature Conservancy and with outside committees. I had so many active collaborators that a study of all official government committees found that no officer in the entire British public service had as many official advisers as I had.

It was also advantageous that several of these new colleagues were heading university science departments. The Nature Conservancy's financial support enabled them to be enlivened as centers of ecological research and training, which allowed them to gain some gifted postgraduate students and train them as future leaders in conservation. They were guided to pioneer fresh studies utilizing our new research stations. We created the stations to investigate serious problems such as the ecology of heathlands, moorlands, and coasts; the dynamics of woodland growth; and the effects of pesticides and agricultural changes.

When I conducted the Oxford Bird Census in my early years, I promoted cooperative efforts among botanists, entomologists, animal ecologists, and others; but the initiative was twenty years premature. It was only now that naturalists from different specialties were working together to examine areas as a whole and deciding what to do about them. We achieved advances by effectively combining the efforts of full-time professionals and organizations of amateur naturalists, whom we introduced to the ecological approach. Field studies were coordinated through carefully organized national inquiries, creating a comprehensive program for the advancement of knowledge. The cooperative relationships among officials, academics, and amateur naturalists was exceptional, especially in comparison to their separation in the United States.

This convergence of diverse groups working on such broad goals was a new experience for all of us, including me. I took on a new role in field studies very different from my early experiences alone in a quiet glade, focusing on a few select inhabitants. Now multiple teams of specialists traversed widespread areas to assess the ecological situation throughout the country. We had to diagnose deviations from ecological health and prescribe possible courses of intervention.

We would have preferred to let nature heal itself, but the ecologically damaged communities of plants and animals needed help to survive. Britain's ravaged landscapes, despoiled by human ignorance, required the improvisation of "field hospitals" to have any hope of recovery. Ecological intervention was necessary to prevent the wholesale destruction of our natural inheritance.

Our ecological and administrative approach proved to be remarkably far-seeing. We developed ecological surveys and management plans of reserves, in addition to a national series of "sites of special scientific interest." Our countrywide listing of the distribution of plant and animal species enabled us to respond effectively to inquiries and requests for advice. It also helped our regional officers and reserve wardens to be knowledgeably involved with their local communities.

In the 1950s most people's perspective hardly reached beyond their daily routine. The majority barely noticed anything but the grossest changes in their surroundings and the countryside. Serious interest in landscapes, habitats, and wildlife was shared by only a small minority. Such now-familiar terms as "conservation" and "the environment" were unknown by the public. Even among scientists, the principles of ecology were generally not known.

During that time, we kept a very low profile. People asked, "Why has no one ever heard of the Nature Conservancy?" I replied, "Because until we have found out exactly what to do and how to do it, we do not want anyone interfering." Owing to my influence, we got a very good start for the Nature Conservancy on the inside track, but I was concerned that politicians would start interfering unless we built up strong support among the voters. Without visible public support, the whole thing was very vulnerable.

When the time arrived for us to go public, around 1960, I started building up the conservation movement publicly. I had already made sure that prominent conservationists like Peter Scott and James Fisher would become the spokespeople for conservation on the BBC. With David Attenborough and others we soon had a first-class media group to convey the message. The public responded wholeheartedly; we increased our supporters from a few hundred in small societies to hundreds of thousands in large, important groups. I think that groups work best as clubs where people become friends. In our organizations, people not only came along to meetings but also formed friendships working together on projects. That happened with the Nature Conservancy and the World Wildlife Fund.

The World Wildlife Fund was organized by a group I chaired in London in 1961. WWF was international but based in Britain. It had a substantial effect on the political status of conservation around the world because there were a number of royals and VIPs who became involved. Prince Philip helped greatly with that and various related undertakings. The urgent threat to nature all over the world demanded an immediate practical response. In many countries awareness of the dangers and a desire to do anything about them were limited to a handful of people without organizations, money, power, or experience. Many of them did wonders within these limits, but the results were pitifully insufficient.

It was a formidable task to try to deal with all these problems on a worldwide basis. It was essential to take emergency steps to gather reliable information about specific problems demanding immediate action, to create an efficient organization for raising funds and routing them to where they were needed, and to communicate the situation through the media. WWF publicized the idea of endangered species, habitat conservation, and environmental protection. We fought publicly to save wildlife wherever we could. A major success was Peter Scott's vigorous fight against the ruthless industry destroying the whales. Handing over to him the leadership of WWF proved a very wise decision.

One of the reasons I started the World Wildlife Fund was my frustration with the problems experienced by the International Union for the Conservation of Nature. Although it had many worthy members and a lot of good scientists, hardly a year went past without them having some desperate crisis, usually financial. So some of us decided we needed a complementary public counterpart to the professional group to support its scientific and ethical endeavors.

The problem with scientific groups was that scientists were holed up in their separate burrows, so we had difficulty persuading them to be interdisciplinary and international. Unfortunately, most of the national academies of science were still dominated by physics and chemistry, which looked down on the life sciences. This situation was exacerbated by the fragmentation of biology and the resulting failure of biologists to recognize the need for conservation and the necessity of doing something about it. When the International Geophysical Year, 1957, finally spurred biologists into parallel action, the International Council of Scientific Unions asked me to undertake the task of reviewing the basis of a world conservation program. I was convener for conservation for the International Biological Programme and continued in that role throughout the 1960s and 1970s.

I was overtaken almost simultaneously by some major unfinished ornithological business, in the shape of an overdue set of volumes to update and supersede Witherby's great five-volume *Handbook of British Birds,* which I helped produce in the 1930s. This now had to be vastly expanded as a multivolume *Handbook of the Birds of Europe, the Middle East, and North Africa: Birds of the Western Palearctic,* published by Oxford University Press between 1977 and 1994. Although I started as chief editor and chair of the board, I was soon forced to hand over much of the burden to others; however, I carried on as habitat editor until the end.

The project involved a substantial, expert, and hard-worked international team. By putting into shape the mass of new data for an important sector of the planet, it helped to open the way toward a global ornithology. This led to a global conspectus of the entire fauna and simultaneous efforts on the flora. It also complemented the broader efforts on the biosphere that had been initiated through the International Biological Programme at the same time.

The challenge of bridging scientific disciplines and synthesizing information was even more compelling because it was becoming clear to us that the dawn of the computer age, with its new potential for storing, retrieving, and analyzing enormous amounts of international data, offered a tool for breaking out of the narrowly bounded horizons in which scientists were trapped. Ecology would thus be able to fulfill its true, universal role. Seeing this early, I tried to utilize the opportunity to further the development of ecological science and its application in conservation and land use.

Public support and involvement is also important for international ecological programs, which is why I became chair of Earthwatch Europe. Earthwatch was started in Boston by Brian Rosborough to support projects of serious scientific value. It brings together scientists involved in international projects and keen volunteers who provide vigorous help. It is worldwide, so in any one year it has teams in about eighty different countries. I was responsible for starting up its European office in Oxford. Its Southern Hemisphere office is in Australia, and the headquarters is in Boston. It does a wonderful job giving people from all countries a chance to do something to conserve the environment and at the same time to learn much about it.

In Majorca, I am involved in a new project to build an innovative scientific center that might serve as a model for future centers around the world. The initial center is in the middle of a Majorcan wetland, pioneering a network in the Mediterranean to undertake scientific studies on the hydrology of wetlands. These complex studies will include all the biotic aspects involving the interactions of animals, plants, and water quality. We are building a field laboratory and database center, with accommodations, where visiting scientists can learn how to assemble data that can be usefully interpreted and applied. Centers such as ours are necessary to get all the required knowledge together.

This collective knowledge will become increasingly important in the future. The UNCED Conventions on Biodiversity were signed by 150 countries, but the politicians did not really understand what it was all about. They instructed their civil servants to carry out the biodiversity treaty, but the bureaucrats were also ignorant, so they had to go to the voluntary organizations the public had created for environmental protection. But even the environmental organizations lacked some of the necessary resources. This is a pervasive problem.

Most people in positions of power cannot comprehend the larger picture. Decision makers are often the last people to understand the background of what they are making decisions about.

In my view, the general public in most countries is ahead of politicians and business management. A lot of ordinary people are saying, "With all these environmental problems happening, what are our children and grandchildren going to do?" Women especially are worried about what sort of world we are bequeathing to our children. Many people in different countries are struggling to protect their environment, even though they encounter serious opposition. They are doing what they can for nature. It is marvelous how many people are getting the message. Although humanity is part of nature, it is no use just saying that. We have to work out how we harmonize with nature.

During the first half of the twentieth century a few gifted ecologists took an imaginative and brilliant lead in integrating and interpreting the discoveries of the life and earth sciences, culminating in the general acceptance of the key role of nature and the need for its care. At the same time, economics, politics, and technology released forces causing enormous damage to natural resources, striking at biodiversity, sustainability, and the healthy functioning of the biosphere.

While the emerging environmental movement earnestly sought to arouse public awareness of these dangers, reception of their message was often frustrated by rooted traditions, prescientific beliefs and assumptions, and the inertia of the status quo. Powerful vested interests dominated our shortsighted, fast-expanding, materialist society. The root ideas of our civilization propagated value judgments that proved disastrous for the environment and sustainability. Scientific information about the origins, capabilities, and limitations of human beings was learned concurrently with that about nature; but they were in separate scientific specialties, leaving misleading assumptions rooted in the past to dominate conduct.

I belong to a small group that is trying to bring together the human and natural aspects. There is a human ecology that is parallel with natural ecology. We are looking at what humanity is doing to the natural resources we depend on and examining human actions in relation to real needs. People have been deliberately misled to believe that human satisfaction consists of having material possessions instead of experiencing personal fulfillment. We are developing a new perspective based on a synthesis of ecology, economics, and the social sciences to design and construct a sustainable and better future.

The time is overdue to integrate our knowledge about humanity with what we know about our environment. We need a comprehensive overview that looks at the human condition the same way we look at ecology as a whole. Now, at the end of my life, I am working in this new group to give primary attention to humanity's problems and the resulting problems we are creating in nature. Human beings have a lot to learn from nature in all sorts of profound ways. It is time for melding humanity with nature.

Further Reading

Max Nicholson. *Bird-Watching in London: A Historical Perspective.* London Natural History Society, 1995.
———. *New Environmental Age.* Cambridge University Press, 1987.
———. *The Environmental Revolution.* McGraw-Hill, 1970.

World Conservation Union

MARTIN HOLDGATE

 I HAVE ALWAYS BEEN AWARE OF THE ENVIRON-
ment and nature because my father was a school-
master who taught biology. I recall being taken very
early in my childhood to the beach near Brighton, on England's south
coast, to collect various kinds of marine life from rock pools and going
inland to find freshwater life lurking in the ponds of the Sussex countryside. As a young child I knew the Latin names of quite a few species
before I was aware they had English ones. Observing nature and
studying living organisms were things I just grew up with.

Like my father, my grandfather was a schoolmaster and biologist.
He was also a mountaineer and an amateur astronomer, and hills and
planets became my own early enthusiasms. The planets fascinated me
because they were other worlds, remarkably different from the one
we live on. My imagination was free to wonder what life there might
be like; at that time there was more speculation about the possibility
of living things on other planets, at least on Mars.

When I was seven years old, our family moved from the south to
the northwest coast of England, where my father became headmas-
ter of a school in the seaside town of Blackpool. We used to go for
holidays to the hill country of a county then called Westmorland,
now swallowed up in Cumbria, and these travels sparked my love of
the hills and the wild country.

As I grew older, I was increasingly fascinated by the patterns of plants and associated life in the hills and along streams. This led to an interest in what I would call the pattern of nature. Looking at a landscape, I tried to work out the interplay of rocks and life. Geological history was visible through the molding of the land in the Ice Ages and the subsequent changes precipitated by human activity. Space, time, and life were woven together in an intricate tapestry. The hills still held faint marks of ancient settlements—three-thousand-year-old villages with their associated field systems. I tried to puzzle out how early people had shaped their living out of the landscape and what changes they had wrought. The complicating factors created by the human component increased my interest in the complexity of it all.

Overall, the interactions and patterns of nature fascinated me much more than detailed analysis of its individual components. When I went to Cambridge University to study biology, I wanted to continue focusing on the whole, rather than being confined to the parts. Ecology was especially fascinating, and I was fortunate that at that time they still taught whole-organism biology—the structure, physiology, and life-cycles of complete plants and animals—rather than the biochemical and genetic disciplines that prevail today.

Reductionist approaches like biochemistry did not interest me, nor was I gripped by laboratory experimentation. Nevertheless, the zoology department was filled with outstanding biologists and was a leading school of experimental science, so I had the chance to learn the discipline of rigorous laboratory research from such gifted people.

In fact, my doctoral research was highly experimental. I studied the structure and composition of the outermost waxy layers of insects, which make them waterproof and determine whether they are easily wetted by other liquids like insecticidal sprays. That work did give me one striking demonstration of the value of reaching across different scientific disciplines. I went out to tea with a former schoolmate and his guest, Michael Seal. Michael was also studying surfaces, those of diamonds, and he was looking at them directly using an electron microscope in reflection, whereas I had to deduce surface properties from how the insect made contact with clean water. Reflection electron microscopes were novel instruments at that time, and it occurred to both of us that his equipment might help solve one of my problems: to determine how the rough, waxy layer of the mealworm beetle pupa is formed.

We developed a technique for preparing bits of insect for the reflection microscope, which showed that whereas the newly molted surface was smooth, the molt one was roughened by fine filaments of extruded material. That was the first time an electron microscope in reflection had ever been used to look at an insect surface. It just happened because a physical scientist and a biological scientist met over a cup of tea at an opportune moment in the development of science.

This experience fixed in my mind the enormous value of looking across the traditional sectors of intellectual disciplines and considering the insights and approaches of people who might be grappling with the same sort of problem in a very different context. I think that is a generally useful approach, especially in our highly compartmentalized world.

My life took a complete turnabout in 1955. I was sitting in my lab looking at insects when somebody came in and said, "Would you like to go to Gough Island?" The island is not exactly on the beaten track; it is located in the middle of the South Atlantic, nearly two thousand miles from the nearest continent. Of course the invitation was very enticing for someone like me, who loves the outdoors and is interested in the patterns of plants and animals and how they relate to the physical structure of the landscape.

Gough Island is about eight miles long, four miles wide, and three thousand feet high (if I stick to the old-fashioned units). It had never been mapped, except around the edges. Its geology, plants, land life, and sea life were little known. What was known was that it had many kinds of seabirds breeding on it and was the home of two kinds of land birds—a moorhen and a small finch—found nowhere else in the world. As it also had a number of unique plant species, we deduced that it ought to have lots of insects that were also peculiar to the island. We knew it had never been permanently inhabited by people and hoped it had not suffered too much from human disturbance.

Ten of us spent six months there, mapping the island and its vegetation, working out its volcanic history, gathering its rocks, collecting numerous insects new to science, counting the enormous populations of seabirds and fur seals, and studying the moorhen and finch. It was exciting scientifically, enormous fun, and even more enjoyable because Gough Island is such a beautiful place. I am happy to say it has now been recognized as a World Heritage Site.

That experience reinforced my interest in ecology and biogeography—the distribution of plants and animals and what causes them to live where they do. From that day on, I gave up the laboratory and experimental zoology and became progressively more involved in field ecology, especially at the southernmost tip of the world.

After Gough Island, I spent a year as a lecturer in zoology at Manchester University, followed by three years at the University of Durham. Professor Jim Cragg had built up a superb group of students and senior academics studying the ecology of the northern English moorlands—my childhood habitat. They were looking at the role of different species within the ecosystems of the northern uplands. It was a congenial environment for me, especially as I could live high up in the tower of Durham Castle, looking across a broad green lawn to the magnificent Norman cathedral, now another World Heritage Site.

Then the Royal Society (the British academy of sciences) invited me to organize an expedition in 1958–59 to celebrate the centenary of Darwin's *Origin of Species.* Initially their intention had been to have a shipload of scientists follow the course Darwin had taken on the *Beagle* across the South Pacific, looking at the interrelationships of life on the various islands on the way.

The ship did not become available, so I was asked instead to prepare and lead a reconnaissance expedition to the southern part of South America. The journey was to take us south from the warm temperate zone, at a big island called Chiloe (then still partly covered in marvelous temperate rain forest), down to the islands at the back of Cape Horn and along the Beagle Channel. This provided another opportunity to see how the patterns of plants and associated life forms interrelated with one another in the landscape.

There are many biological puzzles in that region. For me, one enigma was that on the mainland at the bottom end of South America were some of the same species we had seen on Gough Island and Tristan da Cunha, two thousand miles downwind. Because the young volcanic islands would have been active relatively recently, they must have acquired their resident populations through transoceanic migration. Immigrant species must have crossed two thousand miles of sea by being blown, being carried by birds, or possibly even drifting.

But most of the species we saw in the southern South American forests and moorlands, including the dominant trees and bog plants, had their closest relatives in the forests and wetlands of New Zealand and Tasmania, which were even farther away. There were also many associated insects with a similar distribution pattern. The fact of this puzzling distribution had been known for over a century; the problem was the explanation.

At that time the theory of plate tectonics, explaining the past movement of the continents, had not been worked out fully. But now we can appreciate what must have happened. In South America, Tasmania, and New Zealand we see the fragmented remnants of the forests, wetlands, and other kinds of vegetation and many plant and animal species that once covered the great southern continent of Gondwanaland. It split up millions of years ago, and its pieces moved apart like rafts. One chunk of it drifted all the way down to the South Pole but lost virtually all of its flora and fauna as its icecap expanded.

My interest in Southern Hemisphere biogeography got me involved in Antarctic research. I went back to Cambridge, to the Scott Polar Research Institute, in 1960 and for the next six years organized the biological work of the British Antarctic Survey. Soon thereafter I found myself chairing an international group that brought together biologists from all the countries doing research in the Antarctic. Under the Antarctic Treaty, signed in 1959, the continent was demilitarized and opened to people of all nations for purposes of peaceful scientific exploration.

Everybody thought you went to the Antarctic to study penguins, but we already knew quite a lot about the marine life, particularly birds and mammals. By contrast, there had been very little study of land species. Harsh climatic conditions limited survival, so life on land was meager (just one kind of grass and one other higher plant, and a lot of lichens, mosses, and liverworts). This sparsity of species facilitated our attempts to understand the workings of a naturally simple ecosystem. We looked at the role of various components of the land ecosystem by mapping vegetation and soil, then relating different kinds of plant groupings to soil type; identifying small insects and worms; investigating what was living in the lakes; and looking at marine life in the shallow coastal waters. I became very interested in energy flows and interactions in the polar system.

Working in Antarctica was invaluable because it is a region where both international cooperation in science and international conservation are deeply rooted. All of this prepared me for my later career when I left the field sciences and went into environmental administration and policy and then into world conservation. Comprehending the overall pattern and interactions of life is an essential foundation for conservation.

In 1966, I became deputy director of the British Nature Conservancy and was responsible for its research. I found myself working in an absolutely unique organization that blended scientific research, mainly ecology, with practical action to conserve species and ecosystems. It had been set up in this way by very far-sighted people, led by Julian Huxley and the eminent ecologist Arthur Tansley.

At that time the Nature Conservancy was led by another pioneer, Max Nicholson. He insisted on the blending of research and its application in conservation on the ground. He did not think you could manage a nature reserve unless you had an understanding of the ecology of the plants and animals that lived in the reserves, their dynamics within the system, and their response to human impact on the wider environment.

That approach and background were valuable as I became more and more involved with government policy, beginning in 1969. It happened quite accidentally when the British prime minister, Harold Wilson, and his senior minister, Anthony Crosland, came to our research station at Monks' Wood, not far from Cambridge. Mr. Wilson had just undertaken a great tripartite initiative for the British environment. As part of that he created a standing Royal Commission on Environmental Pollution (like the Council on Environmental Quality in the United States) to do in-depth thinking about pollution and the actions that should be taken. A second step was to appoint Crosland to spearhead government action against pollution. A third step was to give him a scientific team, a Central Scientific Unit in his own office, to support his endeavors.

Anthony Crosland was an intellectual giant in the British Labour Party, highly respected and well placed to coordinate what the whole government machine was doing for environmental protection and regional planning. He was responsible for coordinating activities of the three main departments of government dealing directly with the environment; but he was not a scientist, nor was he particularly interested in technical detail, hence the need for a team of professionals who would examine and explain the nature of the pollution problems he had to address.

When Harold Wilson and Anthony Crosland came to our research station, there was a farmers' demonstration outside, so they were taken away to do some politicking with the farmers. I was left talking to the chief scientific adviser to the government, Solly Zuckerman, who was a very powerful figure during that period and himself one of the architects of the government's new measures for the environment. The two of us went around looking at the research we were doing on the effect of pesticides on wildlife. The British Nature Conservancy had become aware of the troublesome effects of pesticides and was actively researching them well before Rachel Carson published her landmark book *Silent Spring*.

The following day, I got a telephone call asking me to be interviewed to head the Central Scientific Unit in Crosland's office. So the next thing I knew, I was part of the British civil service, attached to the Cabinet Office. Suddenly I found myself appointed to lead a central unit of government that had to look across all sectors at how far a pollutant posed a problem in air, water, or food. You need to have a total ecosystem view of nature in order to truly comprehend such interactions because you have to know what pollutants are, what they do, where they come from, where they go, what they are used for, what they interact with, how they are transformed, and how they are disposed of.

In addition to all the interactions among living systems, I also had to deal with the relations among government agencies. So I found myself getting into dialogue (that is a polite way of putting it) with a huge number of departmental interests and bureaucrats who resented anyone fishing in their particular pond (to say nothing of pointing out its pollution). My position rendered me vulnerable to being universally unpopular as a result of the way the civil service operated. Even more frustrating and disturbing was seeing how the structure of government administration almost guaranteed that we got our pollution control and our environmental policy wrong.

They were all so sectoralized. To use pesticide control as an example, the Ministry of Agriculture was responsible for the productivity of farmland, so it promoted pesticide use and ignored what happened when pesticides ended up on food or washed into watercourses. Purity of the water supply and control of effluents through wastewater treatment were the responsibility of the Ministry of Housing and Local Government. The safety of foodstuffs and contamination in the human food chain were matters for the Department of Health. Needless to say, none of these departments had any connection with each other or with the Department of Trade and Industry, which oversaw pesticide manufacturers.

Predictably, each government sector defended its own interests and resisted pressures to change its policy. So, for example, agriculture's knee-jerk reaction was to shield farmers and the pesticide industry by resisting controls, alleging either that the science was not good enough or that wildlife losses were not really important. If you parcel responsibility for the environment into narrow sectors competing and fighting with one another, as vested interests invariably do, you are certain to get the wrong policies.

Nevertheless, seeing things from inside the government provided me with a window through which to view the problems of the environment. Even at that stage, in the early 1970s, before the United Nations conference raised the issues internationally, it was clear we were suffering from serious environmental problems. They are still with us today because governments and industries took a short-term view and were dominated by narrow interests that did not come together to review the wider picture. In the environmental field, more than any other, it is necessary to have an overview and to take a long-term view. To deal with the most complex systems in existence, you have to think holistically.

As the years went by, my work became increasingly international. I found myself leading British delegations to the Environment Commission of OECD and then organizing our input to the United Nations Conference on the Human Environment in Stockholm in 1972. I chaired the international meeting that negotiated the Convention on the Prevention of Marine Pollution by Dumping of Wastes and Other Matter. In fact, I was drawn into a career in environmental affairs that has lasted since the early 1970s, taking me through a series of jobs in the British government that would be wearisome to detail.

My responsibilities included a vast array of public policies ranging from the conservation of nature and the countryside in Britain, and action to combat pollution and dispose of wastes, to our input into the international environmental debate. I was, as chief scientist, responsible for the quality of research and scientific advice in the Departments of the Environment and Transport and had been given the extra task of overseeing the privatization of the national water industry. Obviously I could not do much of this myself; I was conductor of an orchestra of very capable administrative instrumentalists, and I was confined by the interminable workload and its essentially managerial character.

In 1987 I was in Nairobi, leading the British delegation to the Governing Council of the United Nations Environment Programme, when someone approached me casually by the hotel pool, mentioned that the current director was leaving the International Union for the Conservation of Nature, and then astounded me by asking, "Would you be interested in becoming director general?" When I returned to Britain, to my great surprise and embarrassment, a telegram arrived in the Department of the Environment congratulating me on my appointment as the head of IUCN.

I had not even been to IUCN's headquarters in Switzerland to see what I was in for, but I soon found out. The International Union for the Conservation of Nature, also called the World Conservation Union, is a unique organization. Founded in 1948, when the world was busily inventing the United Nations as the best guarantee of global peace, it now brings together about eighty governments, one hundred government agencies, and seven hundred nongovernmental organizations (NGOs) as a kind of global network for conservation and sustainable development.

When I came to the World Conservation Union in 1988 it was still relatively small, with around one hundred staff, most of them at the headquarters in Switzerland. By 1994, when I left, we had over four hundred staff, most of them in developing countries, and our budget had trebled, to over fifty million Swiss francs a year. Perhaps the most satisfying administrative task was watching the union's program and worldwide range of activities expand steadily. That growth and "southward movement" has gone on. The International Union for the Conservation of Nature is an important world network for tomorrow's environmental challenges.

One of the most interesting aspects of working with IUCN was the diversity of people and places it took me to, often with dramatic juxtapositions. Ministerial meetings in dark suits in capital cities one day and bumpy tracks rising to the mountain mists or winding through the savannah the next. Even the endless formalities had interesting moments, such as sitting with President Bush at the Earth Summit in Rio de Janeiro as a whole series of NGO leaders, including Jacques Cousteau, told him how wrong he and the United States were to abdicate the position of leadership they had advanced at the UN Conference on the Environment in Stockholm twenty years before.

The World Conservation Union is an ongoing global environmental endeavor. Its mission is to "influence, encourage and assist societies throughout the world to conserve the integrity and diversity of nature and to ensure that any use of natural resources is equitable and ecologically sustainable." It works by pooling ideas from its worldwide network of voluntary commissions, involving over ten thousand experts, and utilizing ecological expertise to provide plans, advice, and technical support.

Traditionally, the union has worked to protect nature, and its track record there is long and good. It developed the classification used to rank threatened species and invented the "Red Data Books" and supporting action plans used by conservationists everywhere. It produced a United Nations list of national parks and protected areas and developed the taxonomy of protected areas used by "parks people" around the world.

Several major international conventions, including the Convention on International Trade in Endangered Species and the more recent Convention on Biological Diversity, started on the World Conservation Union's drawing boards. It has helped over fifty countries prepare national conservation strategies. With its sister organization, the World Wildlife Fund (also known as the World Wide Fund for Nature), and with the United Nations Environment Programme, it produced the World Conservation Strategy in 1980 and issued a followup, "Caring for the Earth," in 1991.

While IUCN realizes that wilderness and wildlife need to be conserved because they are invaluable in their own right, it recognizes that they are also precious resources people want to use. Working out how they might be used sustainably, so that their economic importance is maintained and people have an incentive to conserve them, is a more recent challenge. Sometimes this means conflict between people who believe that exploiting wildlife and wilderness is wrong and others who say that using their resources provides the only reason to protect them. Trying to balance conflicting values passionately held by members is problematic, especially on divisive issues such as the use of natural resources—an argument that has rumbled on for a century, since the days when John Muir and Gifford Pinchot battled over the use of America's wilderness.

The World Conservation Union tries to support societies according to need, pooling knowledge across the world, while recognizing that different people and countries have different circumstances. One project serves as an example of how that actually works. In the mountainous region of Gilgit and Hunza, overgrazing of high pastures and destruction of natural forests was threatening Himalayan ecosystems. The villages needed a nondestructive, sustainable source of income.

Our solution was to tap the rivulets that trickled down from the snows to the arid valley floors and use the water to irrigate vegetable gardens and fruit orchards. The Aga Khan Rural Support Programme provided the start-up finance, the villages provided the labor, and IUCN provided the ecological know-how. Community meetings explained to village men and women (separately, of course, in that society) what was in it for them. Enthusiastic participation generated productivity and profits to repay the start-up loan and fund new projects, so the snowball rolled on. Development and conservation joined hands in that marvelous world amid Earth's highest mountains.

Nature conservation is more important now than ever, but the World Conservation Strategy realistically set it in the wider context of human activities. Our species is now the dominant component of the global macrofauna. We are taking over the role of top predator and replacing diverse wild herbivores with a few domesticated animals; altering vegetation patterns and ruining soil fertility; preempting nearly half the flow of energy through ecological systems on land; and transforming biogeochemical cycles.

This momentum will rapidly increase as the human population expands from the present six billion to the predicted twelve billion by the middle of the next century and as all those people demand a higher quality of life. The rapid doubling of our population means we cannot just set aside 10 percent of the world as nature reserves and let market forces do what they will with the rest. It also means that we have to work to end poverty, misery, squalor, illiteracy, discrimination, and inequity—not only because they are morally repugnant but also because they unleash forces of desperation that destroy the future for the sake of transient relief.

Development must be ecologically based if it is to be sustainable. More than ever before we need to be guided by ecological insights, for ecologists are above all concerned with the complex interactions of species and with the living and nonliving components of the biosphere. Ecologists need to explain that human survival depends on the biological systems and natural cycles of the planet and that conserving nature preserves our own life-support system.

We have to conserve the whole biosphere, including humanity. Conservation is therefore a social activity. It has to involve people in deciding the plans and actions that will create their future and that of their children and grandchildren. We are dealing with the relationship between people—all people, now and in the future—and the planet that sustains all of us and all other forms of life.

My time at the World Conservation Union, in particular, convinced me of the importance of committed individuals. The greatest need is for international vision and inspiration. As I wrote in my book *From Care to Action,* human societies down the ages have been led by visionaries rather than functionaries—by poets and prophets. We need to recapture a sense of vision. We need to acknowledge not only that the world of nature is the foundation of our lives but also that it is beautiful, wonderful, an object of reverence, and a manifestation of what people of many faiths have seen as the divine.

Further Reading

Martin Holdgate. *From Care to Action: Making a Sustainable World.* Earthscan, 1996.

Martin Holdgate, Mohammed Kassas, Gilbert F. White, and David Spurgeon, eds. *The World Environment, 1972–82: A Report by UNEP.* Weidner and Sons, 1982.

Martin Holdgate. *A Perspective of Environmental Pollution.* Cambridge University Press, 1979.

Martin Holdgate and Gilbert F. White, eds. *Environmental Issues.* Wiley, 1977.

Martin Holdgate et al. *Forces of Nature.* Edited by Vivian Fuchs. Holt, Rinehart, and Winston, 1977.

Ozone Hole

SHERWOOD ROWLAND

*Although this story is in the third person, Sherwood Row-
land wrote it himself. He used the third person because he
prefers not to express himself in the first person in print.
This is not as unusual as it seems: in professional publications, scientists avoid the first person and subjective observations.*

"THE WORK IS GOING WELL, BUT IT LOOKS LIKE IT MIGHT BE
the end of the world."

Sherry Rowland said these words wearily to his wife after a long
day researching the effects of chlorofluorocarbons at the University
of California, Irvine. Just a few years before, as chair, he had created
the university's new chemistry department, and the challenge had
gone well. But Rowland was also a research scientist. While his specialty was radiochemistry, he felt it was important to move on to
something new every few years. So he resigned the chair, returned to
his position as chemistry professor, and eventually began studying
chlorofluorocarbons. In 1974, Rowland sounded the alarm that these
so-called harmless chemicals were eating a huge hole in the ozone
shield high in Earth's atmosphere.

Chlorofluorocarbons (compounds containing the three elements
chlorine, fluorine, and carbon) had been developed in 1930 as a re-
placement for sulfur dioxide and ammonia, refrigerants known to
be corrosive and toxic. They also smelled. In the old days, sulfur

dioxide and ammonia were okay if they stayed in a refrigerator loop, but when that leaked they had an odor you didn't want in your kitchen.

In comparison, the CFCs, trademarked as Freons by the DuPont company, were considered safe, inert, and odorless. To prove their harmlessness, Thomas Midgley, the research engineer who developed CFCs, inhaled a lungful of CFC-12 and blew out a candle during a press conference.

In the beginning, CFC-11 and CFC-12 went into refrigerators and air-conditioners. Later on, these chemicals were used in aerosol propellants and plastic foams and as solvents in the semiconductor industry. A huge amount, nearly a megaton a year, was being produced by 1973. Most of these CFCs were escaping into the air via aerosol sprays or leaking out from refrigerators and air-conditioners. But at the time no one was tracking their effects in the atmosphere.

In 1972, Rowland attended a meeting in Fort Lauderdale, Florida, at the invitation of William Marlowe, an Atomic Energy Commission (AEC) executive he had met on a trip to a scientific meeting in Austria in 1970. The AEC, seeking to stimulate more interaction between chemists and meteorologists, had started a series of joint workshops.

At the Fort Lauderdale meeting, Rowland heard a presentation that intrigued him. A colleague talked about the observations of James Lovelock, a British scientist who invented the electron-capture gas chromatograph. The instrument detected small amounts of trace gases in the atmosphere. Wherever Lovelock set up his chromatograph, CFC-11 was present.

"We knew that the chlorofluorocarbons are simple molecules designed to be very nonreactive chemically. But even inert molecules can react under some conditions. My thought was, 'Let's see what we can find,'" explained Rowland of his initial decision to investigate chlorofluorocarbons. "Do we know enough about their chemical behavior to predict their fate in the atmosphere?"

The question was basically one of curiosity about how the world works. In retrospect, the main advance was to get out of the lab and into the real world by following a molecule from its release into the atmosphere to its eventual destruction many years later. No one had ever done that before with CFCs.

In 1973, Rowland approached the Atomic Energy Commission, which had funded his research since 1956, for additional support to study chlorofluorocarbons. At the same time, Mario Molina, a Mexican chemist who had been educated in Europe and Mexico and had just completed his Ph.D. at Berkeley, arrived at Irvine to join the Rowland research group. Given a choice of research projects, Molina chose to look for the eventual fate of the CFCs.

Initially, there were no complicated experiments. Rowland and Molina pulled together information from other research. "In principle it was all there, but scattered all over—information about chemical behavior, industrial usage of CFCs, plus the chemistry and meteorology of the stratosphere," Rowland said of their findings. "We used known information in the lab." But the questions they asked were key. How long did the CFC molecule last in the atmosphere? And what did it do there?

They found that the CFC molecule did not break up in a few days or even weeks; it lasted several decades or more, long enough to drift into the stratosphere, eight to thirty miles above Earth's surface. Some CFCs, they estimated, could last 150 years. On rising to the middle of the stratosphere, CFCs encounter ultraviolet radiation from the sun. This ultraviolet radiation can be absorbed by stratospheric ozone, and none of it penetrates to altitudes below fifteen miles. However, at altitudes of eighteen to twenty miles, the CFC molecules are split by the ultraviolet radiation, releasing chlorine atoms.

Rowland and Molina's next quest was to see what happened to the CFC fragments released by the ultraviolet radiation. Ozone formation and its destruction were naturally occurring processes that had always been balanced. Now, with CFC molecules breaking down and releasing chlorine atoms, a major source of chlorine had gathered in the upper atmosphere, throwing off that balance. Ozone was removed faster than by natural processes alone, and less remained. The ozone layer was thinning.

What troubled the researchers was that one chlorine atom destroyed one ozone molecule a minute, without itself being destroyed.

What's more, the chlorine atom remained in the stratosphere for a year. Only when the chlorine diffused into the lower atmosphere did the cycle stop. Imagine the destruction with almost a megaton of chlorofluorocarbons being produced annually.

That's when Rowland made the comment to his wife, Joan. Without that protective ozone shield, life as we know it would change drastically. Radiation from the sun would increase, not only causing skin cancer and cataracts in humans but affecting animals as well, and precipitating changes in the human immune system that could make us sick.

In January 1974, Rowland and Molina sent a paper to the journal *Nature*, which did not appear until June because of personnel problems at the journal. Not until September, when the American Chemical Society had its semiannual meeting and held a press conference, did the press pick up on their discovery. Rowland and Molina predicted an eventual depletion of the ozone layer of 7 to 13 percent.

By that time, working with NASA support, Ralph Cicerone and Richard Stolarski, who had earlier worked out the stratospheric chlorine reaction, now confirmed that a chlorine chain reaction from the CFCs was occurring in the atmosphere.

It is tough to blow the whistle on a $2-billion-a-year industry, even when you are a well-respected chemist. Rowland and Molina's discoveries were based on research and chemical calculations that they felt without question to be correct. The National Academy of Sciences formed a five-member panel, which included Rowland, to decide whether the ozone problem was serious enough for a full-scale investigation.

But DuPont was a formidable company to be up against, and they were not going to give up their profitable product without a fight. They began mobilizing. One DuPont executive who visited Rowland told him he seemed to be an "environmental do-gooder."

"We said two important things about the CFCs," recalled Rowland of his research. "One, CFCs would last for a very long time, long enough to reach the stratosphere; and two, once there they would fall apart. But would they all really last for decades in the lower atmosphere? We wanted to test how rapidly they accumulated.

You have to have measurements around the world, and we started doing that in 1977."

Rowland used a stainless-steel, two-liter canister with a valve through which all the air could be removed in the laboratory. Then he took the canister to a remote location, filled it with air, and headed back to the lab to measure the amounts of CFCs. "We needed a wide variety of latitudes and remote locations. At that time, we were not really funded to do this. So the collections were tacked onto other trips." If Rowland needed samples from Alaska, he arranged a stopover there on a scientific trip scheduled to Oregon. Or he flew to the West Indies on the way to a conference in Florida. "That gave us enough of a geographical spread," he remembers of taking the samples. Fifteen years later, when Rowland's research was expanded, four thousand samples were taken in a two-month period from aircraft.

The next few years were a roller coaster of acceptance, legislation enforcing a ban, then skepticism, political indifference, and no regulation. In 1975 a government committee wrote a strong report supporting the prediction of a 7 percent ozone depletion. In 1976 there was thought to be a flaw in Rowland and Molina's theory—a frustrating, worrisome time. (Their original predictions held up.) In 1978 CFCs were banned in aerosol spray cans in the United States and three other countries, but their use was not banned at all in air-conditioners and refrigerators.

When the Rowlands' son was badly hurt in an auto accident in San Diego that same year, they moved there. Rowland worked as a hospital orderly to be near his son until he was well enough to come home. Except for the five months spent there, he persisted with the CFC issue.

What kind of childhood did Rowland have that lay the groundwork for this resolve? He grew up in Delaware, Ohio. His father was a math professor, and his mother had been a Latin teacher until her marriage. He started school at five, then skipped fourth grade, so that most students in his class were two and a half years older than he was. When that happens, he remembers, "you live by yourself in some respects." His father gave him math problems often and Rowland found that numerical math came easily to him.

He grew up during World War II and liked to build model warships. He and other teenagers played a popular war game with their models, one that emphasized strategies. "The game was written about in *Life* magazine," he recalled. At fifteen, as a senior, he got permission to use the high school gym for a naval war battle with other students. It was a small town and a different time. That was also around the time Rowland experienced his growth spurt and became very athletic. He loved sports, and eventually he played semiprofessional baseball, managed a team, and played basketball in college.

Apparently his early fascination with solving problems helped him with his research. In 1985 the seriousness of his findings on CFCs was supported yet again when the British Antarctic Survey published a report showing a 40 percent depletion of stratospheric ozone over Antarctica. Three expeditions were funded by the United States to Antarctica so that detailed measurements could be taken on the ground and from aircraft. In 1988 NASA reported not only that the Antarctic ozone loss was caused by chlorofluorocarbons but also that ozone loss could be seen at all latitudes, including over the United States.

The Montreal Protocol on Substances That Deplete the Ozone Layer, a United Nations agreement designed to reduce CFC consumption by 50 percent by 1999, was signed by twenty-four nations in 1987. DuPont announced it would phase out the production of CFCs the following year.

With all the ups and downs, Rowland remained calm and persistent, even when President Reagan's first Environmental Protection Agency chief referred to Rowland's work as a scare tactic. The one time he got angry was when a well-known news show asked him to talk about CFCs right after DuPont announced it would stop CFC manufacture. Rowland agreed to do the show. The news show producers then contacted DuPont and asked if a company representative would appear with Rowland. DuPont would only appear, said a company spokesperson, without Rowland. Rowland was bounced.

In 1995, Rowland and Molina were awarded a Nobel Prize for their discovery that chlorofluorocarbon gases were depleting the ozone layer in the stratosphere. Rowland was typically low-key about the honor. (Rumor has it that the morning the Swedish committee called to tell him he was a Nobel Prize winner, he did get excited.)

In spite of all the scientific facts, satellite photos, and the affirmation of the Nobel Prize, disbelief still exists that ozone depletion is caused by CFCs and that it is a serious problem. "Many people just believe what they want to believe. Nevertheless, anyone can now follow on the Internet the startling loss of ozone that occurs over Antarctica every September. It hasn't stopped," he says simply. And Rowland, still at work, hasn't stopped his research.

Climate Change

JOHN FIROR

MOST CHILDREN START OFF BEING REALLY
curious about everything. They love to collect
things like rocks and bugs and want to know all
about them. Whereas a lot of children are fascinated by living things
found outdoors, I was more interested in exploring things indoors. I
was fascinated by electricity, so I built radio sets and other equipment
and experienced great joy when some of them worked. My parents
gave me gifts of things I was interested in, like a chemistry set, astronomy books, and so on. Even in grade school, I knew I wanted to
be a scientist. But because I was self-taught in all these subjects, I did
not know what to study when it was time to go to college. In the end
I registered for electrical engineering because I had been working
with electricity all along.

That was the time of World War II, so after one year of engineering school, at the age of seventeen, I enlisted, and the army
sent me for six months of training. Then I was sent to a parts clerk
school. I jumped at the first opportunity to do something different. I volunteered for a transfer and found myself at Los Alamos,
where they were building the atomic bomb. My job was to take
care of the uranium and plutonium, so I had to learn how to shoot
the gun I carried when I transported plutonium from the vault to
the laboratory. Being there all day guarding the plutonium the

physicists were working on, I realized just how "interesting" physics actually is.

When I came home after my tour with the army, I changed my major to physics. Toward the end of my junior year at Georgia Tech, the chair of the physics department called me in and inquired where I was going to graduate school. When I told him that I had not even thought about it, he said "You should, and you had better start applying now." He handed me a list of the premier physics departments in America, which he had arranged alphabetically, so Chicago was at the top, Harvard in the middle, and Yale at the bottom, even though it was his own school. I went back to the dormitory and immediately wrote to the first on the list—Chicago. Although I made a resolution that I would write to one each night, I never got around to writing to the rest.

Right after the war the University of Chicago had the top physics department in the world, and several of my courses were taught by Nobel laureates. As most of them had worked on the bomb, research concentrated on nuclear physics (which had become the most prestigious field in science as a result). Multimillion-dollar accelerators were built to smash atoms apart so that physicists could study the interaction of high-energy particles. The highest-energy particles could not be created in massive accelerators, but a few of them arrived from outer space. Physicists tried to study those by detecting how they interacted with molecules in the air or on a surface such as a photographic plate. Through my research with cosmic rays, I became more interested in where these mysterious particles were coming from, and so physics led me to astronomy.

After completing my doctorate, I wanted to continue investigating fields broader than microscopic physics, and I was lucky to be able to do that at the Carnegie Institution of Washington, D.C. Among the many institutions Andrew Carnegie endowed were several devoted to scientific research. Carnegie's laboratories were located in different parts of the country. The one in Washington, the Department of Terrestrial Magnetism, was set up around the turn of the century to study Earth's magnetic field.

Studies of Earth's magnetism had tapered off by the time I arrived, and I joined an effort in the new field of radioastronomy, an extension of my cosmic particle research. Two of us were studying radio waves coming in from space, so we divided the universe between us. I took the Sun and he took the rest of the universe, which was a more nearly equal division than it might seem because the Sun is close enough to study in detail, whereas everything else is so distant.

My doctoral research had determined that some cosmic rays come from the Sun, and, after several years of studying its radio waves, I realized that I did not know enough about the Sun as a star. When I said as much to our lab director, he asked me to name the best solar laboratory in the country, and I said the High Altitude Observatory in Boulder. He suggested that I arrange a stay there to see what I could learn, so I moved my family to Colorado and spent half a year working in the observatory.

I learned something about scientific visits. If you just go and wait around for people to tell you things, you will be ignored, whereas if you start working on your own project, you will make mistakes, and everyone will be eager to tell you what you are doing wrong. Using a piece of equipment HAO did not previously have, I started making observations of the sun in infrared wavelengths. Immediately people began telling me how much better I could be doing it, so I learned a lot very fast.

Soon after I left Colorado, a special committee approached the director of the High Altitude Observatory to inquire whether he would be willing to direct a large laboratory devoted to studying Earth's atmosphere. The committee wanted the National Center for Atmospheric Research (NCAR) to attract scientists from many disciplines to atmospheric research. Good scientists were avoiding meteorology and competing in fields with more prestige, such as high-energy physics. Meteorology's reputation was low; the public thought of a meteorologist as the guy on the late TV news forecasting the weather (and getting it wrong).

Walter Roberts agreed to direct the laboratory if they built it in Boulder, which was a choice site for weather observations, and if the large lab absorbed his little observatory. This convenient arrangement solved several of the committee's problems. As the impressive lab was to be operated by a group of fourteen universities, each of which wanted it on its own campus, putting it in Boulder eliminated rivalry. Additional benefits came from absorbing the existing High Altitude Observatory, which had an excellent scientific reputation and so boosted the image of the new center. It also gave the center a head-start on creating the necessary administrative support arrangement.

One of the director's first jobs was to appoint people to direct the major divisions, particularly a reputable scientist to direct atmospheric research. He also needed someone to direct the solar lab, and, rather than a narrowly focused classical solar astronomer, he wanted someone interested in everything about the sun—like that young fellow who had visited. So Walter Roberts phoned to say that he would be in Washington and invited me and my wife to dinner. He spent most of the evening reminding my wife how delightful Boulder was before finally inquiring whether I would like to be associate director of the new national laboratory in charge of solar research.

Later he said that one reason he wanted me was that I had worked at a small, informal lab, which he considered conducive to good science. I had previously told him that the Carnegie Institution had few rules and regulations. The Department of Terrestrial Magnetism bulletin board had a small notice yellowed with age: "We have two rules: 1. Do not spend money we do not have. 2. Do not work with high voltages if you are alone." That was the finest rule book I ever saw, because it says what matters—don't get the organization in trouble, and don't get yourself in trouble. The director wanted that attitude at the National Center for Atmospheric Research. We have a thousand people now, so we need a few more rules, but we got off to a good start by examining what was really needed.

In 1968, after I had been in charge of the solar division of NCAR for eight years, Walter Roberts wanted to retire. He told the board of trustees they ought to select me to replace him as director of the whole laboratory. That is how I changed fields from high-energy physics to astronomy to the sun to Earth's atmosphere. It is atypical that I was made director of an astronomical laboratory without ever having had a course in astronomy, and then became director of a meteorological laboratory without ever having studied meteorology. I have been forced to scramble to learn new things as I go along. That is not a bad thing; I believe the world needs people who can see beyond their narrow specialty to the broader range of science and the social context in which it functions.

Working at NCAR has given me some instructive experiences with the interactions between science and society. Once the government asked us to see if we could modify the weather to decrease the amount of hail damaging crops. The Soviet Union had reported success in this endeavor, so the U.S. government thought we should try, too. We put together a program with several universities cooperating, in addition to government labs such as the National Oceanic and Atmospheric Administration.

As director of NCAR, I was responsible for the program, but the more I thought about it, the clearer it became that two questions needed to be answered: Can we modify damaging hail? And *should* we modify it? When I raised the latter question, the scientists turned away in disgust. Their reflexive response was, Why answer the second question before we have answered the first? My reply was that because it is more difficult, we have to start earlier on the "should." Over their objections, I took some money out of the field sciences to create a small environmental impacts group whose job was to answer the question, "Should we?"

The group took two different approaches. The first was environmental: Do the chemicals used to seed clouds do anything harmful? At the time, the effect appeared to be negligible. The second was economic: What would the program cost, and how much would it save the farmers? We hired a bright young Canadian economist who did a thorough study. He looked at the value of land in the affected counties in Kansas, Wyoming, Nebraska, and Colorado, and he obtained records of how much hail fell in each county and what the land value was, so he could estimate how much hail damage was holding back the value of land. After asking field scientists how much hail they thought they might be able to reduce, which was about 15 percent, he estimated how much land value would increase if hail were decreased by that amount.

Then he looked again at his data and realized that the land values were more sensitive to lack of rain than to excessive hail, which led him to figure out that the value of a 15 percent decrease in hail would be canceled by a 3 percent decrease in rainfall. He went back to the scientists to ask if they could guarantee no loss in water. They could not, of course, so it seemed we were working on the wrong problem. Trying to increase rain, rather than decrease hail, might help farmers more. So the project was terminated. That was an important episode in changing my own and the laboratory's view of things. It became clear to me that we needed to ask such questions. Consequently, we kept the impacts group that I had set up and made it a regular part of the laboratory.

I directed NCAR for a dozen years. As rewarding as it was, management wears you out after a while, so I went to the board of trustees and said I would prefer to do something less demanding. They asked me to run the group that brought young scientists for working visits to NCAR, and I accepted. Over the years, as director of different groups, I remained a continuous member of the directors committee from the time it was set up, in 1962, until 1996. Management problems are never solved completely; every decade you have to reconsider the same problems. After over thirty years in management, I figured I had solved each management problem three times, and I did not want to go through it all a fourth time. So I officially retired, even though I am still there.

After retirement, I chose to have my office in the middle of the impacts group I had formed years earlier, because they take the broadest view. I had in fact prepared myself for this transition by taking a sabbatical leave to work with a group of economists in Washington, D.C., and then a group of political scientists at the University of Minnesota. That helped me see where societal problems lie and just how pervasive they are. I learned, for example, the extent to which neoclassical economics has exacerbated many of our problems. Economists have tried to transform their field into increasingly complex mathematics, and some have become so enamored of their abstract mathematical formulas that they have forgotten they are dealing with complex human and environmental problems.

For example, economists measure progress by gross national product; but GNP has no explicit value judgments in it at all, just implicit ones, including the assumption that it does not matter who gains and who loses. So it cannot indicate genuine progress. GNP accounting makes $10 million used to destroy the environment equivalent to $10 million used to save it. Headlines boast, "Good news—GNP grew 5 percent," but that does not tell you whether what grew was good or bad. Growth is good—no matter how bad it is! That mentality pervades much of what we do. CEOs try to expand their businesses and measure success by the rate of growth, not necessarily by doing something better. What we value is skewed, and the societal systems we have created as a result further distort our values and perpetuate our problems. Unfortunately, those problems are not confined to the systems we create but also affect natural systems—like the atmosphere.

Having worked so long at one of the great laboratories studying atmospheric phenomena, I have seen what has been happening to the atmosphere and watched the signs of climate change progressing. To fully comprehend what is involved, it helps to understand our relationship to the atmosphere. People think of the air as merely a transparent substance, without realizing that it has an intimate connection with everything on Earth. Our atmosphere is created by living organisms that absorb and emit air, altering the air's composition as it is processed through organic systems.

Over time, the nature of organisms has been changed by the atmospheric composition created by them. The original life on our planet subsisted on gases produced by geologic processes, such as volcanic hydrogen compounds. Eventually organisms evolved that could utilize the sun's energy to convert carbon dioxide and water into carbohydrates. This process of photosynthesis released oxygen, which accumulated in the atmosphere, creating conditions for a new form of life to evolve—organisms that absorb oxygen and emit carbon dioxide. For the past ten thousand years these and other processes have been in balance so that the amount of carbon dioxide in the air has remained nearly constant.

Carbon dioxide warms the air because it traps heat within the atmosphere. Almost two hundred years ago a scientist likened this trapping of heat radiation to the way glass keeps the sun's warmth inside a greenhouse, so it is sometimes referred to as the "greenhouse effect." Heat-trapping gases warm the planet by about 33° C (59° F). If these gases were present in the air but trapped no heat, the average temperature of Earth's surface would be below freezing, about −18° C (0° F), instead of safely above, about 15° C (59° F).

Heat-trapping gases have warmed the planet throughout history, so it is obvious that adding more of them to the atmosphere, as we are doing today by burning fossil fuel and destroying forests, will heat the planet even more. We are releasing around six billion tons of carbon as carbon dioxide to the atmosphere annually—which is the equivalent of one ton per person every year.

Scientists have detailed measurements of the increase in heat-trapping gases over time because they have been recording atmospheric carbon dioxide concentrations since the middle of this century. They have been able to compare this recent increase with past concentrations over thousands of years by taking deep core samples of polar ice and measuring the amount of heat-trapping gases contained in the air that is frozen in the ice. Heat-trapping gases began increasing noticeably with the growth of the human population during the industrial revolution, and this increase accelerated further in the latter half of this century.

These historic measurements provide an observable close correlation between human activities and heat-trapping gases, particularly between our domestic and industrial activities and increases in carbon dioxide concentrations and between our agricultural activities and increases in methane and nitrous oxide concentrations. Methane is released from decay in landfills, rice paddies, cattle ranching, and such, whereas nitrous oxide is a byproduct of nitrogen-based substances such as fertilizers.

Because all fossil fuels contain carbon, burning them inevitably releases carbon dioxide. A solid fuel like coal is almost all carbon, so it releases a lot of carbon dioxide, along with other noxious gases like sulfur dioxide and nitrogen oxides. Liquid and gaseous fuels are hydrocarbons that release water vapor and carbon dioxide during combustion. Thus the burning of carbon-based fuels to generate electricity, heat buildings, and power vehicles loads the atmosphere with carbon dioxide.

Occasionally I try to explain the complete role of fossil fuels to the public, but I have not been too successful. I start off a talk with what fossil fuel has done for us before mentioning that it has a few drawbacks. Then I list some detrimental effects of fossil-fuel energy production and use, starting with what happens when we take it out of the ground and damage vast areas with procedures like strip mining. After that we have to transport it and spend millions cleaning up when it is spilled. When we burn it, it forms acid rain, which gets into our water, destroys fish, kills trees, disturbs soil, and damages buildings and other things. It reduces visibility over the East Coast and the Grand Canyon, generates ozone smog that permanently damages children's lungs, and creates sulfur pollution that causes respiratory difficulties in urban residents.

In addition, it grossly increases our national trade deficit: our largest import is oil. And we have been known to go to war, incurring deaths and suffering, to protect foreign sources of oil. So I say that for all those reasons, I think we should diminish our use of fossil fuels as much as we possibly can. At the end of this talk, someone in the audience always blurts out, "But I thought you were going to talk about climate change." . . . Oh yes, that too. The point I am trying to make is that each harmful substance causes multiple damages, and we need to deal with the multiplicity of interactions if we are going to solve the problems.

The combined changes we are making to the biosphere are distorting natural forces. The cumulative effects of the substances we are emitting into the atmosphere are altering the ongoing relationships between climate and life. We have pumped so much heat-trapping gas into the atmosphere that it has disturbed the equilibrium of heat gain and loss from Earth's surface. The more heat-trapping gas we eject, the hotter it will get. It is not going to heat up just a few degrees and then stop. In fact, it will get progressively worse the longer it goes on. The 1980s were the hottest decade on record, and the 1990s have been even hotter; and the heating will accelerate if we continue to put large quantities of heat-trapping gases into the air.

As long as we continue unbalancing natural forces, climate change will keep escalating, and the effects will intensify. Not all consequences are predictable, but many are, given what we already know. Certain repercussions for human health are known: heart failures increase with heat, and respiratory complications worsen with air pollution. Diseases spread more easily and expand their range as regions warm, allowing tropical and subtropical pestilence to invade formerly temperate zones.

Fires also spread as areas become hotter and drier, and deliberate burning of forests releases carbon stored in the trees, heating climate even more. Forests cannot survive rapid climate change because they cannot migrate fast enough to areas where conditions match their needs. Agricultural crops are also subject to limited ranges determined by temperature and precipitation, so changes in crop patterns and schedules will be required, which could be difficult. As the climate warms, rainfall increases, but evaporation also increases, redistributing surface and ground water now used for irrigation and drinking.

Oceans expand as they warm, and their volume enlarges as glaciers melt into them, raising sea level above coastal lands and inundating islands. Of even greater global consequence are differences in the distribution of land and water in the Northern and Southern Hemispheres. The North's continental masses heat up more than the South's extensive oceans, and the greater the temperature difference between hemispheres, the more it will unbalance weather systems and alter general global circulation of oceanic currents and atmospheric winds.

Given such potential change, why aren't we doing what we can to slow and stop it? Scientists have been warning about these changes for a long time, but they are ignored, even though the changes are already happening. Why? Because the economic and political systems that should be doing something about it are part of the problem. Scientists can inadvertently add to the difficulty by not understanding the actual political situation that is holding up progress.

That became clear to me with the acid rain problem. In 1980 the U.S. government set up the National Acid Precipitation Assessment Program and provided money for ten years of research. But a year before the study was completed, suddenly Congress passed the 1990 Clean Air Amendment. Of course people wondered why they did not wait until they had the conclusions of the study that had been funded specifically to research the problem.

Afterward, I was asked to look into this sequence of events, and I had been close enough to the various steps to put together a reasonable picture of what happened. Congress had already been convinced that sulfur in the air was bad and that it caused acid rain, but they had been unable to construct a way of paying for the cleanup that did not anger representatives from either districts with high-sulfur coal or those with low-sulfur coal. The acid rain research program that Congress funded was designed at least in part to give it time to solve this political dilemma.

Therefore, as soon as one of the environmental groups sold the White House and Congress on a plan that allowed the marketplace to determine how much was paid and who paid it, Congress immediately acted on it. The plan not only got Congress off the hook, it was an outstanding success. Prior estimates of how much it would cost to eliminate sulfur emissions were very high, but when it was actually done, the cost was so low it was not even noticeable.

Improving energy efficiency generally saves money for corporations and consumers. Energy-efficient equipment and appliances, building insulation, and waste energy recovery for power plants can pay back the extra investment in a few years and afterwards generate savings. Even in individual homes energy efficiency can pay off. Most people do not realize that their refrigerator uses a quarter of their electricity and that they could cut one-half to two-thirds of that expense with an energy-efficient refrigerator. And heating, too, can be made much more efficient.

Transportation, including automobiles, consumes one-third of all the energy used in our country. The average American car goes roughly twenty miles on a gallon of gas; in Europe and Japan, where gas is much more costly than it is here, the average is near thirty miles. Cars are available that get fifty miles per gallon—in fact, I have one.

In general, American energy use is wasteful compared to use in other industrialized countries. Both Europe and Japan use about half as much energy to generate a dollar of gross domestic product as does the United States. This fact suggests that it will be easier for the United States to reduce its use of fossil fuels than for these more efficient overseas competitors.

Many environmental problems, including climate change and air pollution, have worsened over the past few decades. This negative trend has forced some changes in the role of the National Center for Atmospheric Research. NCAR was created with the goal of improving old activities, such as weather forecasting, and perfecting new technologies, such as weather modification, that might be used to advantage. As atmospheric conditions have worsened, however, our role has expanded from suggesting new and better things people could do to telling them about old things they should quit doing. While people welcome scientists' new inventions, they are less happy with scientists' warnings about the consequences of overusing natural resources and the careless disposal of waste. People want scientists to solve the problem for them, not tell them to stop creating the problem.

Many Americans think that all our problems can be solved by technology, despite the fact that the unbridled expansion of technology helps create the problems. Personally, I do not think that technology can solve our most serious problems, because when I look deeply at these problems, I find that underlying the technological defects are societal flaws. Science cannot provide solutions to society's failings.

There was a big debate among ecologists a few years ago after three of them wrote a paper questioning recommendations for more research to solve worldwide ecological problems, such as the exhaustion of resources and extinction of species. They pointed out that we already know what the real problem is: our multiplying population and rising use of resources. They said that scientists should not distract people from the truth—that there are so many of us using so much—by implying that perhaps more scientific research can solve the problem without the rest of us having to change our ways.

Even with the overall resistance to facing environmental problems, many Americans today are attempting to behave in a more environmentally favorable way. But they find that it is not simple or easy. Economic and social systems limit people's ability to make environmentally sound choices. So not only do individuals need to change their damaging activities, but societal systems also need to be changed from motivating destructive actions to mobilizing constructive activities. Structures such as pricing arrangements push people in the wrong direction. A conspicuous example is our subsidization of fossil fuels and automobiles. We fight to keep the price consumers pay for energy as low as possible, but with gasoline cheaper than bottled water, we are in deep trouble.

Economists and energy experts tell us that we will not make progress toward reducing fossil-fuel use until we get the prices right. And getting the prices right means that consumers should pay not only the cost of mining or drilling, processing, and transporting the fuel but also the cost to society as a whole of the damages resulting from the use of fuels. These externalities, as they are called, are quite large for fossil fuels, involving urban smog and ground-level ozone production, oil spills and land degradation, and, for the United States, a very large proportion of its international trade deficit from importing petroleum. With such costs included in the price, consumers would have motivation to become more efficient in their use of these fuels, and alternative energy sources such as wind and solar power would have a level playing field on which to compete.

To achieve this result by taxing carbon in fuels does not meet with much favor, perhaps because voters believe that Congress will not use the extra revenue in a sensible way. One proposed way of avoiding this difficulty is a revenue-neutral tax shift. If carbon is taxed enough to pay its own way and other taxes, for example payroll or income taxes, are reduced by the same total amount, government revenues would not change, and the average American would benefit despite paying higher fuel costs. Economists add that if we select the tax to reduce from among those that distort the economy, this step will actually give a boost to the national economy and involve some gain to the country.

I know that taking such a step, even if all kinds of experts endorsed it, would not be easy. Although Americans in general could gain, certain groups, such as coal miners and mine owners, would be disadvantaged, so the tax shift would need to be introduced gradually to allow such groups a smooth transition to more diversified activities, with perhaps some government aid in making the transition. There are lots of studies about how effective this tax shift would be, but I have not seen any proposals about how the disadvantaged workers and sectors would be handled. With the overall economy prospering there should be some way of managing the transition equitably.

I give frequent public speeches about climate change and other atmospheric problems, so I get a lot of feedback from people. Many have heard of obvious problems like the ozone hole and acid rain, and they sense changes in climate through more violent storms, severe cold spells, heat waves, droughts, floods, and such. Even though they do not see how all these problems are connected, they are convinced that we are messing up the atmosphere. So they are concerned about the consequences, but they do not know what to do about it.

Surveys show that most Americans label themselves as environmentalists. But ask them, "What do you do?" and the response is, "I am an environmentalist; I want clean air and water." Ask them, "What do you do personally?" and the hesitant reply is, "Well, uh, I recycle." Although recycling is an important step, bigger changes will have to occur to make real progress on our climate problems.

This is related to a dreaded question that is always asked at the end of my public talks, "But what can I do about it?" I used to say, "Write to your representative in Congress," but people do not seem confident that this will do any good. So I give a list of steps in the right direction—more efficient appliances, better cars, and so on—which, if taken by enough people, can make a difference. Just recently, the last time I was asked that question, I took a chance with an additional answer. I ended the list of things to do with the suggestion that if you are going to have a family, consider limiting it to one or two children. I expected moans, but was surprised with applause. Apparently, they had been waiting for someone to say that out loud.

My wife is my teacher about population. Being the national president of Zero Population Growth, she speaks to all kinds of audiences. She participated in the United Nations Conference on Population, where a consensus emerged on what needs to be done. We know how to slow population growth voluntarily, because surveys have shown that women almost everywhere want fewer children. Thus we have to take all of the steps to allow women to have opportunities to become educated, have jobs outside the home, control their own resources, and otherwise become full citizens wherever they live. Limiting our procreation is one of the three most important things each of us can do for the world—the others being to reduce consumption of natural resources and improve equity and social justice.

Only by changing our political and economic systems and our behavior can we prevent climate change. Most of what we do as a society affects the atmosphere, just as our society is dependent on the atmosphere for what we do. My avocation, flying sailplanes above the Rocky Mountains, is a simple example of that dependency. Updrafts over the Rockies lift my glider thirty thousand feet above Boulder, so far up that I can see all along the mountains from Wyoming to New Mexico. Winds flowing over the top of the mountains, down the other side, and bouncing back up lift me high above the mountain range. Without any mechanical power, I am totally dependent on atmospheric dynamics to stay aloft and experience the feelings of success for the flight and awe at the earth laid out below me.

Further Reading

John Firor, ed. *Global Warming.* American Association of Physics, 1995.
———. *The Changing Atmosphere: A Global Challenge.* Yale University Press, 1992.
John Firor and Judith Jacobsen, eds. *Human Impact on the Environment: Ancient Roots, Current Challenges.* Westview, 1992.

Worldwatch

LESTER BROWN

I GREW UP ON A SMALL FAMILY FARM THAT WAS not very profitable. When we were young, my brother and I started our own farming venture. I was fourteen and my brother was eleven when we bought our first tractor, an old one that we managed to fix up and get running well enough to plow and cultivate. It was exciting to have our own equipment and be farming on our own. We were not allowed to work on our field until we had completed all the tasks for the family farm, like milking the cows. Time was scarce, but my brother and I were energetic and entrepreneurial. During the harvest we had most of our schoolmates helping to pick the tomatoes. We started on a small scale, but ten years later we were marketing 1.5 million pounds of tomatoes a year.

Being a farmer, I worked with the interrelationships among numerous environmental factors and their changing dynamics: plants, nutrients, water, soil, insects, weather, and growing cycles, in addition to market economics. So, early on, I learned to analyze disparate, detailed information, synthesize the effects of multiple interactions, and evaluate the eventual outcome. I am still doing that, only now on a global scale.

The other invaluable experience early in my life was school. I probably relied more on teachers than some students did, partly because my parents did not have much formal education themselves; they were farmers who had not graduated from elementary school. Fortunately, I had a number of good teachers who encouraged me and pointed me in the right direction. We lacked books at home, but I hurried my schoolwork so I could read on my own, reading all the books for my grade, the next grade, and then whatever I wanted.

I found biographies fascinating. Our school library had a whole series on people such as Abraham Lincoln, Patrick Henry, Ben Franklin, Thomas Jefferson, Marie Curie, Clara Barton, and George Washington Carver. Probably I subconsciously identified with the people in these biographies because they accomplished something with their lives, as I wanted to with mine, so it was personally inspiring. Although I was unaware of it at the time, I think my reading also led me to an inherently broader view of the world. As I look back on the way things have unfolded, those experiences were influential in my development.

Another experience that greatly affected me came just after I graduated from Rutgers in 1955. Through the 4-H Club's International Farm Youth Exchange Program, I had a chance to go to India and spend six months living in villages. That experience expanded my view of the world enormously. My brother took care of the tomato harvest while I was gone, and when I returned to the farm, I grew tomatoes for a couple more years before deciding that doing the same thing for the rest of my life would not be very challenging.

From living in India I became interested in the world food problem and wanted to join the Foreign Agricultural Service. To do that I needed a degree in agricultural economics (my undergraduate degree was in agricultural science), so I wintered over in College Park at the University of Maryland and got a master's degree in 1959. Then I started working as an international agricultural analyst with the U.S. Department of Agriculture during Eisenhower's presidency. After that, one thing led to another, and in 1961 I went to Harvard for an additional degree, this time in public administration.

When I returned to the government, I ended up doing the first systematic projections of world population, land, and food trends to the end of the century. It was called *Man, Land and Food: Looking Ahead at World Food Needs.* That study got a lot of attention because it was the first time global agricultural projections had been correlated with population growth forecasts. *U.S. News & World Report* did a cover story on it, "Why Hunger Is to Be the World's Number One Problem." In 1963, when it came out, even the term "world food problem" was new.

Not long after, I was given a special, newly created position as adviser on foreign agricultural policy to the secretary of agriculture, Orville Freeman. In those early years I worked really hard just getting to know world agriculture. I had some advantages in that process, because in addition to a degree in agricultural science I had practical experience farming in this country and living in Indian villages. I worked closely with the agriculture secretary, advising him on international trade and aid issues.

Then they created a new agency called the International Agricultural Development Service. Its purpose was to mobilize professional resources in the Department of Agriculture, which is an impressive collection of professions and agencies. I headed the agency from 1966 to 1969, and we did some exciting things. The day before Nixon took office in 1969, I left to help Jim Grant start the Overseas Development Council. I remained there for the next five years, and Jim later became head of UNICEF.

Working on international issues, I realized the need for an analysis and overview of the global environmental situation. The Rockefeller Brothers Fund saw the same need, so they provided a start-up grant of $500,000 to launch the Worldwatch Institute. We began by producing the *Worldwatch Papers* and a series of books. In 1982, I was asked by the Rockefeller Brothers Fund to spend some time with them as they thought through the transition of the fund from the brothers' generation to that of their children.

One of the things I suggested they do was a report card on progress toward a sustainable future. They liked the idea, so they started looking for someone to do it; then they came back and asked me. I was hesitant, because annual reports squeeze everything else in the organization to meet deadlines, and it can become boring doing the same thing year after year. But I decided to give it a try, and the result was our annual *State of the World* reports, which are now translated into all major languages and are such widely read public policy documents that they have achieved semiofficial status.

By 1988, I thought we needed to get information out more frequently, so we published a bimonthly magazine called *World Watch.* A few years later, we decided to do some topical books because there were people on the staff who were developing extensive knowledge of specific issues, such as water, energy, and population. We had already provided an impressive volume of issue analysis for the *State of the World,* so we extended that analysis by creating the Environmental Alert book series, beginning with the book *Saving the Planet: How to Shape an Environmentally Sustainable Economy.* Not long after that, I looked around and realized the trends were still all heading in the wrong direction, so I asked myself what else we could do with the resources we had. Then it occurred to me that the data we gathered for our publications could be put in simple graphic form. The result was our second annual publication, *Vital Signs: The Trends That Are Shaping Our Future.*

It is a challenge to one's intellectual creativity to find the best way to present information. I spend a lot of time trying to figure out how to present issues in ways that will engage people and capture the interest of the media. It is crucial for our data to reach as many people in as much of the world as possible, and for that we have to rely heavily on the communications media. We work closely with all the world's news organizations, including national and international wire services and radio and television networks.

We are engaged in a worldwide educational endeavor to raise public understanding of global issues, and we produce an impressive volume of information. We are cited in, or by-line, about forty stories a day in major newspapers and magazines around the world. Many more stories are inspired by our information. We are probably the most widely cited research institute in the world, although there are hundreds larger than we are.

Our effectiveness is due to the quality of research we do and its accessibility and relevance to so many people in so much of the world, including government agencies, universities, corporations, and environmental organizations. It is an ironic situation, because by almost any meaningful criteria you could use to evaluate the success of the Worldwatch Institute, we do very well; yet the planet itself is not doing very well. Its capacity to support life is deteriorating. We are still adding another ninety million people every year and eliminating countless numbers of other species. Our forest cover is shrinking, and our soils are eroding. Deserts are expanding, and our water is disappearing. Greenhouse gases are increasing, and the planet is becoming more polluted all the time. The world will fatally overtax its natural systems if we do not change. The only thing that will matter in the end is whether we turn around the destructive trends. We are failing to do that.

We win occasional battles here and there. We have reduced CFC production, so we might be able to save the ozone layer. What helped that was the discovery of the hole in the ozone layer over Antarctica. The interesting question is, What will be the climate equivalent of the ozone hole—what will really scare us to the point where we start phasing out fossil fuels? No one knows.

I have a feeling we are moving toward a major scare, a wake-up call of some sort. Exactly what form it will take is not clear. Most people realize that the trends of the last few decades cannot continue, that as population grows, everything else suffers. Less clear is what will stop those trends and turn them around.

Behavior changes in response to either new information or new experiences. There used to be many cigarette smokers in this country, but every few weeks there has been another story linking smoking with health deterioration, from skin wrinkling to heart conditions and lung cancer. It never seems to stop. A lot of people, reading more and more of these articles, finally reach the point where they say, "Enough," and throw their cigarettes away. Others do not; they keep smoking until one morning they cough up blood. Then they are scared, but it is too late. This is a metaphor for what we are doing in relation to the planet. Worldwatch is trying to provide enough information to get people to stop smoking before they reach the point of no return. That is basically what we are about. So far, we have them reading the articles but not scared enough to change their behavior.

I suppose another thing that handicaps industrialized people is that we are removed from things. The cause and effect chains are so long that we do not perceive the links anymore. When people talk about the need for a new set of values, those values have to be based on information and understanding. We do not understand the consequences of the things we do.

A simple example is the gold wedding band many of us wear. To mine the amount of gold in a ring requires digging a huge hole. If we had to have the hole in our front yard, we might not want the ring. But the way the world is organized, the hole is in someone else's yard, not ours. How many people purchasing their wedding rings think about the environmental consequences? Yet gold mining displaces almost as much earth as iron ore mining. It is not essential to the survival of civilization.

One of the challenges for us is to present information in ways that will engage people. If you look at the literature on biodiversity, most of it is about the loss of millions of species. People cannot relate to these enormous numbers, so how do you put them in terms people can relate to? An issue of *World Watch* magazine had an article on what is happening to the world's birds. There are nearly ten thousand species of birds, and of those about three thousand appear to be holding their own. Close to seven thousand are declining in numbers, and of those around one thousand are now threatened with extinction. Those are numbers we can relate to somewhat.

But when you say that an individual bird is almost extinct, it means more to people. For example, the stork has always been an integral part of European culture and folklore. Europeans can relate to the stork disappearing because they have close associations with it. They understand that its demise occurs during its migration to and from Africa: the birds might be shot, the places where they winter over might have lost habitat, the water might be gone, the food sources might no longer be there. It is important to put things in terms people can understand. In North America, people can relate to the declining duck populations or the diminishing songbirds. If you talk about specific birds that people know and can recognize, it brings the problem home.

It is harder to relate to global climate change unless it directly affects your local weather in obvious ways. So one article we did, about climate change and the imminent doubling of greenhouse gases, looked at it through the eyes of the insurance industry. Insurance companies around the world, including Lloyds of London, are in serious trouble because of the increase in storm intensity. When Hurricane Andrew went through Florida in 1991, taking down thousands of buildings, it also took down eleven insurance companies. Lloyds is insolvent now because recently Europe has had too many destructive storms with winds of one hundred miles per hour. Storms of a severity that only came once in a century are now coming more frequently.

Insurance companies realize they need to understand what is happening, and they have to get it right. It is such a contrast with the oil companies, who continue to say that we do not know for sure whether rising levels of greenhouse gases cause global warming. Of these two major industries, one is scared enough to want to know what to do, and the other is still trying to deny the link between fossil-fuel burning and global warming because they make money selling fossil fuels.

Another area of denial is world food supplies. Official projections of food supplies by the UN Food and Agriculture Organization or the World Bank are hypothetical delusions. The economists who do these models and projections merely take the grain yield per acre in 1960 and 1990, draw a line between the two points, and extrapolate it into the future. They rationalize their method by claiming the past is the only guide we have to the future.

They refuse to acknowledge the entire body of literature on S-shaped growth curves in biology. Any biological growth process in a finite environment will eventually conform to an S-shaped growth curve, showing rapid increase followed by a decline. Food production on Earth is a biological process in a finite environment, so it will follow this curve. But economists are not biologists, so they are oblivious to reality. According to them, natural resources should be infinite; we will never run out of anything. Using their projection techniques, we would not be running out of fish in the world's oceans as we are now, because if you graph the catch between 1960 and 1990 and extend the line, it is still rising, even though, in fact, the fish are diminishing. No problem. They have these "no-problem" projections for world agriculture and food supplies.

We directly challenged them in our book *Full House: Reassessing the Earth's Population Carrying Capacity.* The foreword to the book recounts an experience I had in India as a prelude to understanding this situation. In 1965, I was asked by the Agency for International Development (AID) to go to India and evaluate their next five-year plan. When I arrived, I immediately began to question the estimate of nearly one hundred million tons for their grain harvest that year.

By reading many Indian newspapers every day, I realized drought was pervasive. Although some part of India is always drought-stricken or flooded, the entire country seemed dry. The awareness I gained from extensive reading was verified by personal encounters, such as with an oil company executive who said irrigation fuel sales had doubled because farmers were pumping water continually in an effort to save their crops.

After compiling information from multiple sources regarding crop failure in various parts of the country, I had the strange feeling I might be the only person who realized it. Convinced that India would have a huge grain shortfall, I cabled the secretary of agriculture in Washington, mobilizing the movement of one-fifth of America's wheat harvest—ten million tons of grain—in six hundred ships to India.

The largest movement of food ever conducted between two countries avoided one of the most massive potential famines in history. India's crop production was eighteen million tons short of predictions, and the country had no reserves for such an emergency. Asked about the situation, an Indian government official stated that "our reserves are in the grain elevators in Kansas."

As the food crisis escalated, I was assigned by the U.S. government to assist India in creating an agricultural policy that would provide greater food security. The result was a highly successful agricultural development strategy that doubled India's wheat harvest in seven years, the first time a major food-producing country doubled the grain harvest so quickly. It kept millions of Indians from starving to death.

Unfortunately, India was not as committed to its family planning program, so its population doubled from half a billion to nearly one billion people in the interim. Consequently, I have the same feeling of dread for their future now as I did then. The difference between then and now is that now the whole world is at risk.

The reason we did the book *Full House* was to help people understand that we are moving into a new era when we can no longer assume the rapid growth in food production that characterized most of the last half-century. It is difficult for people to grasp because we are conditioned by unprecedented growth during our lifetime.

We need to realize there are many new factors emerging that will directly affect the food prospect—major factors like water scarcity. There is growing competition between countries for water, which could lead to international conflicts. Even within nations there is competition between the cities and the countryside.

Another critical factor is loss of cropland. When countries are already densely populated before they begin to industrialize, they use large areas of cropland for their new industries. That has happened in Japan, South Korea, and Taiwan. It is now happening in China, although the authorities try to deny it. Of over one billion Chinese, three hundred million live in the urban industrial centers, and nine hundred million live in the rural agricultural sector.

China is shifting one hundred million farm workers into industry. If the average factory employs about one hundred people, which is what they do in the private sector, then one hundred million people require one million new factories. Every factory needs a warehouse to store the incoming raw materials and outgoing products; it also needs other infrastructure support, such as access roads and highways.

That development is creating an enormous loss of land, especially in the southern part of the country, where the land is double- and triple-cropped in rice. They are losing some of the most productive land in the world to the construction of factories. They will also be losing it to the construction of houses necessitated by population growth of half a billion more people over the next few decades. If each family has five people, consisting of two adults, one child, and one set of in-laws, then five hundred million additional people require one hundred million more houses. There is no way of escaping the amount of land one hundred million housing units and one million factories are going to take, and the result is a shortage of cropland.

When you think about the numbers in China, they are really staggering. We are not accustomed to dealing with numbers that large in a human context. The thing we are discovering in analyzing China is that whenever you multiply one billion times anything, it is a lot: another egg, pound of pork, bottle of beer per person. When I was in Norway launching the Norwegian edition of the *State of the World,* I pointed out that one bottle of beer for every Chinese takes nearly four hundred tons of grain. Someone there pointed out that two bottles of beer for everyone in China would consume the entire Norwegian grain harvest. It is amazing. We do not have any experience in assessing what is happening on as gigantic a scale as China and the claims it is going to make on the world's resources.

Most people who think about these things have said for a long time that the world cannot reasonably aspire to an American standard of living. But that is what everyone wants. The Chinese are figuring out how to get it. The same things happening in China are happening in Indonesia and India. They are just not moving as fast yet. That trend is going to force us to rethink the distribution of resources at the international level and to consider population policy in a way that we have not done before. China's economic growth rates in the last few years were over 10 percent. Its economy grew 56 percent in four years. Population grew 4 percent, so income per person went up by half in four years. That requires enormous increases in grain, which they cannot produce because they are losing their cropland.

We did an article in a 1994 issue of our magazine titled "Who Will Feed China?" It looks at the prospect of over one billion more people moving up the food chain at an unprecedented rate. What is the effect of over a billion people eating higher on the food chain at the same time? It takes incredible amounts of meat, poultry, eggs, and beer, all of which take more grain. This demand, combined with China's delay in checking its population growth, will affect the entire world.

Obviously it will create an enormous demand for grain that will eventually create intense competition among importing countries and overwhelm the export capacity of the United States and other exporting countries. At that point, world food prices will escalate dramatically. China's scarcity of food, water, and land will be everyone's problems. Their rising food prices will become our rising food prices. We will find ourselves competing with over a billion Chinese for our own grain. Their trade surplus with us totaled over $50 billion in just one year. That is more than enough to buy all the grain we exported last year. The question is not whether China can afford to buy our grain, but whether we can supply as much as they need.

Consider the consequences if we have another summer like 1988, when intense heat and drought reduced our grain harvest below the level of domestic consumption for the first time in our history. It did not pose serious problems then because we had huge reserves, but those reserves have never been rebuilt. Today, if that were to happen again, there is no way we could satisfy the import needs of the hundred or so countries to whom we export grain. We account for half of all world grain exports.

If we had another summer this year like that of 1988, by September there would be total chaos in world grain markets. Prices would double, then triple, and keep escalating because of intense competition among the importing countries to get enough grain to keep skyrocketing prices from destabilizing their political systems.

During my lifetime, the population of the planet has doubled. We are gaining nearly a hundred million people every year—the equivalent of the United Kingdom, Denmark, Sweden, Norway, and Belgium combined. Each month the world adds another New York City. Each day there are another quarter of a million people more than there were the day before. Each hour we gain over ten thousand more human beings.

Of the over ninety million additional people every year, more than eighty million are added in the Third World. In 1950, Western Europe had more people than Africa; now Africa has twice as many people. Western Europe has the lowest population growth rate; Africa has the highest, with the Middle East almost as high. Within the next four decades, at their current growth rate, India and China together will add another billion people to the two billion they already have.

Obviously this cannot go on forever. Once populations expand to the point where they overwhelm the local life-support systems, they begin consuming their resource base. Environmental degradation creates such devastating poverty that desperate people deplete their increasingly diminished resources. Water is pumped until water tables fall and wells go dry. Land is overfarmed until soils erode and crops fail to grow. Grasslands are overgrazed, firewood cut, and forests felled until nothing remains. Environmental deterioration and economic decline feed into each other, pulling everything into a downward spiral of disintegration.

The challenge in the analysis we do is to look at how the various systems interact: how the environmental system affects the economic system, which in turn affects the political system. There is no economic indicator that is more politically sensitive than food prices. At some point, environmental constraints are going to restrict the production of food, which will dramatically affect availability and prices. There will be enormous pressure on global food supplies. Then the panic will begin.

If I had to guess now, I would guess that is where the wake-up call is going to come from. I think we are moving into a period that is very different from anything we have known in the past, and we are not prepared for it. That is why we are doing our research and writing, to try to get the information out so people will understand what is happening and do something about it—before events spiral out of control.

Further Reading

Worldwatch Institute. *State of the World: A Worldwatch Institute Report on Progress toward a Sustainable Society.* Norton, annual.

———. *Vital Signs: The Trends That Are Shaping Our Future.* Norton, annual.

Lester Brown, Gary Gardner, and Brian Halweil. *Beyond Malthus: Nineteen Dimensions of the Population Problem.* Edited by Linda Stark. Norton, 1999.

Lester Brown and Ed Ayres, eds. *The Worldwatch Reader on Global Environmental Issues.* Norton, 1998.

Lester Brown. *The Agricultural Link: How Environmental Deterioration Could Disrupt Economic Progress.* Worldwatch Institute, 1997.

———. *Tough Choices: Facing the Challenge of Food Scarcity.* Norton, 1996.

———. *Who Will Feed China? Wake-Up Call for a Small Planet.* Norton, 1995.

Lester Brown and Hal Kane. *Full House: Assessing the Earth's Population Carrying Capacity.* Norton, 1994.

Lester Brown, Christopher Flavin, and Sandra Postel. *Saving the Planet: How to Shape an Environmentally Sustainable Global Economy.* Norton, 1991.

Global Security

NORMAN MYERS

I WAS BORN ON A HILL FARM IN WEST YORK-
shire in northern England. It was a small sheep
farm, less than one hundred acres, where we lived
partly outside the cash economy. We were what the World Bank
would call "semi-subsistence peasants." The area was lovely and the
natural environment quite beautiful, but at the time I did not appreciate it much because I did not like the eight-day working week
of a farmer. As a result, I had very little interest in the outdoors, let
alone in wild nature.

I went to school in a neighboring town and then on to Oxford
University. After finishing my studies in foreign languages, I decided
to go to Africa because people said Kenya was a beautiful place to
live. I had no ambitions or career plans; I just wanted to find a good
part of the world to live in.

So at age twenty-three I left for Africa. In the 1950s, Kenya was a
sea of wildland with a few islands of human settlements. Today it is
a sea of human settlements with just a few islands of wildland. Then
there were only a few million people; today there are around thirty
million.

When the plane came in to land, it had to circle a couple of times
to chase giraffes and buffalo off the airfield. Black-maned lions sat at
the edge of the tarmac that I walked across to the terminal. Huge

herds of wildebeest and zebra lined the road into Nairobi, which was then just a large village surrounded by grazing gazelles. This immediate introduction to African animals elated me.

The evening of my arrival, my new colleagues took me for a ride in the local game park, just a few miles away. We soon encountered a giraffe—not a particularly splendid giraffe, in fact rather a moth-eaten specimen. But there it was, marching along the horizon, entirely free and able to go wherever it wanted. We were the ones caged in a motor vehicle. Experiencing a wild animal in its own environment really stirred me; I couldn't wait to go and see more.

Fortunately, part of my work with the Kenya civil service in those days was in Masailand, a large sector of East Africa encompassing the finest wildlife area. There were huge herds of wildebeest, impala, gazelle, zebra, buffalo, and elephant. I was thoroughly hooked on the wildlife; it was marvelous, some of the best work I have ever done in my life. I spent half the year living in a tent and helped set up game reserves and national parks.

Three years after I arrived in Kenya, the country became independent, and my work as an administrator ended. I liked living in Kenya and wanted to stay on, so I became a citizen. I still had no career plans and just took whatever work was available, which happened to be as a high school teacher. I happily spent all my vacations in game parks enjoying the wildlife and taking photographs.

Park fees, camping costs, and photographic expenses added up, so I entered one or two photos in competitions. Much to my surprise, I won. A magazine wanted to publish one of my pictures and gave me $50 for it. Encouraged, I sent some pictures off to magazines and got more published. After a few years of that I became a full-time photographer, eventually making films and television programs.

I spent months on end in game parks, which was fantastic. But to make money photographing wildlife, you had to get action photos. It was not good enough to take a picture of lions lying in a plain; you had to get lions jumping on a zebra or wildebeest. To do that I went to the water holes where the wildebeest and zebra came down to drink. Arriving before dawn, I often found a lioness lying among the bushes in ambush. When the zebra or wildebeest came to drink, the lioness attacked, but she failed time after time. I would wait for days, watching dozens of attacks, with no real action.

To pass the time, I started to read every popular article I could find on what made a lion function, what made a zebra function, and how they functioned together. Then I started reading scientific papers and books on wildlife by experts like George Schaller. As a result, I effectively put myself through an undergraduate degree in wildlife biology. The more I learned, the more interested I became in the science of wildlife management and conservation biology.

When I went on a lecture tour in the United States, a wildlife specialist at the University of California asked me if I was interested in graduate work. So after twelve years in Kenya, I went off to Berkeley. Working like crazy for two years, I completed the equivalent of a bachelor's degree in my new discipline, on top of all the coursework for a Ph.D. Then I went back to Kenya, did my field research in a year, and completed my dissertation the following year.

From then on, I worked as a consultant scientist. My first assignment was for the World Wildlife Fund and its sister organization, the International Union for the Conservation of Nature. Disturbed by reports that leopards and cheetahs were endangered by the fur trade, they engaged me to do a survey to assess their status. So I explored forty countries in sub-Saharan Africa to find out what was happening. I discovered the fur trade was not the worst problem for the cats, although they certainly would have been better off without being hunted for their spotted skins. More important was their loss of habitat. Commercial ranchers were moving into the grasslands, squeezing out the wild animals with domesticated beasts. At the same time, multitudes of pastoral herders were spreading into the savannah. The main threat to both leopards and cheetahs was not from direct hunting, but from people expanding into animal habitats.

Realizing that, I wondered which other creatures were also becoming threatened. The official rate of extinction at that time was considered to be no more than one species per year. But the investigative researchers were looking only at species they knew were in trouble. That meant just a few plants, mammals, birds, amphibians, and reptiles, and fewer insects and invertebrates, even though they make up the majority of species.

So I did some work on my own, at my own expense, and came up with an estimate that the real extinction rate was not one species per year but more like one per day. My estimate was immediately derided as gross exaggeration. But my critics were vastly underestimating the situation. Now the estimate is more like one hundred species per day becoming extinct.

Initially I investigated tropical forests, because I wanted to understand why they were declining faster than any other ecological zone. They cover an area about as large as the United States (6 percent of Earth's land surface) and contain at least half of all species. According to my survey, they had already lost half of their expanse, and the rest was disappearing at the rate of about 1 percent per year. Once again I brought down a firestorm of criticism on my head until remote sensing surveys from satellite analysis revealed that my estimate was actually too low.

Tracking the complex causes of tropical deforestation, I discovered multiple sources. For example, American demand for cheap hamburger beef resulted in Central America's demolishing its national forests. Ranchers bought forest from the government for very little money, then torched the forest and raised beef for export to the United States. The root cause of deforestation originated in the north, one thousand miles away from tropical forests. I called it the "hamburger connection" to point out how material consumption and lavish lifestyles in rich nations were causing deforestation and species extinction in poor countries.

But this was not the whole story. For every acre of land taken by commercial ventures, ten more were taken by displaced peasants who found themselves landless. Heading off with machete and matchbox, they torched the forest to clear land on which to grow their subsistence crops. In tropical forests around the world, migrant cultivating was the number one cause of deforestation.

The problem was not the traditional shifting cultivators who had lived in the forests for centuries. They did not cause long-term injury to their ecosystems, and they had plenty of forest to shift around in.

But by the early 1980s there was only half as much forest; and instead of a few million traditional shifting cultivators, there were several hundred million "shifted" cultivators.

So then I began to look at issues of population growth and poverty in poor countries. By the mid-eighties, most developing countries were convinced their population growth rates were too high, and they wanted to reduce family sizes as quickly as they could. Not only governments were saying that, but a great majority of their citizens as well. Over one hundred million couples in poor countries (one couple in five) wanted no more children, but they lacked birth control.

I felt these people should have their needs met for humanitarian reasons, even if there were no population problem. It could be readily resolved if the rich nations were to put more funds into population planning in poor countries. The cost to rich countries would only be a penny a day per citizen, the equivalent of a couple of beers a year for taxpayers. The savings to all countries would far exceed the expenditure because it would take two billion people off the global total.

By the time the United Nations Conference on Population and Development was held in 1994, the rich nations were prepared to provide the necessary money and pledged to do so. Unfortunately, since that time, the rich nations have protested that they have never been poorer, and they have reneged on almost all their promises. The opportunity being lost is unimaginable.

Realizing the environmental effects of industrialized living, I also considered the population problem in developed countries. Industrialized countries have an effect on biodiversity and environment in many parts of the world, not only at home. Great Britain has an annual population growth rate of 0.2 percent, which is relatively low, but it still creates an extra hundred thousand Britons each year.

That number is not much compared with growth in Bangladesh, which has an annual population growth rate of 2.4 percent, producing an extra two and a half million people every year. But because of the profligate way people in Britain consume fossil fuels, at this time the extra thousands of people in Britain damage the atmosphere more than the extra millions in Bangladesh.

In Britain we have not even discussed whether we have a population problem. We have never asked ourselves how many people we want on our crowded little island: how many people are good for Britain, and how many Britons are good for the world. We have no population policy; no developed country does.

We could get to zero population growth just by eliminating half the unwanted births in Britain, where every ninth child is unwanted. We could prevent that at very little cost. In fact, it would boost our economy because it would reduce welfare payments. It would help families by allowing parents to have only children they want. Most important for everyone's welfare, we would reduce our population growth rate to zero.

The global population is now over six billion people. One billion live in developed countries, and all the rest live in developing nations. The top billion have the lowest reproduction rates, and the bottom billion have the highest. Of the extra ninety million people added every year to the world, over 90 percent are in developing countries. They already double their population every generation and will continue to increase even faster, because half their population are children who will reach reproductive age together, resulting in explosive population growth.

Even now half of all births in poor countries are unplanned, and one-quarter are unwanted. Of the one billion women most at risk of having too many children, almost half do not use any form of modern contraception. Several hundred million of them want to limit their fertility but lack birth control. The need and demand for it is now greater than ever. Since the 1950s, family planning in the developing world has been responsible for the decline from over six children to under four per family. It eliminates the births of nearly fifty million unwanted children every year.

Family planning also reduces serious health problems. Each year at least half a million women in poor countries die of pregnancy-related problems, and several million more barely survive childbirth. Women's health in poor countries is much worse than men's because of their inferior treatment by society. Women suffer severe physical stress and their financial plight can be desperate. They are rarely paid for work, own little property, and have meager or no inheritance rights. Without family support, there is often no way for them to survive.

Girls receive only half as much schooling as boys, if they are given any at all. As a result, there are twice as many illiterate women as men in poor countries. We know that women with seven years of schooling reduce their family size by an average of two to three children. As the United Nations Conference on Population concluded, women's education and equality are crucial to solving the world's population problems.

The preponderance of problems in poor nations is due to excessive population growth. Generally, the poorer a nation, the worse its population problem—and the more its population grows, the poorer it becomes. This downward spiral is exacerbated by poor nations' limited capacity to cope with the economic and environmental consequences of rapid population growth. Even a rich nation like Switzerland would have difficulty dealing with twice as many Swiss every generation.

Unfortunately, the more people there are, the less food there is and the less land to grow it on. Land shortage is widespread in most poor countries, where agriculture provides the livelihood for three-fifths of people. With more people trying to survive on less land, they overwork their croplands, clear forests, and try to cultivate arid lands and mountain slopes. When their lands fail, they move to the only ones left, marginal lands that are too dry, too wet, or too steep for subsistence agriculture.

Marginal lands are occupied by over 50 percent of poor people in Africa, 60 percent in Asia, and 80 percent in Latin America. The one billion additional people we gained in the past decade were born mostly into impoverished communities having to migrate into marginal environments. There are already over one hundred million people threatened by severe desertification and over half a billion subject to chronic water shortages.

As increasing numbers of impoverished people press harder on overloaded environments, it becomes increasingly difficult for them to make a living on the land because of drought, soil erosion, desertification, deforestation, and other environmental problems. As bad as it is now, it will be far worse when climate change exacerbates such problems and severely impairs the world's capacity to grow food. Global warming will increase droughts and disrupt rainfall regimes such as monsoon systems. It will increase extreme temperatures and escalate destructive storms, eventually raising sea levels and flooding the coastal communities where most of the world's population lives, displacing hundreds of millions of people.

Already, millions are forced to abandon their homelands without hope of returning and go wherever they can. Fleeing rural areas for urban slums, they find multitudes more suffering from unemployment, exploitation, crime, violence, malnutrition, pandemic diseases, and death. Lacking adequate water, food, shelter, and health, they barely survive in absolute poverty. Of those who can earn anything, over one billion people earn less than one dollar a day, and another billion people earn just that much.

Cities and countries cannot absorb unending throngs of environmental refugees. As outsiders multiply, they are perceived as threats to social cohesion and national identity. Immigrants become excuses for outbreaks of ethnic tension, civil disorder, and political upheaval. The resulting economic, social, and political crises are a destabilizing factor in international relations and will be more so when the world is battling an overload of other environmental problems at the same time.

The ever-increasing demands of growing numbers of people on decreasing resources are a predominant factor in problems of environmental decline. All countries, rich and poor, are having difficulty sustaining their populations on their natural resources. Since the end of the last world war, we have chewed up more raw materials than all our ancestors combined.

In just the past year, we gained ninety million people, almost equivalent to another Mexico. We lost billions of tons of topsoil, which means millions more starving people. We desertified an area the size of Ireland so badly it cannot grow food. We felled tropical forests on an area the size of England, reducing species habitats, watershed services, and climate stability. Our greenhouse gas emissions increased global warming, decreased the ozone shield, and increased ultraviolet radiation, which attacks marine food chains and crop plants as well as humans. In a single year, we made thousands of our fellow species extinct.

As human communities continue expanding in numbers and demands, they will exert increasing pressures on overburdened ecosystems. There are already so many of us that we are endangering the environment's capacity to sustain us. Paul Ehrlich defined our global carrying capacity as the number of people the planet can support without irreversibly reducing its capacity to support people in the future. Unfortunately, we are already exceeding our carrying capacity.

Although humans have exploited resources for a long time, our population growth is increasing exploitation so much that our needs are exceeding the planet's sustainable yield. At this point, resources become depleted with surprising rapidity. Accelerated destruction also occurs when ecosystems absorb stresses over long periods without obvious signs of damage, then reach a point when the cumulative consequences of stress become critical—and the system breaks down suddenly. Degraded ecosystems are inherently unstable and lack resistance to environmental dislocations, so they break down much faster and more easily than intact systems.

The biggest environmental problem will probably consist of interactions between smaller problems. The combination of compounded interactions can be many times greater than the sum of the component effects. One problem combines with another in a way that is not merely additive but multiplicative, and the result is not a double problem but a superproblem.

To give an example of a single synergism, the compounding interaction between air pollution, contaminated water, and food shortages already undermines public health. But when our immune systems are depressed by increased ultraviolet radiation from ozone depletion, we will have severely reduced resistance to all the new pathogens which will arise in a greenhouse-affected world.

It is certain that the multiple insults we are imposing on the environment will surprise us with significant problems. The mutually amplifying effects of synergistic interactions will create extraordinary impacts. Simultaneous multiple impacts will be incalculably worse than our single-problem scenarios. Consequently, environmental destruction will be far greater and arrive more rapidly than is currently predicted. The planetary ecosystem will be disrupted much more profoundly than we can presently foresee.

As far back as the 1970s, I was attempting to anticipate the implications of environmental breakdown for global security. I realized early that runaway population growth degraded environments in many developing countries. Living in Kenya, I watched its northern neighbor, Ethiopia, deplete the soil in its highlands. Starving Ethiopian peasants migrated toward their border with Somalia, resulting in war between the two countries. I observed that in African countries there is an ongoing connection between population pressures, environmental ruin, and war.

Looking at countries within Africa and around the world, I noted that decline of the environmental basis of agriculture creates food shortages that lead to riots. Resulting civil disorders and military eruptions overthrow governments, several times over in some countries. Problems over food supplies occur among rich nations as well as poor, as evidenced by current international conflicts over marine fisheries. Such disputes are a portent of what will be frequent phenomena in the future.

As too many people make too many demands on too few natural resources, they increasingly resort to force to ensure their share. If we continue ruining the environment around the world, environmental problems will become predominant causes of conflict. National security is no longer primarily about fighting forces and weapons. It is more and more about protecting water, soil, lands, forests, and other natural resources. If they are depleted, the nation's economy declines, its social fabric deteriorates, and its political structure destabilizes. The outcome will be conflict within a nation and with other nations.

The principal threat to national and international security is environmental breakdown and the need for natural resources that are increasingly scarce as more people make greater demands on them. The oil wars have begun, the water wars are beginning, and resource wars of all kinds will soon follow. That will be our future world war: a war of us all against us all, a war we are waging against Earth!

We cannot dispatch tanks to counter the advancing desert, we cannot launch submarines to resist the rising seas, we cannot fire the smartest missiles against the ozone hole and changing climate. Obviously, security strategy that relies on military force to safeguard nations' interests is obsolete. Yet the world still acts as though security is achieved only through military activities.

Military expenditures are $730 billion a year, $2 billion dollars a day, $2 million a minute. The annual total equals the collective incomes of the poorest half of humankind. Since the end of World War II, the United States has spent over $10 trillion on military activities, far more than the value of all America's tangible assets except the land itself.

Every time political leaders and military strategists allocate a dollar for armaments, they choose not to spend that dollar for health and the environment. The more than $100 billion a year spent on development of new weapons of destruction is more than all research on health and environment. To provide family planning for all couples who need it would cost $3 billion a year, equal to just a day and a half of military spending. Real security could be accomplished through the transfer of a tiny fraction of total military expenditure to the environment. The problem is not a shortage of money; it is a shortage of vision.

By focusing on the various environmental components of security, eventually I was able to see the big picture of global security. I wrote up my analysis in a series of articles in scientific journals, and the idea began to take on a legitimacy of its own. I was invited to present it to security experts in the United States government, including the State Department and the Pentagon. The North Atlantic Treaty Organization also arranged a workshop for me to explain my ideas to defense experts in NATO. Then the scientific organization Pugwash organized a conference in Russia that included Soviet military leaders too.

I was invited to a workshop with fifty people from the State Department, the National Security Council, the Central Intelligence Agency, and other security organizations in the U.S. government. In the front row sat generals, admirals, and chiefs from the Pentagon. They were all there to discuss environmental security and listen to a new appointee at the Pentagon, a general whose sole responsibility is to look out for environmental security. She assesses whether the

United States could buy more real security by spending another $100 million for yet another fighter plane to add to hundreds of existing fighter planes or by putting the same money into energy efficiency, desert reclamation, soil conservation, forest restoration, and so on. That is a big breakthrough, right in the heart of the Pentagon.

A smaller breakthrough occurred in the 1980s, when the United Nations created the World Commission on Environment and Development to review the state of the planet with regard to economic growth. Typically, it was composed of politicians, policy makers, bankers, financiers, industrialists, trade experts, and lawyers. I was a senior adviser to the commission, and when I introduced the importance of environmental security, members were predictably skeptical. But when they prepared their official report several years later, they had me do a whole section on it. Their final report concluded: "Humankind faces two great threats. The first is that of a nuclear exchange. Let us hope it remains no more than a diminishing prospect for the future. The second is that of environmental ruin worldwide—and far from being a prospect for the future, it is a fact right now."

Although the concept of environmental security is becoming accepted on the international scene, nations are not yet cooperating to ensure their collective security. The Earth Summit sponsored by the United Nations in 1992 brought together more nations than had ever assembled over anything. One hundred and seventy nations argued and negotiated, producing piles of recommendations pandering to their own individual interests. One hundred and twenty heads of state attended, but hardly a single leader spoke up substantively for the world or Earth. Quite the opposite. President Bush even declared that American lifestyles are not up for negotiation on ways to change. American lifestyles may not be negotiable, but they will definitely change. Their unsustainability ensures that the change will be as momentous and disastrous as it is inevitable.

Changes in the future will be worldwide. Nations cannot insulate themselves from environmental impacts, no matter how economically, technologically, or militarily powerful they might be. No nation can protect itself from the environmental actions, or inaction, of others. Activities in one locality affect other localities, sometimes all the way around the planet.

This seismic shift in international relations portends a bigger change for the nation-state than any since its emergence four hundred years ago. The confrontations between nations that characterized past international conflicts will not resolve global environmental problems. "We" are only as safe as "they" are. The fundamental assumption that I gain what you lose, and vice versa, is invalid. From now on, we shall all win together, or we shall all lose together. We are all in the same environmental boat: we shall all get wet as it springs leak after leak, and we shall all go under when it sinks.

As we cannot yet manage the world as an indivisible unit, we split it into manageable packages, such as nations, economic sectors, and ecological zones. Each makes final sense only through the context of the bigger picture. We no longer live apart from each other; we are a part of each other. Rather than malfunctioning as disjunct parts, we need to relate parts to the whole and ensure that they function as a whole. All nations are components of a planetary unity far greater than the sum of its parts.

Global security means not just individual or national security but our collective security and survival. The entire community of nations needs a public trust doctrine for basic principles of collective living in the global village so that we can protect the single biosphere that sustains life for us all. Global society should reflect our environment, which is a seamless web of interactions operating in a continuum wherein everything is connected to everything else. Whether we realize it or not, our world is becoming one.

The World Commission on Environment and Development opened its report with the statement: "Our Earth is one, our world is not." At a remote-sensing conference, I saw the oneness of Earth on a global map composed of Landsat images. There were no political boundaries on the planet. Yet unnatural, human-made divisions are a major reason why tropical forests are shrinking and deserts are expanding visibly on that map.

Beside the satellite-image map was the photograph of Earth taken from the Moon. Even though I had seen it many times before, I realized then that what I was looking at is a planetwide experiment. We are experimenting with the entire planetary ecosystem. The experiment is completely unplanned, and we have no idea of its outcome, except that evidence so far indicates that it is harming us and might kill us. We are like a bunch of Neanderthals trying to pilot a spacecraft. We behave as though we have a spare planet parked out there in space to which we can move when we destroy this one.

Our planetary ecosystem faces unparalleled threat. We have the capacity right now to impoverish Earth, but we also have the capacity to save Earth. Just as we can eliminate millions of species, we can preserve millions of species. We can devastate the planetary ecosystem, or we can save it at a time of unprecedented risk to the planet and terminal threat to the future of human life. No human community of the future will ever have our opportunity: if we fail, they will not exist.

What we do today will affect future generations extending for millions of years. We need to make the greatest change since we came out of our cave and create an entirely new mode of Earthling existence. The challenge is to redesign our societies so that we can be a truly global society based on Earth. We can all play our part, each and every one of us. Indeed we must, or we shall fail. The challenge is right now, and it is ours.

Further Reading

Norman Myers. *Ultimate Security: The Environmental Basis of Political Stability.* Island Press, 1998.

Norman Myers and Jennifer Kent. *Global Exodus: An Emergent Crisis in the Global Arena.* Climate Institute, 1995.

Norman Myers, ed. *Gaia: An Atlas of Planet Management.* Gaia Books, 1993.

———. *The Primary Source: Tropical Forests and Our Future.* Norton, 1992.

———. *The Gaia Atlas of Future Worlds: Challenge and Opportunity in an Age of Change.* Anchor Books, 1991.

———. *A Wealth of Wild Species: Storehouse for Human Welfare.* Westview, 1983.

———. *The Sinking Ark: A New Look at the Problem of Disappearing Species.* Pergamon, 1979.

The End

JOSEPH ROTBLAT

IT HAS BEEN GENERALLY ASSUMED THAT human life will continue indefinitely on this planet. Of course there is the possibility of the extinction of the human species by some sort of cataclysmic occurrence, like a collision with a comet or an exceptionally violent volcanic eruption. It is believed that the extinction of some species of animals that once dominated the planet, such as the dinosaurs, was due to an event of this nature. Nevertheless, the fact that such a violent catastrophe occurred more than sixty million years ago and has not been recorded since has meant that, for all practical purposes, we have put this possibility out of our minds.

That such a catastrophe should be caused by the actions of human beings has never been considered seriously. Of course history is full of terrible carnage in war, with mass exterminations of whole communities by invaders. Actually, the largest number of people killed in wars occurred in this century. Nearly nine million people were killed in World War I, and about sixty million in World War II. The worst single crime of genocide was committed during World War II, by the Nazis. They had almost a scientific program for the elimination of whole categories of people. Their attempts never succeeded in full, mainly for technical reasons, but now the technical obstacles have been overcome.

I see the nuclear age as beginning with the bombing of Hiroshima and Nagasaki. The main characteristic of the nuclear age is that for the first time in the history of civilization, it became possible for humans to destroy their own species and to accomplish it in a single act, either deliberately or accidentally. I do not believe that people have realized the enormity of this development. We continue our petty squabbles, which often lead to bloody wars, without considering the fact that such trivial disputes might escalate into war with large-scale hostilities—potentially leading to a nuclear war with catastrophic consequences.

This dire situation came about as the result of scientists' inventions. Scientists invented the weapons of war and developed the atom bomb by their own volition. They were fully aware of its potential for destruction. People might ask, Why did they do it? Most of the scientists who initiated the work on the atom bomb during World War II, first in England and then in the United States, were responsible members of the community. It is therefore difficult for the average person to understand why they embarked on such highly irresponsible activity. Of the original scientists who were actually involved in starting work on the bomb, only a few of us are left. I am one of those people. So I will speak about my own involvement.

From my early youth, I wanted to be a scientist. I was also conscious of the social responsibility of science. I believed that although the primary impulse for pursuing scientific research is the intellectual satisfaction of enlarging knowledge and understanding the laws of nature, science could also be of service to the community. Yet I became involved in the undertaking to develop a nuclear bomb. In fact, I was one of the initiators in 1939. The reason for this was a strange coincidence of history: the crucial discovery that led to the atom bomb occurred just before the outbreak of World War II, a war between democracy and a ruthless totalitarian regime.

That discovery was the fission of uranium atoms. I was then still in Poland, my native country. In February 1939 I read a scientific report by Otto Frisch and Lise Meitner about the discovery of fission: if you hit a uranium atom with a neutron, an elementary particle, it breaks into two particles and releases energy. It occurred to me that, in addition, some other neutrons are also emitted. At the time I was doing an experiment on the scattering of neutrons by uranium, so it did not take me more than a few days to complete this experiment and find out that indeed, in this process of fission, more neutrons are emitted. The same observation was made independently in several laboratories. This is the way science works; when an idea is ripe, it occurs to many scientists more or less simultaneously.

The importance of this observation about the emission of new neutrons was that it opened a way for a chain reaction. The new neutrons can be made to hit more uranium atoms, producing more fission and releasing more energy. These reactions in turn create an exponential increase in the number of fissions, so in a very short time one can get an enormous release of energy. This discovery gave us access to the vast stores of energy contained in the nucleus of the atom.

But then another idea occurred to me: if all this energy is released in a very short time (a millionth of a second or less), it will be a mighty explosion. In other words, an atom bomb. When this idea occurred to me, I immediately put it out of my mind because my concept of science did not include work on a weapon of mass destruction, or indeed on any weapon. It was unthinkable to me that I should be involved in such work.

Nevertheless, despite my conscious decision, at the back of my mind a fear kept gnawing away: the fear that other scientists might not have the same moral scruples. In particular, I was afraid German scientists might develop the bomb and enable Hitler to win the war. Living in Poland, I knew war was inevitable.

This knowledge created for me a terrible dilemma, a choice between the devil and the deep blue sea. On the one hand, the idea of working on a weapon of mass destruction went against the basic ideals of science. On the other hand, these very ideals of science were in danger of being eradicated if the evil doctrine of Nazism were to prevail through Germany's development of the bomb. I struggled with this dilemma throughout the summer of 1939, and I came to a decision after the outbreak of war on September 1. The Germans invaded Poland, overcoming the entire country within a few days. This manifestation of the enormous military power of Germany made me realize that if they also had the bomb, then they were bound to win the war. I could not accept that outcome because I was convinced that civilization as we understand it would be destroyed.

Consequently, I made the decision to start work on the bomb. But even though I decided it was necessary, I still needed to remain true to my moral ideals. My rationale for the work was that if a nuclear bomb could be made, and if Hitler acquired it, the only way we could prevent Hitler from using his bomb would be the threat of retaliation with a bomb of our own. It was the classic concept of nuclear deterrence. I could not have known then that although my fears were valid, the Germans would not succeed. As it turned out, the Germans did start working on the bomb, but they made the wrong calculations, did faulty experiments, and gave up the project in 1942.

Moreover, my reasoning was wrong in one critical respect: the belief that scientists, having created a weapon, could influence military and political leaders regarding its use. Once these leaders got the bomb, they just did what they wanted. Their concepts differed from ours all along. I found out when I was at Los Alamos that for some of the military leaders the purpose of the project was not what we scientists believed, to prevent the Germans from using the bomb against us. From the very beginning their purpose was quite a different one: to subdue the Russians, even though the Russians were our allies during the war. This was told to me in private by General Groves, who was head of the Manhattan Project. So I found out fairly early that the military's purpose was very different from ours.

When I was at Los Alamos, I came to see that the war in Europe would be over before the bomb was made. It was much more difficult than we imagined initially. Late in 1944 the Germans were nearly beaten militarily. They suffered defeat in Russia and were forced to retreat. Nevertheless, I was still worried that they would develop the bomb. I had no idea they had given up the project until I was informed of this fact at the end of 1944. As soon as I learned that, the whole purpose of my work on the project evaporated. I resigned and left the Manhattan Project immediately.

I went to England and changed my profession from nuclear to medical physics. Eight months after I had left the project came the destruction of Hiroshima and Nagasaki. This was a terrible shock to me because I had still hoped they would just test the bomb and not use it. When I found out it was used as soon as it was made, and used against a civilian population, I realized the enormous political significance of this event. If, as I understood at the time, the main purpose of the bomb was to demonstrate that it made America the most powerful military force in the world—and therefore able to subdue anyone, particularly Russia—then the Russians would feel compelled to make their own bomb. The inevitable outcome would be an international arms race.

I was also aware that the fission bomb used on Japan was only the beginning. I knew that work was already being done in Los Alamos on the hydrogen bomb, the so-called "super bomb," a thousand times more powerful than the atom bomb. I realized that once a nuclear arms race began, then the whole of civilization would be at stake, indeed the entire existence of the human species.

That was when I began my activities to inform the scientific community about the danger. After World War II, a number of scientists who were involved in the project decided nuclear weapons should never be used again. We organized ourselves in groups like the Federation of American Scientists in the United States and the Atomic Scientists Association in Great Britain. We made an effort to educate the public about these new developments and thereby to influence governments. Of course the governments ignored our warnings, and, as we foresaw, nuclear weapons development escalated. When the Russians developed their own atom bomb, then the Americans, having lost the nuclear monopoly, produced the hydrogen bomb—and so it went on and on, a race toward oblivion.

We decided something must be done by scientists from both sides of the Iron Curtain. But it was very difficult during the Stalin regime for any of the Soviet scientists to talk to scientists from other countries on such matters. We had to wait until after Stalin's death in 1953 before we could begin talking to Soviet scientists.

The initiative for an international meeting of scientists came from the British philosopher and mathematician Bertrand Russell. I had been in touch with him earlier and had enlightened him about the effects of nuclear weapons development, including the health hazard from continuous testing of nuclear bombs in the atmosphere. He became very worried about this and deeply involved in the issue.

Soon after the first atomic bombs were exploded, Russell gave a speech in the House of Lords forecasting the threat to civilization and suggesting that a meeting between Western and Soviet scientists might provide the best opportunity for the establishment of a system of international controls. Russell later gave a powerful radio talk, called "Man's Peril," evaluating the dangerous situation that resulted from the development of nuclear weapons and the catastrophic consequences of a future nuclear war. The broadcast made a great impact on public opinion but not on government policy.

Russell thought scientists should do something about the situation, so he initiated an appeal by eminent scientists to the scientific community and to the world. The preeminent scientist living then was Albert Einstein, so Bertrand Russell wrote a letter to Einstein, suggesting scientists issue a proclamation and hold a conference to discuss these problems. Einstein very eagerly assented, saying he would endorse such a proclamation if Russell would write it. So Russell wrote it and sent it to Einstein for his signature.

Russell told me that soon afterward he was flying from Rome to Paris when the pilot of the aircraft informed the passengers that he had just heard Einstein had died. Russell was shattered; without Einstein's endorsement, he feared, the whole project would collapse. But when he arrived at his hotel in Paris, there was a letter waiting for him that had been sent from London. It was a letter from Einstein with his signature to the statement—one of the last acts of Albert Einstein's life.

Bertrand Russell then collected the signatures of nine other eminent scientists, mostly Nobel laureates, and issued the proclamation that became known as the Russell-Einstein Manifesto. I am the only one of the signatories left; all the others have passed away. I chaired the international press conference in 1955, when the manifesto was issued. The manifesto called on scientists to come together in a conference to appraise the perils resulting from the development of weapons of mass destruction. It was hoped that if the peril of universal death were understood, we might collectively avert it.

At that time, though, it was very difficult to get the finances for such a meeting. Fortunately, we received a letter from Cyrus Eaton, a Canadian industrialist, who offered to pay for the conference if it was held in Pugwash, the village in Nova Scotia where he was born and where he had set up a trust to support such meetings. We accepted his invitation and met in 1957.

This first conference of scientists was something of a gamble. In the atmosphere of the cold war, with all its hostile propaganda, there was a real possibility that the meeting would break up in disarray. As it turned out, it was a great success. It was quite a small meeting, with only twenty-two scientists, but they came from both sides of the Iron Curtain: from the Soviet Union, China, the U.S.A., Britain, France, and so on. We were able to discuss what was essentially a political issue—how to deal with nuclear weapons under the conditions of the cold war—because everyone came as an individual, rather than representing a government or an institution, and we talked to one another as scientists. We approached the problems in the spirit of scientific objectivity.

Although we disagreed on certain issues because we approached them in different ways, we believed we could reach agreement. Therefore we decided to convene regular meetings. We created the movement that became known as the Pugwash Conference on Science and World Affairs. The Pugwash movement gradually developed over the years.

Nevertheless, we were bitterly attacked from the beginning and have continued to be maligned. In the beginning, it took a great deal of courage for Western scientists to come to a meeting with Russian scientists to talk about peace. We were immediately branded as a Communist front organization. In fact, the U.S. Senate conducted an investigation into our activities. People said that at best we were idiots; we were dupes. Even recently, in Britain's House of Lords, there was a discussion in which our Pugwash group was called Soviet dupes.

This ignorance is a result of people not understanding what we are trying to do. The Soviet government did try to influence our discussions, but we were always very careful to prevent this happening. A few years later, when the Western governments realized the importance of our Pugwash movement, they tried to influence us as well. I received directives from them about what we should discuss and whom we should invite. We had to resist the overtures from all governments. Throughout the years we kept on the path of neutrality—a very narrow path, but we managed to keep on it.

After all these years, we have finally been recognized with the Nobel Peace Prize. We have managed to achieve quite a lot, particularly during the cold war, when the world was threatened with complete catastrophe. We successfully influenced the policies of Mikhail Gorbachev to stop the arms race. He told us that himself. In that respect, I believe that what we have been doing over the years has been successful, despite the obstacles we have had to overcome.

But our task is not finished yet, although nuclear arms are being reduced gradually. Even if weapons dismantlement goes in accordance with current agreements, there will still be some fifteen thousand nuclear weapons left in the arsenals. We do not believe the dangers will truly cease as long as nuclear weapons exist. Therefore our main work now is to find a way to eliminate all nuclear weapons. In fact, we have made a good study of the task and published the results in our book, which has appeared in eight languages. The foreign minister of Australia told me it influenced the Australian government to create the Canberra Commission on the Elimination of Nuclear Weapons and put it before the United Nations.

Yet even if we manage to achieve this objective of eliminating nuclear weapons, the world still will not be safe. Safer than now, but not absolutely safe, because we cannot erase the knowledge of how to make these dangerous weapons. We cannot disinvent them; the genie is out of the bottle, as the saying goes. A dispute between major powers, say China and India, might result in the building up of nuclear weapons again. In other words, it is not enough just to eliminate them, although this is an essential step.

Our aim now is to go much further, to eliminate not just nuclear war, but all war. This is necessary because science might develop other methods of self-destruction. We must prevent them. As the destiny of humankind now depends on science and technology, it is imperative for scientists to be aware of their social responsibility. We must continually be on the alert to ensure that what science is doing will not harm the whole of humankind and our environment.

Ending war sounds utopian, but I believe it is possible nevertheless. Consider the two world wars that occurred in this century, where Britain and France were on one side and Germany on the other. A war between them is now unlikely because Europe has become so interdependent. That is why I feel even the abolition of all war could be accomplished. I hope we will achieve it.

In order to prevent war, we have to remove the causes of war. Of course ultimately our problems depend on population control because we cannot continue indefinitely multiplying ourselves and using up all the resources. By ravaging our environment, eventually we will destroy ourselves simply by the numbers of people consuming so much. We need to resolve these urgent problems, because they put us in danger of a nuclear war. We are trying to inform and educate the public to ensure that this ultimate environmental catastrophe does not happen. We can go down with a whimper, as Paul Ehrlich says, from environmental degradation, or with a bang in a nuclear explosion. It is possible that environmental deterioration would lead to nuclear destruction, and our whimper would end with a bang!

As the original manifesto for the Pugwash Conference on Science and World Affairs stated:

> Here, then, is the problem which we present to you, stark and dreadful and inescapable: Shall we put an end to the human race; or shall mankind renounce war?
>
> There lies before us, if we choose, continual progress in happiness, knowledge, and wisdom. Shall we, instead, choose death, because we cannot forget our quarrels? We appeal, as human beings, to human beings: remember your humanity, and forget the rest. If you can do so, the way lies open to a new Paradise: if you cannot, there lies before you the risk of universal death.

Further Reading

Joseph Rotblat. *Nuclear Weapons: The Road to Zero.* Westview, 1998.

———. *World Citizenship.* St. Martin's Press, 1997.

Joseph Rotblat, Jack Steinberger, and Bhalchandra Udgaonkar, eds. *A Nuclear Weapon-Free World: Desirable? Feasible?* Frank Blackaby, executive editor. Westview, 1995.

Joseph Rotblat, M. P. Fry, and N. P. Keating, eds. *Nuclear Non-proliferation and the Non-proliferation Treaty.* Springer-Verlag, 1990.

Joseph Rotblat and J. Altman, eds. *Verification of Arms Reduction.* Springer-Verlag, 1989.

Joseph Rotblat and John Holdren, eds. *Building Global Security through Cooperation.* Springer-Verlag, 1989.

———, eds. *Strategic Defense and the Future of the Arms Race: A Pugwash Symposium.* St. Martin's Press, 1987.

Joseph Rotblat, ed. *Scientists, the Arms Race, and Disarmament.* Taylor and Francis, 1982.

Union of Concerned Scientists' Warnings

HENRY KENDALL

THE NOBEL FOUNDATION, WHOSE RESPONSI-
bilities are the administration of the Nobel prizes
and the activities related to their award, asked if I
would participate in a debate in Stockholm being planned as part of
a celebration of the ninetieth anniversary of the first awards, the
Nobel Jubilee. It was an invitation that I could not refuse, for the
subject was whether the human race was using its collective intelligence to build a better world—a subject that was clearly very close to
my heart. I was selected as the spokesperson for the negative side of
the proposition to be debated. Archbishop Desmond Tutu was selected as the opposing spokesperson.

I chose for my subject a synoptic review of the environmental pressures, resource management, and population issues, and the ways in
which a continuation of current practices would affect succeeding
generations. I spent several months collecting material and talking to
a wide variety of scientists, especially from the life sciences.

Two unexpected matters surfaced in the course of this effort. The
first was how stressed the global food-producing sector was. The second was the grave concern expressed by those biologists whose interests were in ecosystem studies, population dynamics, and other fields
that touched on the consequences of the destruction of species and
resulting loss of global biodiversity. These revelations made a deep

impression on me. I concluded that this scientific community appeared ready to speak out publicly.

My preparation for the debate set the stage for two continuing activities. In the months after the event, I searched out a potential collaborator to help in preparing a synoptic analysis of global food problems. By the middle of winter 1992, I and David Pimentel, a Cornell University entomologist and agricultural expert, were at work on our paper, "Constraints on the Expansion of the Global Food Supply" (*Ambio* 23:3, May 1994).

Also that winter I began preparation of a declaration, the "World Scientists' Warning to Humanity," having concluded that others besides just the biologists were distressed and that many other scientists would support a broad statement of concern. In its final form, it was signed by over 1,700 scientists from 71 countries, including 104 Nobel laureates, and it was released in November 1992 by the Union of Concerned Scientists.

The warning, as one of my colleagues remarked, has "had legs," real, lasting power. It has, over the ensuing years, become UCS's most widely requested publication, with an estimated 150,000 copies distributed. It has been and continues to be quoted and referenced extensively both in scientific and popular publications and has become the document of record in setting forth the consensus of the scientific community on some of the most vexing problems facing humanity.

I and my Union of Concerned Scientists colleagues launched another warning on the eve of the international meeting on climate change held in Kyoto, Japan, in December 1997. It was titled "World Scientists' Call for Action at the Kyoto Climate Summit." While it addressed directly the subject of the meeting and the need to reduce worldwide emissions of carbon into the atmosphere, it also contained an update to the 1992 warning. Like the 1992 statement, it gained the support of a powerful segment of the global scientific community. It was signed by 109 Nobel laureates, including 104 of the 178 Nobel winners in the sciences.

It is through such statements as these that the Union of Concerned Scientists is able to speak for the world's senior scientific community and, in an important sense, be its voice on critical issues.

Five years ago, in the World Scientists' Warning to Humanity, 1,600 of the world's senior scientists sounded an unprecedented warning:

> Human activities inflict harsh and often irreversible damage on the environment and on critical resources. If not checked, many of our current practices put at serious risk the future that we wish for human society and the plant and animal kingdoms.

Addressed to political, industrial, religious, and scientific leaders, the Warning demonstrated that the scientific community had reached a consensus that grave threats imperil the future of humanity and the global environment. However, over four years have passed, and progress has been woefully inadequate. Some of the most serious problems have worsened. Invaluable time has been squandered because so few leaders have risen to the challenge.

The December 1997 Climate Summit in Kyoto, Japan, presents a unique opportunity. The world's political leaders can demonstrate a new commitment to the protection of the environment. The goal is to strengthen the 1992 Framework Convention on Climate Change by agreeing to effective controls on human practices affecting climate.

This they can and must do, primarily by augmenting the Convention's voluntary measures with legally binding commitments to reduce industrial nations' emissions of heat-trapping gases significantly below 1990 levels in accordance with a near-term timetable. Over time, developing nations must also be engaged in limiting their emissions. Developed and developing nations must cooperate to mitigate climate disruption. The biosphere is a seamless web.

Completion of an effective treaty at Kyoto would address one of the most serious threats to the planet and to future generations. It would set a landmark precedent for addressing other grave environmental threats, many linked to climate change. It would demonstrate that the world's leaders have now recognized, in deed and words, their responsibility for stewardship of the earth. The stark facts carry a clear signal:

> There is only one responsible choice—to act now.

We, the signers of this declaration, urge all government leaders to demonstrate a new commitment to protecting the global environment for future generations. The important first step is to join in completing a strong and meaningful Climate Treaty at Kyoto. We encourage scientists and citizens around the world to hold their leaders accountable for addressing the global warming threat. Leaders must take this first step to protect future generations from dire prospects that would result from failure to meet our responsibilities toward them.

The Web of Environmental Effects

Atmospheric Disruption

Predictions of global climatic change are becoming more confident. A broad consensus among the world's climatologists is that there is now "a discernible human influence on global climate."

Climate change is projected to raise sea levels, threatening populations and ecosystems in coastal regions. Warmer temperatures will lead to a more vigorous hydrologic cycle, increasing the prospects for more intense rainfall, floods, or droughts in some regions. Human health may be damaged by greater exposure to heat waves and droughts, and by encroachment of tropical diseases to higher latitudes.

The developing world is especially vulnerable to damage from climatic disruption because it is already under great stress and has less capacity to adapt.

Climate Change: Linkages and Further Damage

Destructive logging and deforestation for agriculture continue to wreak havoc on the world's remaining tropical forests. The burning of the Amazonian rain forests continues largely unabated. Other forests in developed and in the developing nations are under heavy pressure. Destruction of forests greatly amplifies soil erosion and water wastage, is a major source of loss of species, and undermines the environment's natural ability to store carbon. It releases additional carbon to the atmosphere, thereby enhancing global warming.

Fossil-fueled energy use is climbing, both in industrial nations and in the developing world, adding to atmospheric carbon. Efforts to enhance energy conservation and improve efficiency are much hindered by low energy costs and by perverse incentives that encourage waste. Without firm commitments, most industrial nations will not meet the carbon-emission goals they agreed to at the 1992 Rio conference. The transition to renewable, non–fossil-carbon-based energy sources is feasible but is not in sight for lack of aggressive political will.

The insurance industry has recognized the risks posed by climate change. Leading economists have identified viable policies for reducing these risks. Markets undervalue ecosystems worldwide and inflict few penalties against practices that do long-term environmental and resource damage. Political leadership must introduce incentives that reward sound practices.

Water Scarcity and Food Security
Humanity now uses over one-half of the total accessible freshwater runoff. Freshwater is the scarcest resource in the Middle East and in North Africa. Efforts to husband freshwater are not succeeding there, in East Asia, or in the Pacific.

Global food production now appears to be outpaced by growth in consumption and population. There is broad agreement that food demand will double by 2030. Most land suitable for agriculture is already in production. Sub-Saharan Africa's increase in agricultural production is one-third less than its population growth. The region now produces 80 percent of what it consumes, and per capita production is declining. Projections indicate that demand for food in Asia will exceed the supply by 2010.

Thus, food consumption levels in many countries are likely to remain totally inadequate for good nutrition. Widespread undernutrition will persist unless extraordinary measures are taken to ensure food for all, measures not now even contemplated by governments. Climate change is likely to exacerbate these food problems by adversely affecting water supplies, soil conditions, temperature tolerances, and growing seasons.

Destruction of Species
Climate change will accelerate the appalling pace at which species are now being liquidated, especially in vulnerable ecosystems. One-fourth of the known species of mammals are threatened, and half of

these may be gone within a decade. Possibly one-third of all species may be lost before the end of the next century.

Biodiversity gives stability to the ecosystems that we are so dependent on, enhances their productivity, and provides an important source of new foods, medicines, and other products.

WORLD SCIENTISTS' WARNING TO HUMANITY

Introduction

Human beings and the natural world are on a collision course. Human activities inflict harsh and often irreversible damage on the environment and on critical resources. If not checked, many of our current practices put at serious risk the future that we wish for human society and the plant and animal kingdoms, and may so alter the living world that it will be unable to sustain life in the manner that we know. Fundamental changes are urgent if we are to avoid the collision our present course will bring about.

The Environment

The environment is suffering critical stress.

The Atmosphere

Stratospheric ozone depletion threatens us with enhanced ultraviolet radiation at the earth's surface, which can be damaging or lethal to many life forms. Air pollution near ground level, and acid precipitation, are already causing widespread injury to humans, forests, and crops.

Water Resources

Heedless exploitation of depletable ground water supplies endangers food production and other essential human systems. Heavy demands on the world's surface waters have resulted in serious shortages in some 80 countries, containing 40 percent of the world's population. Pollution of rivers, lakes, and ground water further limits the supply.

Oceans

Destructive pressure on the oceans is severe, particularly in the coastal regions which produce most of the world's food fish. The total marine catch is now at or above the estimated maximum sustainable yield. Some fisheries have already shown signs of collapse. Rivers carrying heavy burdens of eroded soil into the seas also carry industrial, municipal, agricultural, and livestock waste—some of it toxic.

Soil

Loss of soil productivity, which is causing extensive land abandonment, is a widespread by-product of current practices in agriculture and animal husbandry. Since 1945, 11 percent of the earth's vegetated surface has been degraded—an area larger than India and China combined—and per capita food production in many parts of the world is decreasing.

Forests

Tropical rain forests, as well as tropical and temperate dry forests, are being destroyed rapidly. At present rates, some critical forests will be gone before the end of the next century. With them will go large numbers of plant and animal species.

Living Species

The irreversible loss of species, which by 2100 may reach one-third of all species now living, is especially serious. We are losing the potential they hold for providing medicinal and other benefits, and the contribution that genetic diversity of life forms gives to the robustness of the world's biological systems and to the astonishing beauty of the earth itself.

Much of this damage is irreversible on a scale of centuries, or permanent. Other processes appear to pose additional threats. Increasing levels of gases in the atmosphere from human activities, including carbon dioxide released from fossil fuel burning and from deforestation, may alter climate on a global scale. Predictions of global warming are still uncertain—with projected effects ranging from tolerable to very severe—but the potential risks are very great.

Our massive tampering with the world's interdependent web of life—coupled with the environmental damage inflicted by deforestation, species loss, and climate change—could trigger widespread adverse effects, including unpredictable collapses of critical biological systems whose interactions and dynamics we only imperfectly understand.

Uncertainty over the extent of these effects cannot excuse complacency or delay in facing the threats.

Population

The earth is finite. Its ability to absorb wastes and destructive effluent is finite. Its ability to provide food and energy is finite. Its ability to provide for growing numbers of people is finite. And we are fast approaching many of the earth's limits. Current economic practices which damage the environment, in both developed and underdeveloped nations, cannot be continued without the risk that vital global systems will be damaged beyond repair.

Pressures resulting from unrestrained population growth put demands on the natural world that can overwhelm any efforts to achieve a sustainable future. If we are to halt the destruction of our environment, we must accept limits to that growth. A World Bank estimate indicates that world population will not stabilize at less than 12.4 billion, while the United Nations concludes that the eventual total could reach 14 billion, a near tripling of today's 5.4 billion. But, even at this moment, one person in five lives in absolute poverty without enough to eat, and one in ten suffers serious malnutrition.

No more than one or a few decades remain before the chance to avert the threats we now confront will be lost and the prospects for humanity immeasurably diminished.

Warning

We the undersigned, senior members of the world's scientific community, hereby warn all humanity of what lies ahead. A great change in our stewardship of the earth and the life on it is required, if vast human misery is to be avoided and our global home on this planet is not to be irretrievably mutilated.

What We Must Do

Five inextricably linked areas must be addressed simultaneously.

1. *We must bring environmentally damaging activities under control to restore and protect the integrity of the earth's systems we depend on.* We must, for example, move away from fossil fuels to more benign, inexhaustible energy sources to cut greenhouse gas emissions and the pollution of our air and water. Priority must be given to the development of energy sources matched to Third World needs—small-scale and relatively easy to implement.

   We must halt deforestation, injury to and loss of agricultural land, and the loss of terrestrial and marine plant and animal species.

2. *We must manage resources crucial to human welfare more effectively.* We must give high priority to efficient use of energy, water, and other materials, including expansion of conservation and recycling.

3. *We must stabilize population. This will be possible only if all nations recognize that it requires improved social and economic conditions, and the adoption of effective, voluntary family planning.*

4. *We must reduce and eventually eliminate poverty.*

5. *We must ensure sexual equality, and guarantee women control over their own reproductive decisions.*

The developed nations are the largest polluters in the world today. They must greatly reduce their overconsumption, if we are to reduce pressures on resources and the global environment. The developed nations have the obligation to provide aid and support to developing nations, because only the developed nations have the financial resources and the technical skills for these tasks.

Acting on this recognition is not altruism, but enlightened self-interest: whether industrialized or not, we all have but one lifeboat. No nation can escape from injury when global biological systems are damaged. No nation can escape from conflicts over increasingly scarce resources. In addition, environmental and economic instabilities will cause mass migrations with incalculable consequences for developed and undeveloped nations alike.

Developing nations must realize that environmental damage is one of the gravest threats they face, and that attempts to blunt it will be overwhelmed if their populations go unchecked. The greatest peril is to become trapped in spirals of environmental decline, poverty, and unrest, leading to social, economic, and environmental collapse.

Success in this global endeavor will require a great reduction in violence and war. Resources now devoted to the preparation and conduct of war—amounting to over $1 trillion annually—will be badly needed in the new tasks and should be diverted to the new challenges.

A new ethic is required—a new attitude towards discharging our responsibility for caring for ourselves and for the earth. We must recognize the earth's limited capacity to provide for us. We must recognize its fragility. We must no longer allow it to be ravaged. This ethic must motivate a great movement, convincing reluctant leaders and reluctant governments and reluctant peoples themselves to effect the needed changes.

The scientists issuing this warning hope that our message will reach and affect people everywhere. We need the help of many.

We require the help of the world community of scientists—natural, social, economic, political;

We require the help of the world's business and industrial leaders;

We require the help of the world's religious leaders; and

We require the help of the world's peoples.

We call on all to join us in this task.

Sponsored by the Union of Concerned Scientists
26 Church Street, Cambridge, MA 02238

GLOSSARY

acid rain

Precipitation that is acidic as a result of atmospheric pollutants, specifically sulfur dioxide from power generation and industrial facilities, nitrogen oxides from car exhaust, and particulate matter. It acidifies water and soil, killing aquatic organisms such as amphibians and fish, damaging plants, and contributing to forest decline and dieback. In addition to precipitation, pollutants can also be deposited as gases or particles in the form of dry fall.

adaptation

Organisms' adjustments to accommodate themselves to their environment; the evolutionary changes in structure, function, or behavior that allow populations to survive and that result in genetic modifications over successive generations.

algae

Aquatic organisms that contain chlorophyll and are thus capable of photosynthesis. The primary producers of food and oxygen in water environments, algae form the base of the aquatic food chain.

benthos

The bottom of a body of water; also refers to the organisms dwelling in the lowest depths of the sea or lakes.

bioaccumulation

The buildup of nonbiodegradable chemicals in biological tissues. Persistent pesticides such as DDT accumulate in organisms and increase in concentration along the food chain through the process of biomagnification.

bioamplification   The increase in concentration of toxins in organisms higher up the food pyramid, with every level of organism consuming the accumulated toxins of multiple organisms below it in the food chain.

biodegradable   The capacity to be decomposed into natural substances by biological processes, usually bacterial action.

biodiversity   The variety of living organisms and ecological systems at all levels: genetic diversity, species diversity, and ecological diversity. High biological diversity is important for the stability and longevity of ecosystems.

biogeochemical cycle   The cyclical movement of elements such as carbon, nitrogen, sulfur, and phosphorus between the organic and inorganic components of the biosphere. It is also referred to as the nutrient cycle because elemental nutrients are continually recycled.

biogeography   The geographical distribution of organisms and habitats over space and through time.

biology   The study of living organisms and life processes, including their origin and evolution, classification, structure, functioning, activities, interrelationships, and distribution.

biomass   Total mass of living matter (dry biological material) within a specific unit of measurement from a single organism to an ecosystem.

biome   A large ecosystem maintained by distinct climatic conditions, with distinctive vegetation and animals. For example, desert, grassland, woodland, and rain forest are terrestrial biomes; coral reefs, estuaries, and floodplains are marine and freshwater biomes.

bioregion   An area with distinct natural characteristics, including climate, landforms, watershed, and wildlife.

bioremediation   The process in which microorganisms are utilized to detoxify toxic wastes.

biosphere   Earth's total ecosystem; the limited region in which life exists, a thin layer from a short distance below to a little above Earth's surface.

biota   The species of a given region or period.

biotic community	All the living organisms sharing a common environment, including producers, consumers, and decomposers.
boreal forest	Northern coniferous forest, including fir, hemlock, and spruce; can also contain deciduous species such as aspen and birch.
carbon cycle	The cyclical transfer of carbon between the environment and organisms: for example, the conversion of atmospheric carbon dioxide to carbohydrates by photosynthesis in plants, which are eaten by animals, metabolized into carbon dioxide, and then exhaled into the atmosphere.
carbon dioxide	Gas molecule with one atom of carbon bound to two of oxygen. Oxygen is released from carbon dioxide by plants during photosynthesis, and carbon dioxide is expired by animals during respiration. It is also released by organic decomposition and combustion.
carbon monoxide	Gas molecule with one atom of carbon to one of oxygen; an extremely poisonous gas formed by incomplete combustion of carbon, commonly from automobile gasoline.
carbon sink	Ecosystem that absorbs more carbon dioxide than it releases. For example, trees bind carbon as they grow, so forests absorb some of the excess carbon dioxide humans produce and help adjust the resulting atmospheric imbalance.
carcinogen	A cancer-causing agent.
carrying capacity	The number of organisms of a species an environment can support indefinitely without degeneration. When the carrying capacity is exceeded by overpopulation, the environment deteriorates and population declines.
chlorinated hydrocarbons	A category of synthetic chemical compounds formed by bonding chlorine and carbon, including aldrin, chlordane, DDT, dieldrin, endrin, heptachlor, and lindane. These chemicals, used as insecticides that poison the nervous system, persist in the environment for years.
chlorofluorocarbons (CFCs)	Chemical compounds consisting of chlorine, fluorine, carbon, and hydrogen, used as refrigerants and aerosol propellants before some restrictions were placed on their use. CFCs deplete atmospheric ozone.

chlorophyll	Green pigment in plants that absorbs light and enables photosynthesis to occur.
coevolution	The evolution of complementary adaptations in species as a result of mutual influence, such as the changes that have occurred in both plants and insects to enable pollination.
community	Populations of all species living together and interacting in their habitat.
conservation biology	The study of the maintenance of biodiversity, particularly in relation to human intervention.
DDT	Dichlorodiphenyltrichloroethane, a chlorinated hydrocarbon and broad-spectrum pesticide capable of killing other organisms in addition to the targeted pest. It concentrates in animal fat and milk because it is fat-soluble and chemically stable. The most widely used pesticide, this toxic pollutant has migrated all over the planet.
deforestation	The permanent removal of forests and conversion of the landscape for nonforest use, such as exploiting natural resources, clearing land for crops and pasture, and development.
desertification	Land degradation resulting in loss of vegetation and biological productivity. Overcultivation and overgrazing cause so much soil erosion that vegetation cannot grow. Salinization and waterlogging from irrigation are also contributing factors.
diatom	Microscopic unicellular alga with siliceous cell walls; a major constituent of marine plankton.
DNA	Deoxyribonucleic acid, a chromosomal constituent of cell nuclei that determines individual hereditary characteristics and is the genetic material passed from one generation to the next.
ecology	Study of the functions and dynamics of living systems, of organisms in relation to one another and their natural environment.
ecosystem	An ecological community of organisms within a particular environment.
endangered species	Species whose populations have been reduced to the point of immediate danger of extinction.
environment	The surrounding external physical, chemical, and biological conditions affecting organisms.

environmental impact	Change in the natural environment, usually with reference to human activity.
estuary	Coastal ecosystem where a river flows into the sea, mixing silted freshwater with salt water that changes with the tides, creating highly productive wetlands.
evolution	Biologically, a change in the genetic constitution of a species' population through successive generations. Generally, the process by which species develop through changes in inherited characteristics.
evolutionary biology	Study of the evolutionary process in species and the development of biological diversity.
externalities	Social benefits and costs of producing and using an economic item that are not included in its market price.
extinction	Permanent disappearance of a species.
fauna and flora	All the animals (fauna) and plants (flora) in a habitat.
food chain	A sequence of organisms, each providing food for the next, in the feeding chain of a food web.
food or energy pyramid	An ecosystem's levels of energy production and consumption. Plants and phytoplankton, the primary producers, form the base of the energy pyramid and supply energy for everything else in the food web. All consumers are dependent on them, including the many organisms that eat plants directly and the far fewer predators that eat plant-eaters. The number of organisms shrinks at each functional level because available energy diminishes. An organism utilizes most of the energy it consumes in order to live, and thus only a fraction of its energy is available to whatever eats it. Herbivores obtain only 10 percent of a plant's energy; carnivores only 10 percent of that; and predators preying on carnivores only 10 percent of that.
food web	Who eats what: all the feeding relationships in an ecological community.
fossil fuels	Combustible hydrocarbon materials derived from organic matter altered by high temperatures and pressure underground, such as coal, petroleum, and natural gas.
Gaia hypothesis	Theory suggesting that Earth is a self-regulating system that maintains the planet in a stable balance favorable for life.

gene	The component of chromosomal DNA that transmits hereditary traits.
genome	All the genes contained in a single set of chromosomes, organism, or species.
Gondwanaland	Postulated supercontinent that formed from the southern segment of the single protocontinent Pangaea in the late Paleozoic era. During the Mesozoic era, it broke apart to form the land masses that became Africa, Antarctica, Australia, India, Madagascar, New Zealand, and Sri Lanka.
greenhouse effect	The trapping of heat near the earth's surface, caused by Earth's absorption of solar radiation and reemission of infrared radiation. This energy is subsequently absorbed by atmospheric water vapor, carbon dioxide, and other "greenhouse gases," preventing its dissipation into space and thus increasing atmospheric temperature and global warming.
habitat	Specifically, the physical environment in which an organism or biological population naturally lives: its home. Generally, an environment characterized by its physical features or dominant plant types.
homeostasis	Physiological equilibrium produced by a balance of internal functions within an organism and adjustments to the external environment.
hydrologic cycle	Continuous circulation of water on the planet, as a liquid, solid, and vapor. For example, water vapor is transferred from the atmosphere to the earth through precipitation and returns to the atmosphere through evaporation and transpiration.
hydrosphere	The layer of water on the planet, covering nearly 75 percent of Earth's surface, including oceans, lakes, rivers, and ice, in addition to groundwater under the surface.
ionizing radiation	Radiation with enough energy to ionize matter, making it unstable. The spectrum includes streams of subatomic particles such as electrons and short-wave radiation such as X rays. Because ionizing radiation can cause extensive damage to molecular structures, exposure can be dangerous to organisms.
lianas	High-climbing plants, especially tropical woody vines that grow up tree trunks.

limnology	Study of the biological, physical, and chemical conditions of freshwater organisms and their habitats.
lithosphere	The solid part of the planet, the rigid outer layer of Earth's crust and upper mantle.
meteorology	The study of atmospheric phenomena, especially weather and climate.
monoculture	Planting of a single species crop for harvest over a large area, such as many acres of wheat in place of a naturally diverse ecosystem. The lack of biodiversity and profusion of a single species creates conditions for the rapid development of diseases and pests specific to that crop.
mutagen	Agent capable of producing genetic changes through DNA alteration or chromosomal damage, causing biological mutation.
mutation	Inheritable alteration of an organism's genes or chromosomes.
mutualism	A symbiotic relationship in which both organisms benefit from their partnership. Such mutually beneficial relationships are common between plants and insects.
organism	A unicellular or multicellular living body whose components work together as a whole to carry out life processes.
ozone	A molecule containing three oxygen atoms. *Stratospheric* ozone is formed when oxygen gas (containing two oxygen atoms) in Earth's outer atmosphere is exposed to ultraviolet radiation. *Tropospheric* (ground-level) ozone is formed by combustion gases from fossil fuels, particularly car exhaust. This air pollutant forms smog, resulting in respiratory and other health problems as well as damaging plant chlorophyll and growth.
ozone layer	The ozonosphere, a region of the stratosphere containing gaseous ozone that absorbs harmful solar ultraviolet radiation and provides a protective shield for life on Earth.
photosynthesis	The process by which green plant cells containing chlorophyll convert light to chemical energy by synthesizing organic compounds from inorganic compounds, creating carbohydrates from carbon dioxide and water, and releasing oxygen.
phytoplankton	Microscopic floating aquatic plants, such as algae.

population	Ecologically, organisms of the same species living within a specific habitat. All the species together in the habitat form a community.
recycling	Recovering and reprocessing a used resource so that it can be made into a new product and reused.
S-curve	Growth pattern of a population, whereby the growth rate decreases as density increases. When population expands to a point beyond which the environment cannot support further growth, population levels off or declines.
species	Generally, a population of closely related similar organisms. In organisms that reproduce sexually, a species is a population that naturally interbreeds and produces fertile offspring.
succession	The process of development in an ecosystem resulting from changes in species populations, particularly progression from initial stages of colonization to a more stable, mature climax community.
sustainable	Capable of being sustained, supported, saved, or preserved without diminution. Sustainable development is supposed to maintain an environment's natural resources in perpetuity.
symbiosis	The relationship of different organisms living together in close association.
synergy	A net effect greater than the sum of the independent effects of combined individual factors.
taxonomy	Classification of organisms, on the basis of similarities and differences, into hierarchical groups representing relationships among them. Taxonomic categories include species, genus, family, order, and phylum.
transpiration	Process in which water is absorbed by plant roots, passed through their stomata, and evaporated into the atmosphere.
trophic level	Functional level in the food chain, such as plant producers or animal consumers.
watershed	The drainage basin surrounding a body of water, such as a river or lake, which is the source of the runoff supplying its water.
wetland	Land covered with surface water, such as bogs, marshes, and swamps. Wetlands are exceptionally productive and

biodiverse, providing rich habitat for wildlife, including nesting areas for birds and nursing areas for most commercial and game fish.

wildlife   Wild animals and vegetation living in a natural, undomesticated state.

These brief descriptions necessarily omit many of these scientists' important achievements, awards, publications, and administrative contributions. Note, too, that the Nobel Prize is not awarded in the life sciences.

LESTER BROWN was an international agricultural analyst with the United States Department of Agriculture's Foreign Agricultural Service, adviser to secretary of agriculture Orville Freeman on foreign agricultural policy, and administrator of the department's International Agricultural Development Service. He helped establish the Overseas Development Council, of which he became a senior fellow. In 1974 he founded the Worldwatch Institute to analyze global environmental issues. He continues to run the institute and oversee its research. In addition to books, a magazine, and periodic reports, it publishes the widely read *State of the World* reports.

PAUL EHRLICH, professor of population studies and president of the Center for Conservation Biology at Stanford University, has researched ecology, entomology, evolutionary biology, and behavior, doing fieldwork all over the world. With Peter Raven, he developed the concept of coevolution. Of his thirty books, the best known is *The Population Bomb,* which led him to found the organization Zero Population Growth. He is internationally known for presciently warning of the dangers of overconsumption and overpopulation for the carrying capacity of the planet.

JOHN FIROR researched cosmic particle physics at the University of Chicago and then studied radioastronomy at the Carnegie Institution of Washington. His study of solar radio waves led him to the High Altitude Observatory in Boulder, which later became the base of the National Center for Atmospheric Research (NCAR). After being associate director in charge of solar research, Firor became director of NCAR and remained in management for over thirty years. His research contributions include solar-terrestrial relations, the physics of Earth's atmosphere, the impact of climate change, and policy use of scientific information.

MARTIN HOLDGATE was chief biologist of the British Antarctic Survey, deputy director (for research) of the British Nature Conservancy, and first director of the Institute of Terrestrial Ecology. In Britain, he was the first director of the Central Unit on Environmental Pollution and then chief scientist of the Departments of Environment and Transportation. He was president of the Governing Council of the United Nations Environment Program and director general of the International Union for the Conservation of Nature/World Conservation Union. He is president of the Zoological Society of London.

HENRY KENDALL won the Nobel Prize in physics for the discovery of quarks. A professor at the Massachusetts Institute of Technology, he researched meson and neutrino physics, nucleon structure, and high-energy electron scattering. He warned of safety hazards in the nuclear power industry, the dangers of nuclear weapons, and the impracticality of space-based weapons. He led the scientific community in assessing and developing means to control the adverse effects of advanced technologies. Until his untimely death, he was chair of the Union of Concerned Scientists, which he cofounded to conduct technical studies and provide public education to advance responsible public policies on issues in which science and technology play a critical role. He initiated the "World Scientists' Warning to Humanity" to bring public attention to the threats of global environmental degradation to Earth's life-support systems.

THOMAS LOVEJOY directed the science program of the World Wildlife Fund–United States and undertook a giant experiment in Brazil's rain forest, the Minimum Critical Size of Ecosystems Project, which became the Biological Dynamics of Forest Fragments Project. Later he originated innovative debt-for-nature swaps for international conservation. He also started the popular public television series *Nature*. He is head of Biodiversity and Environmental Affairs for the Smithsonian Institution, science adviser to the U.S. secretary of the interior, and chief biodiversity adviser at the World Bank.

JAMES LOVELOCK, who has a Ph.D. in medicine and a D.Sc. in biophysics, worked at the National Institute for Medical Research in London. Later he collaborated on lunar and planetary research with NASA's Jet Propulsion Laboratory. His interdisciplinary research covers such broad fields as medicine, biology, geophysiology, and instrument science. He has filed over fifty patents for his inventions, and one, the electron-capture detector, first revealed the ubiquitous distribution of pesticide residues, PCBs, nitrous oxide, and the CFCs responsible for atmospheric ozone depletion. He is best known for originating the Gaia hypothesis.

NORMAN MYERS initially documented the destruction of the world's rain forests and then identified and originated the strategy of conserving biodiversity "hot spots." As a conservation biologist and ecologist and international consultant on sustainable development, he has worked in over eighty countries on issues as varied as mass extinction of species, tropical forests, savannahs, and grasslands, global warming, population growth in developing countries, resource waste in developed countries, environmental economics, and the environmental dimensions of national and international security.

MAX NICHOLSON, renowned conservationist, helped establish the Edward Gray Institute and the British Trust for Ornithology. He drafted "A National Plan for Britain," the basis of a socioeconomic group PEP (Political and Economic Planning). After World War II he was head of the office of the deputy prime minister. When the government created the British Nature Conservancy, he became its director general. Later he was a founder of the World Wildlife Fund/World Wide Fund for Nature. He also started and was chair of Earthwatch Europe and was head of the world conservation section of the International Biological Programme.

ELLIOTT NORSE was a marine biologist with the Environmental Protection Agency before becoming staff ecologist for the President's Council on Environmental Quality. Later he became public policy director of the Ecological Society of America and opened its Washington, D.C., office. He then compiled two books on American forests for the Wilderness Society. After being chief scientist at the Center for Marine Conservation, he founded the Marine Conservation Biology Institute to advance interdisciplinary research and collaboration in the emerging field of marine conservation biology. For further information, contact the Marine Conservation Biology Institute, 15806 NE 47th Court, Redmond, WA 98052.

RUTH PATRICK's extensive research on diatoms led her to expand her study of their taxonomy, physiology, and ecology to an analysis of the aquatic environments that they inhabit. She invented the diatometer to detect pollution in freshwater conditions. Her field research focused on the biodiversity of rivers and how these ecosystems function under natural and polluted conditions. She founded the Limnology Department (now the Environmental Research Division) at the Academy of Natural Sciences in Philadelphia and later became chair of its board of trustees.

PETER RAVEN is director of the Missouri Botanical Garden, where he has developed botanical field research programs undertaken around the world, as well as the Center for Plant Conservation, a national consortium to preserve endangered species. In addition to heading a variety of international projects and committees, he is home secretary for the National Academy of Sciences and has convened studies for the National Science Foundation and the National Research Council on systematic and evolutionary biology and ecology, biodiversity, and other related interdisciplinary research.

JOSEPH ROTBLAT, a nuclear physicist, was the only scientist to leave the Manhattan Project on principle. Ever since resigning, he has campaigned for nuclear disarmament and organized scientists for arms control. He chaired the press conference for the Russell-Einstein Manifesto, was cofounder of the Atomic Scientists Association, organized and still heads the Pugwash Conferences on Science and World Affairs, cofounded the Stockholm International Peace Research Institute, and was president of the International Science Forum, in addition to heading organizations in the field of nuclear medicine. In 1995 Joseph Rotblat and Pugwash were awarded the Nobel Peace Prize.

SHERWOOD ROWLAND created and was the first chair of the chemistry department of the University of California's Irvine campus. Previously he researched radioactive atoms and developed the subfield of tritium "hot-atom" chemistry. When his interest in chemical kinetics and photochemistry led him to determine the atmospheric fate of chlorofluorocarbons, he discovered that they were destroying stratospheric ozone. Realizing the environmental consequences of ozone depletion, he testified in legislative hearings to regulate CFC production. In 1995 Rowland and his colleague Mario Molina won the Nobel Prize in chemistry.

DAVID SUZUKI was a professor at the University of British Columbia, doing genetics research, before he began his syndicated newspaper column, the radio program *Quirks and Quarks*, the television series *Suzuki on Science*, and the ongoing TV series *The Nature of Things*. In addition to producing over one hundred major research papers and textbooks, he has written twenty-five popular books. In 1989 his five-part Canadian Broadcasting Corporation radio series about the global environment, *It's a Matter of Survival*, brought such an impassioned public response that he started the David Suzuki Foundation to find solutions and create sustainable communities. For more information, contact the David T. Suzuki Foundation, 2211 West Fourth Avenue, Vancouver, B.C., Canada V6K 4S2.

GEORGE M. WOODWELL studies the structure and function of natural communities and their role as segments of the biosphere. He also investigates biotic impoverishment, especially the circulation and effects of persistent toxins, the ecological effects of ionizing radiation, and biotic interactions related to global warming. He was the founder and director of the Ecosystems Center at the Marine Biological Laboratory in Woods Hole, Massachusetts, and also of the Woods Hole Research Center for global environmental research and policy. He was a founder of the Environmental Defense Fund and a founding trustee of the Natural Resources Defense Council and the World Resources Institute. He has headed many groups and was chair of the World Wildlife Fund and president of the Ecological Society of

America. He also headed the Nuclear Winter Symposium, the conference on the long-term biological consequences of nuclear war. An expert on the basic metabolism of ecosystems and the global carbon cycle, he contributed substantially to the "Framework on Climate Change" adopted at the Earth Summit in Rio de Janeiro, and he established a World Commission on Forests to protect all of Earth's forests.

ACKNOWLEDGMENTS

I THANK THE REMARKABLE INDIVIDUALS PROFILED IN THIS BOOK FOR trusting me with their life stories. As these scientists have superhuman schedules—lecturing, teaching, researching, heading organizations and projects, serving on major committees, attending national and international meetings, constantly traveling all over the world—they have no time to write about their activities. (Unfortunately, several profiles of scientists, including additional women, had to be omitted because the subjects did not find time to review their chapters.) The only way this book could be written was by someone else putting it all together, as I have attempted to do. I am grateful for their cooperation in creating *Life Stories*.

As I was unable to afford the innumerable books and articles needed for this project, I depended on libraries for the information. I am indebted to the university and public libraries that provided access to the documents that enabled me to research what is happening to the planet. I also thank the University of California Press for publishing this book, and everyone involved in that process, especially Doris Kretschmer. I appreciate having been given total freedom to create the book from conception through completion.

My greatest gratitude is for remaining alive all the years I worked "total-time" on this project without any income, not knowing how I could—or whether I would—survive. My gratitude extends to my mother, for her lifelong, selfless giving; my father, who was stoically dying of environmentally induced cancer; my "sister" Marion, whose generous response saved me and the book; and James Compton of the Compton Foundation, and the founders of the New England Biolabs Foundation, who, in the end, provided some funds to help to complete it.

INDEX

Aberly, Doug, 64
aboriginal peoples, 61–62
Academy of Natural Sciences, Philadelphia, 46, 87–92
acid rain, 149, 151, 154, 198; defined, 203
adaptation, defined, 203
Africa: agricultural production, 197; population growth and security, 178; wildlife, 43, 169–72
Aga Khan Rural Support Programme, 132
Agency for International Development (AID), 163
Ages of Gaia (Lovelock), 12, 13
agriculture: biodiversity in, 36–37; Brown's work on, 156, 157–58, 163–66; China's industrialization and, 164–66; climate change affecting, 150, 196; commercial ranchers and, 171, 172; genetic engineering in, 38; global projections, 157–58, 163–65, 193, 194, 197, 199; "green revolution," 36; in India, 163–64; monoculture, 36, 63, 209; Myers and, 169; pesticides and, 77, 80–81, 83–84, 128; population growth and, 165, 166, 175–76, 178. *See also* food supply

air: connected with everything, 147; humans linked by, 72; pollution, 13–14, 72, 75, 82–84, 149, 151–52, 173, 196–97, 198. *See also* atmosphere
Air Force, 99
algae, 36, 46; defined, 203. *See also* diatoms
Amazon: Patrick expedition to, 91; rain forests, 43–46, 47–49, 53–54, 196; senators' trips to, 44–46; Suzuki visit, 60–61
American Association for the Advancement of Science, 87
American Chemical Society, 137
Ancient Forests of the Pacific Northwest (Norse), 96, 102
Antarctica, 125–26; ozone hole over, 139, 140, 160
Antarctic Treaty (1959), 125
ants, Wilson's work on, 18
artemisin, 37–38
astronomy, Firor and, 143, 144–45
Atlantic Refining Company, 87–88
atmosphere: carbon dioxide, 27, 49, 148–49, 196; CFCs, 4, 134–38, 139–40, 160; Earth's organisms and, 25; ozone hole, 4, 134, 136–40, 154, 160, 176–77,

atmosphere (*continued*)
198; radioactive residues, 82; research, 143–44, 147–49, 152, 154, 155; ultraviolet radiation, 136, 137, 176–77, 198. *See also* air; climate change; greenhouse effect; meteorology
Atomic Energy Commission (AEC), 135–36
Atomic Scientists Association, 187
Attenborough, David, 116
Australia: Canberra Commission on the Elimination of Nuclear Weapons, 190; Ehrlich in, 19; Suzuki in, 61
automobiles, 13–14, 151–52, 153

Baldwin, Malcolm, 98–99
Ballantine, Ian, 19
barndoor skate, 106
Bay checkerspot butterflies, 17
BBC, 49–50, 116
beef, rain forest decline and, 14, 172
Benchley, Peter, 45
benthos, defined, 203
Berry, Wendell, 64–65
bioaccumulation, defined, 203–4
bioamplification, defined, 204
biodegradable, defined, 204
biodiversity: of birds, 161; defined, 100, 204; global view on, 52, 102, 118–19, 193–94, 198; human disconnection from, 59, 63, 72–73, 107; Kendall on, 193–94; Lovejoy on, 44–54, 100; Norse on, 99–108; Raven on, 34, 35–40; in sustainable communities, 64; tropical, 34, 43–46, 47–49, 53–54, 91. *See also* extinction
biogeochemical cycle, defined, 204
biogeography, defined, 124, 204
bioindustry, 50
Biological Dynamic of Forest Fragments Project, 47–49
biology: defined, 204; disconnection from, 58–65, 161; evolutionary (defined), 207; specialized/fragmented, 7, 117; S-shaped growth curves, 162–63; useful and bad organisms, 100; wildlife, 171. *See also* biodiversity; biogeography; conservation; field studies; marine biology; nature

biomass, 36; defined, 204
biome, defined, 204
bioregions, 64; defined, 204
bioremediation, defined, 50, 204
biosphere, defined, 204
biota, defined, 204
biotechnology, 50. *See also* genetic engineering
biotic community, 26–27, 39–40; defined, 205
Birch, Charles, 19
birds: Lovejoy collecting, 43; Nicholson and, 109, 110–12, 114, 117; Worldwatch on, 161
Birds in England (Nicholson), 110
Black Sea, coastal nations, 104–5
Bloome, Mark, 103
Bloome, Sharon, 103
boreal forests: DDT spraying of, 74–77; defined, 205
Bradlee, Ben, 45
Brandegee, Katharine, 31
Brazil, rain forests, 47–49, 53–54
British Antarctic Society, 125, 139
British Columbia: bioregions, 64; forests, 68
British Museum, 32
British Trust for Ornithology, 111, 112
Brixton, Lovelock in, 2
Brookhaven National Laboratory, Long Island, 77
Brooklyn, The Canal, 95
Brooklyn College, Norse at, 96
Brower, Dave, 19, 21
Brown, Lester, 156–68, 213
budworm, spraying, 74–75
Bush, George, 130, 180
butterflies, 16–18, 28, 32

Cadwalder, Charles, 88
California Academy of Sciences, San Francisco, 29, 30–31
Cambridge University, Holdgate at, 122, 125
Canada: elders, 62; Pugwash, 189; Suzuki family, 55–58, 62–63. *See also* British Columbia

Canberra Commission on the Elimination of Nuclear Weapons, 190
Cannon, Walter, 11
carbon cycle, defined, 205
carbon dioxide: in atmosphere, 27, 49, 148–49, 196; defined, 205
carbon monoxide, defined, 205
carbon sink, defined, 205
carcinogen, defined, 205
"Caring for the Earth" (1991), 131
Carnegie, Andrew, 142
Carnegie Institution, Washington, D.C., 142–43, 144
carrying capacity: defined, 205; global, 24, 177. See also life-support systems
Carson, Johnny, 20
Carson, Rachel, 46, 82; Silent Spring, 4, 75, 97, 127
Carter, Jimmy, 99
Center for Environmental Education, 99, 101
Center for Marine Conservation (CMC), 99, 102–3
Central Intelligence Agency, 179
Central Scientific Unit, British, 127–28
CFCs. See chlorofluorocarbons
Challinor, David, 46
Chernobyl, nuclear accident, 72
Chesapeake Bay, oysters, 107
China: Ehrlichs in, 22; industrialization and food supply, 164–66
chlorofluorocarbons (CFCs), 4, 134–38, 139–40, 160; defined, 134, 205
chlorophyll, defined, 206
chromatography: Lovelock and, 4–5, 135; toxins measured by, 76, 78
Cicerone, Ralph, 137
Clark, Colin, 105
Clarkia franciscana, 31–32
Clean Air Amendment (1990), 151
clearcutting, 106–7
climate: global ecosystem, 27. See also climate change
climate change: Brown on, 162, 166; Firor on, 147–55; Myers on, 176; "World Scientists' Call for Action at the Kyoto Climate Summit," 194, 195–98. See also

greenhouse effect; weather modification
Clinton, Bill, 101
coevolution, 26–27; defined, 32, 206
Coker College, South Carolina, Patrick at, 86
Cold Spring Harbor, Long Island, 86
cold war, scientists vs. nuclear weapons in, 189, 190
collections: butterfly, 16–18; Conestoga watershed aquatic species, 89; diatom, 86, 87; Lovejoy's, 43; Patrick's early, 85, 86; Raven's, 28–31; Suzuki's, 57
Commonwealth Club, Ehrlich's speech to, 19
communities: biotic, 26–27, 39–40, 205; defined, 206; as survival unit, 63–64; sustainable, 27, 64. See also life-support systems
computer age: international ecology and, 117–18; military and, 93–94
conservation: biodiversity, 99–108; cooperative aspect, 114–15; debt-for-nature swaps, 51–52; governmental organization, 112–13, 127–29; international management of, 112, 116–18, 126, 129–33; Lovejoy on, 43, 47–52; marine, 96, 98–108; Nature Conservancy, 113–20, 126; and pesticides, 75–76; reserves (early British), 114, 115, 126; Ripley on, 42; wildlife, 171–72. See also endangered species; extinction; preservation
conservation biology: defined, 206. See also conservation
Conservation Foundation, 75–76
Conserving Biological Diversity in Our National Forests (Norse), 100, 101
"Constraints on the Expansion of the Global Food Supply" (Kendall and Pimentel), 194
consumption, 153; Ehrlich on, 24; energy, 151–52, 153, 196–97, 201; rain forest decline and, 172; Suzuki on, 64–65, 67; UCS on, 196–97, 201; war elimination and, 191; water, 197. See also food supply

and, 172–73; and security, 180; Suzuki on, 63–69; war, 93, 202; of weather modification, 145–46; World Conservation Union, 130. *See also* consumption; industry

ecosystem, defined, 206

Ehrenfeld, David, 107–8

Ehrlich, Anne, 18, 19, 21–24

Ehrlich, Paul, 16–27, 50, 69, 191, 213; on global carrying capacity, 24, 177; *Population Bomb*, 19, 20, 33, 97; Raven and, 21, 23, 32–33

Einstein, Albert, 188

Eisenhower, D. D., 157

elders, wisdom of, 61–62, 65

electron-capture detector, Lovelock's invention, 4, 135

Elton, Charles, 110

endangered species, 33–34, 61, 131, 161; defined, 206. *See also* conservation; extinction; preservation

Endangered Species Act (1970s), 100

energy: efficiency, 151–52, 153–54, 196–97, 201; food or energy pyramid (defined), 207. *See also* fossil fuels

environment: Brown on, 156–67; compounding interactions in, 177–78; defined, 206; Ehrlich on, 17–27; Firor on, 145–55; Holdgate on, 122–33; Kendall on, 193–94; Lovejoy on, 43–54; Lovelock on, 4, 7–15; Myers on, 171–82; and National Center for Atmospheric Research, 145–47; Nicholson on, 110–20; Norse on, 97–108; nuclear threat and, 191; Patrick on, 87–92; Raven on, 29–40; Rotblat on, 191–92; Rowland on, 135–40; Suzuki on, 57–73; Union of Concerned Scientists on, 195–202; Woodwell on, 74–84. *See also* biology; ecology; environmentalism; nature

Environmental Alert book series, 159

Environmental Defense Fund (EDF), 82

environmental impact, defined, 207

environmentalism: Americans', 154; formation of, 4; knowledge held by general public/politicians/business, 119; NCAR impacts group, 145–47; Nichol-

son's, 110–20, 126; Norse's, 98–102; nuclear threat and, 191; Patrick's, 46, 87–92; Raven's, 32–33; during Reagan years, 100–101, 139; of Suzuki's foundation, 64. *See also* conservation; ecology; environment; pollution; preservation

Environmental Protection Agency (EPA), 82, 90, 98, 99

Environmental Quality 1980 (CEQ), 100

environmental security, 179–80

Environment Commission, OECD, 129

estuary, defined, 207

Ethiopia, population growth and security in, 178

evolution: coevolution, 26–27, 32, 206; defined, 207; Ehrlich course, 19; Gaia hypothesis and, 11–12; plant, 30, 31, 32, 39; Suzuki on, 71–72

evolutionary biology: defined, 207. *See also* biodiversity; evolution

externalities, defined, 207

extinction: Brown on, 161; defined, 207; Lovejoy on, 54; Myers on, 171–73, 177; Norse on, 100, 106; Raven on, 38–39; Rotblat on, 183–84, 191; Suzuki on, 61; UCS on, 197–98, 199–200. *See also* endangered species

farming. *See* agriculture

fauna and flora: defined, 207. *See also* biology; nature; plants; wildlife

Federation of American Scientists, 187

"field hospitals," in Britain, 115

field studies: Nature Conservancy, 114–15. *See also* collections

fire ants, spraying, 18

fires: climate change increasing, 150; rain forest, 49, 53–54

Firor, John, 141–55, 213–14

fish: economic forces and, 105–7, 162–63; Ehrlich's early interest, 16; food, 105–6, 199; Norse's early studies, 96; pesticides and, 72, 75, 81; Suzuki and, 57–58, 61. *See also* marine biology

Fisher, James, 116

fishing techniques, 106–7

fission: discovery of, 184–85. *See also* nuclear physics
Fitzer Institute, 7
Flower Garden Banks, 98
food chain, 26; defined, 207
food or energy pyramid: defined, 207; salt marsh, 78
food supply, 73; disconnected from nature, 58–59, 64–65; plant, 36; population growth and, 19, 157–58, 165, 166, 178, 197, 200; from sea, 19, 105–6, 198–99; shipment of, 64–65; world, 157–58, 162–67, 175, 176, 193, 194, 197. *See also* agriculture; food webs
"The 'Food from the Sea' Myth" (Ehrlich), 19
food webs: defined, 207; fishing down, 105; toxic, 74–84
Foreign Agricultural Service, 157–58
Forest in the Clouds, 49
forests, 27; "ancient," 102; boreal, 74–77, 205; British Columbia, 68; clearcutting, 106–7; climate change affecting, 150, 196; DDT spraying on, 74–77; Norse and, 96, 100, 101–2, 106–7; "old growth," 101–2; UCS on, 199. *See also* rain forests
fossil fuels, 148–49, 153–54, 201; defined, 207; pollution, 148–49, 152, 173, 196–97
4-H Club, International Farm Youth Exchange Program, 157
Freeman, Orville, 158
Freons, 135. *See also* chlorofluorocarbons (CFCs)
Frisch, Otto, 184–85
From Care to Action (Holdgate), 133
fruit flies, DDT resistance, 18
Full House: Reassessing the Earth's Population Carrying Capacity (Brown and Kane), 163, 164
fur trade, 171

Gaia: A New Look at Life on Earth (Lovelock), 13
Gaia hypothesis, 9–13, 15, 73; defined, 9, 207
Garth, John, 97

gender. *See* sexual equality; women
genes, 38; defined, 208. *See also* DNA
genetic engineering, 38, 71
genetics, all life forms related, 61
genocide, 183
genomes, 38; defined, 208
Georgia Tech, Firor at, 142
Global Marine Biological Diversity (Norse), 102
global security, 178–82
global view: of agriculture, 157–58, 163–65, 193, 194, 197, 199; on biodiversity, 52, 102, 118–19, 193–94, 198; Brown's, 158–67; Ehrlichs', 23–27, 177; Gaia, 9–13, 15, 73; Holdgate's, 129; monoculture, 63; Myers's, 173–82; Nicholson's, 112, 117; ocean, 104, 198–99; ornithology, 117; on population growth, 24, 173–77; Raven's, 33–35; of security, 178–82; Suzuki's, 72–73; UCS, 70, 194–202. *See also* internationalism; life
global warming. *See* greenhouse effect; heat-trapping gases
Godfrey, Arthur, 20
Golden Gate Park, Raven and, 28, 29
Gondwanaland, 125; defined, 208
Gorbachev, Mikhail, 190
Gore, Al, 45
Gough Island, 123–24, 125
Governing Council of the United Nations Environment Program, 129
government, 99; and biodiversity, 52–53, 99–100, 118–19; Bush, 130, 180; conservation organization, 112–13, 126–29; Environmental Protection Agency (EPA), 82, 90, 98, 99; and food supply, 157–58, 163–64; and pesticides, 18, 77, 80–81; President's Committee of Advisors on Science and Technology, 34; President's Council on Environmental Quality (CEQ), 98–101, 127; Reagan, 100–101, 139; and scientists' warnings about nuclear weapons, 187, 189–90; security concerns, 179; and weather modification, 145. *See also* military; politics
grain, 36, 163–64, 166
Grant, Jim, 157

inventions: Lovelock's, 3–4, 6, 8–9, 135; nuclear weapons, 184, 185–86, 190
ionizing radiation, 82, 83; defined, 208

Japanese beetle, spraying, 80–81

Kansas University, Patrick at, 86
Kendall, Henry, 193–202, 214
Kenya: Lovejoy in, 43; Myers in, 169–71
Kew, Royal Botanical Gardens, 32

Lake Michigan, dieldrin spraying, 80–81
land and water distribution: climate change affecting, 150, 176; population growth and, 175–76
Lear, Linda, 82
Lepidopterists' Society, 16–17, 19
Lewis, Harlan, 31–32
Lewis, Ivy, 86, 91
Lewis, Margaret, 31
lianas, 44; defined, 208
life: Lovelock and study of, 6–13, 15. See also ecology; evolution; life-support systems
life-support systems, 24–27, 50, 133, 167. See also carrying capacity; food supply; nature; sustainability
limnology, 88, 92; defined, 88, 209
lithosphere, defined, 209
Lloyds of London, 162
London: Lloyds of, 162; Lovelock in, 1, 2, 5; Natural History Museum, 32, 109; Raven in, 32; World Wildlife Fund, 116–17
London Times, 110
Long Island, pesticide effects, 77–80
Los Alamos: Firor in, 141–42; Rotblat in, 186
Lovejoy, Thomas, 42–54, 100, 214
Lovelock, James, 1–15, 73, 135, 214–15
Ludwig, Daniel, 43

MacLane, Louis A., 81
magnetism, Earth's, 142–43
Maine, DDT spraying, 74–77
Majorca, scientific center, 118
Maldive Islands, corals, 107
Manchester University, Holdgate at, 124

Manhattan Project, 186
Man, Land and Food: Looking Ahead at World Food Needs (Brown), 157–58
"Man's Peril" (Russell), 188
Manual of Flowering Plants of California (Jepson), 29
Margulis, Lynn, 10
marine biology, 96–100, 102–8, 176–77; Antarctic, 125–26; conservation, 96, 98–108; national sanctuaries, 99. See also fish; oceans
Marine Conservation Biology Institute (MCBI), 103, 106
Marlowe, William, 135
Mars, Lovelock and, 6–9, 10
Masailand, Myers in, 170
McManus, Roger, 102
McVay, Scott, 49
media: and CFCs, 139; conservation message through, 49–50, 116; Ehrlich in, 20–21; and pesticide court cases, 80, 81–82; photography (Myers's), 170–71; and UCS, 70. See also television
medicinal compounds, plants', 37–38
Meitner, Lise, 184–85
Mendez, Chico, 45
meteorology, 143–44, 145–46, 152; defined, 209. See also atmosphere; climate change
methane, 148
Michener, Charles, 16, 17–18
Michigan Conservation Department, 81
microscopes: Patrick's early, 85; reflection electron, 123
Midgley, Thomas, 135
military: Air Force missiles, 99; scientists' purpose differing from, 186–87; security role of, 179–80; technology, 93–94. See also nuclear weapons; war
Millbrook School, 42
Minimum Critical Size of Ecosystems Project, 47–49
mining: gold, 161; strip, 149. See also oil industry
Ministry of Agriculture, 128
Ministry of Housing and Local Government, 128

Ministry of Shipping, Nicholson in, 111
Missouri Botanical Garden, 33
Molina, Mario, 136–38, 139–40
monoculture, 36, 63; defined, 209
Montreal Protocol on Substances That
    Deplete the Ozone Layer, 139
Montrose Chemical Company, St. Louis,
    81
Mooney, Hal, 23
Morrison, Herbert, 112
mosquitoes, salt marsh, 77–80
moths, gypsy, spraying, 77
Mountain Lake, Virginia, 86
Muir, John, 131
Murphy, Dennis, 21
Murphy, Robert Cushman, 77
mutagen, defined, 209
mutation, defined, 209
mutualism, defined, 26–27, 209
MX missiles, 99
Myers, Norman, 169–82, 215
mysticism, Lovelock accused of, 12–13

National Academy of Sciences, 34, 91–92,
    137
National Acid Precipitation Assessment
    Program, 151
National Aeronautics and Space Adminis-
    tration (NASA), 6–9, 137, 139
National Biological Survey, 52–53
National Center for Atmospheric Re-
    search (NCAR), 143–46, 152
National Institute for Amazon Research in
    Brazil, 47
National Institute for Medical Research,
    5–6, 7
National Medal of Science, Patrick's, 92
National Oceanic and Atmospheric Ad-
    ministration, 145
National Parks and Access to the Coun-
    tryside Act (1949), British, 113
"National Plan for Britain" (Nicholson), 111
National Research Council, 34
National Science Foundation, 34, 75
National Security Council, 179
Natural History Museum, London, 32, 109
Natural History of Selborne (White), 109

nature: dependence on, 35, 40, 60, 83–84,
    119–20, 133; disconnection from, 58–65,
    68, 71–72, 161; economically motivated
    destruction of, 105–7, 119–20, 132, 147,
    153, 162–63, 172–73; life-support sys-
    tems, 24–27, 50, 133; patterns of, 122;
    television programming, 49–50, 59, 60.
    See also biodiversity; biology; collec-
    tions; conservation; ecology; environ-
    ment; environmentalism; life; nature—
    early interests; plants; wildlife
nature—early interests: Brown's, 156;
    Ehrlich's, 16–17; Holdgate's, 121–22;
    Lovejoy's, 42; Lovelock's, 2–3; Nichol-
    son's, 109–10; Norse's, 94, 95–96;
    Patrick's, 85, 86; Raven's, 28–31;
    Suzuki's, 55–58, 60. *See also* science
    learning, early
Nature (journal), 8, 137
Nature (television series), 49–50
Nature Connection (television series), 59
Nature Conservancy, British, 113–20, 126,
    127
The Nature of Things (television series), 60
nature reserves, early British, 114, 115, 126
Nature's Services (Daily), 21
Nazis, 183, 185–86
NBC, 20
NCAR. *See* National Center for Atmos-
    pheric Research
New York Times, 51, 70
New Zealand, 125
Nicholson, Max, 109–20, 126, 215
nitrous oxide, 148
Nixon, Richard M., 158
Nobel Jubilee, 193–94
Nobel laureates: Chicago physics depart-
    ment, 142; vs. nuclear weapons, 188;
    "World Scientists' Call for Action at the
    Kyoto Climate Summit," 194; "World
    Scientists' Warning to Humanity," 194
Nobel Prizes, 193; for Chicago economist,
    67; Crafoord Prize and, 18; in National
    Institute for Medical Research, 6; for
    Pugwash movement vs. nuclear
    weapons, 190; for Rowland and Molina,
    140. *See also* Nobel laureates

spiritual experience, Lovelock and, 12–13
Stalin, Joseph, 187
Stanford University: Ehrlich at, 18–19, 24;
  Raven at, 32
State Department, U.S., 179
State of the World (Worldwatch), 159, 165
Stebbins, George Ledyard, 30
Stein, Charles, 88, 89, 90
Stolarski, Richard, 137
storks, endangered, 161
The Stork and the Plow (Ehrlich, Ehrlich,
  and Daily), 24
students, Ehrlich on, 21
succession, 48–49; defined, 210
Sun Oil, 90
sustainability: defined, 64, 210; Ehrlich on,
  27, 177; environmental security and,
  180; international, 158–59; population
  growth and, 177; Raven on, 34–35. *See
  also* food supply; life-support systems
Suzuki, David, 55–73, 216
Swedish Academy of Sciences, 18
symbiosis, defined, 210
Symposium on Marine Conservation Biology, first, 103
synergy, defined, 210

Tansley, Arthur G., 110, 112, 126
Tasmania, 125
taxol, 37
taxonomy, defined, 210
technology: illusions about capacities of,
  59, 60, 152; international ecology and,
  117–18; military, 93–94
television: conservation message, 49–50,
  116; Ehrlich on, 20–21; nature programming, 49–50, 59, 60; *Planet for the Taking*, 68
Tonight Show, 20
"Toxic Substances and Ecological Cycles"
  (Woodwell), 82
toxins: food web, 74–84; zero-release of,
  83–84. *See also* pesticides; pollution
"Trans-Amazonica: Highway to Extinction" (Lovejoy), 43
transpiration, defined, 210

transportation, energy consumption,
  151–52, 153
trawling, 106–7
Trevor, Frank, 42
Tristan da Cunha, 125
trophic level, defined, 210
tropics: biodiversity, 34, 43–46, 47–49,
  53–54, 91; extinction rate, 172; Raven
  focus on, 33, 34. *See also* Amazon; rain
  forests
Troubled Waters: A Call for Action
  (MCBI), 103
Tutu, Desmond, 193
Tyler (John and Alice) Award in Ecology,
  92
Tyler Prize for Environmental Achievement, 22

UCS. *See* Union of Concerned Scientists
UNICEF, 158
Union of Concerned Scientists (UCS), 70,
  194–202
United Nations, 130; Canberra Commission on the Elimination of Nuclear
  Weapons, 190; Conference on Population and Development, 70, 155, 173,
  175; Conference on the Human Environment, 128–29, 130; Earth Summit,
  70, 130, 180; Environment Program,
  129, 131; Food and Agriculture Organization, 162; list of national parks and
  protected areas, 131; Montreal Protocol
  on Substances That Deplete the Ozone
  Layer, 139; quality of life indicators, 67;
  Sasakawa Environment Prize, 22; on
  total population growth, 200; UNCED
  Conventions on Biodiversity, 118–19;
  UNICEF, 158; World Commission on
  Environment and Development, 180,
  181
University of British Columbia, 105;
  Suzuki at, 216
University of California, Berkeley: Myers
  at, 171; Raven at, 31
University of California, Irvine, Rowland
  at, 134, 136

University of California, Los Angeles, Raven at, 32
University of Chicago, Firor at, 142
University of Durham, Holdgate at, 124
University of Iowa, Norse at, 98
University of Kansas, Ehrlich at, 17–18
University of Maine, Woodwell at, 74–77, 81
University of Manchester, Lovelock at, 5
University of Maryland, Brown at, 157
University of Pennsylvania: Ehrlich at, 17; Patrick at, 92
University of Southern California (USC), Norse at, 97, 101
University of Victoria, 103
University of Virginia, Patrick at, 86
U.S. News & World Report, 158

Van Dusen, Lewis H., 90
Variation and Evolution in Plants (Stebbins), 30
vision, recapturing sense of, 133
Vitousek, Peter, 23

war: cold, 189, 190; eliminating all, 191; nuclear, 184, 187–91; UCS vs., 201–2. *See also* military; World War I; World War II
Washington Post, 70
Washington State Department of Natural Resources land, 101
water: British privatization, 129; Brooklyn (The Canal), 95, 96; climate change and, 150, 176, 197; diatomic studies, 87–88, 90, 91; in forests, 27; humans linked by, 72–73; pollution, 61, 72, 75, 80–84, 87–92, 198; scarcity, 164, 198. *See also* marine biology
watershed, defined, 210
Watling, Les, 106
Watson and Crick, DNA studies, 38
weather modification, 145–46, 152. *See also* climate change
Weber, Michael, 99
wetland, defined, 210–11
whales, 107
White, Gilbert, 109

"Who Will Feed China?," 168–69
Wilderness Society, 101–2
wildlife: Amazon, 44–45; defined, 211; sub-Saharan Africa, 43, 169–72. *See also* biodiversity; birds; ecology; fish; insects; nature; plants; zoos
Wild Life Conservation Special Committee, 112–13
Wilson, Edward O., 18
Wilson, Harold, 126–27
Wirth, Timothy, 21, 35, 45
Wirth, Wren, 21
Wisdom of the Elders (Suzuki), 65
women: health of in poor countries, 174–75; and population growth, 155; as scientists, 87, 88, 91–92; UCS on sexual equality, 201
Woods Hole Oceanographic Institute, Massachusetts, 86
Woodwell, George M., 74–84, 216–17
World Bank, 162, 169, 200
World Commission on Environment and Development, 180, 181
World Conservation Strategy (1980), 131, 132
World Conservation Union. *See* International Union for the Conservation of Nature
World Heritage Sites, 124
"World Scientists' Call for Action at the Kyoto Climate Summit," 194, 195–98
"World Scientists' Warning to Humanity," 194, 195, 198–202
World War I: casualties, 183; Nicholson and, 110
World War II: atomic bombings, 184, 185–87; casualties, 183; Firor during, 141; Lovelock in London during, 5; Norse and, 93, 94; Rowland childhood during, 139; Suzuki relocated during, 56
Worldwatch Institute, 158–65
World Watch magazine, 159, 161, 165–66
Worldwatch Papers, 158
World Wildlife Fund (WWF), 116–17, 131, 171; U.S. (WWF—US), 46–47
Wurster, Charles, 78

Yannacone, Victor, 79, 81
Yarn, Jane, 99

Zero Population Growth (ZPG), 20, 155, 174

zero-release of toxic substances, 83–84
zoos: Detroit, 6; Millbrook School, 42; Toronto, 61
Zuckerman, Solly, 127

Compositor:	Binghamton Valley Composition, LLCA
Text:	12/14.5 Adobe Garamond
Display:	Perpetua and Adobe Garamond
Printer and binder:	Edwards Brothers, Inc.
Index:	Barbara Roos